Negotiating
with a
Sovereign Québec

Negotiating with a Sovereign Québec

Edited by
Daniel Drache and Roberto Perin

James Lorimer & Company, Publishers
Toronto, 1992

James Lorimer & Company Ltd. acknowledges with thanks the support of the Canada Council, the Ontario Arts Council and the Ontario Publishing Centre in the development of writing and publishing in Canada.

Cover photo: Confederation Chamber, Province House, Charlottetown, P.E.I. (Courtesy P.E.I. Tourism/Gord Johnston)

Canadian Cataloguing in Publication Data
Negotiating with a sovereign Québec

Includes bibliographical references and index.
ISBN 1-55028-343-6 (bound). ISBN 1-55028-392-8 (pbk.)

1. Quebec (Province) - History - Autonomy and independence movements. 2. Federal-provincial relations - Quebec (Province).* 3. Federal-provincial relations - Canada.* 4. Federal government - Canada. 5. Canada - Constitutional law - Amendments. 6. Quebec (Province) - Politics and government - 1985- .* 7. Canada - Politics and government - 1984- . I. Drache, Daniel, 1941- . II. Perin, Roberto.
FC2925.9.S37N43 1992   971.064'7   C92-094669-0
F1053.2.N43 1992

James Lorimer & Company, Publishers
Egerton Ryerson Memorial Building
35 Britain Street
Toronto, Ontario
M5A 1R7

Printed and bound in Canada

Contents

Acknowledgements

The initial support for this volume came from Tom Meininger, acting Dean of Atkinson College, York University. Without his enthusiasm and confidence, we would not have had the means to hold a workshop on negotiating new political and economic relationships with Québec. York University President Harry Arthurs, Vice-President Stephen Fienberg, and the Robarts Centre for Canadian Studies also provided the workshop with generous financial backing. We are particularly grateful to them. Many of the chapters of this book were originally presented in draft form at that time. Those who helped make the workshop a success as well as contributed to the editorial work on the book include: Harry Glasbeek, Daniel Latouche, Andrée Lajoie, Alain-G. Gagnon, Denis Smith and Daniel Salée. A special thank you is also due to Diane Young, our editor. She has been both vigilant and patient in the preparation of the manuscript. The hard work of editing was done by Cy Strom. All the contributors have benefited from his watchful eye. Needless to say, we accept all responsibility for the errors that remain.

D.D.
R.P.
July 1992

Introduction

Daniel Drache and Roberto Perin

Constitutional Fatigue

Yet another book on Canada's ongoing constitutional saga? Canadians are justified in reacting with a mixture of weariness, irritation and boredom to a thirty-year-old crisis that tenaciously reappears as soon as it is apparently resolved. Politicians of various stripes have led us to believe over the years that a final constitutional settlement is within reach and that they alone can bring it about. They have usually done so in apocalyptic terms: either my way or chaos. The latest version of this scenario has the government of Brian Mulroney presenting Canadians with a neo-conservative and decentralist recipe for saving Canada. Apparently there is no other way to square the circle: meeting Québec's demands for more power requires Ottawa to devolve power to all ten provinces. Failure to follow this foolproof recipe, we are assured, will lead to the breakup of the country.

The Nature of Québec's Dissatisfaction

For their own reasons, political observers in the media and in academia have accepted the parameters set by a succession of political leaders on the constitutional question. Commentators have spent a great deal of physical and intellectual energy following the debate in its most minute, not to say most trivial, detail. Their implicit assumption is that there is no alternative other than the agenda that they have defined. As a result, political analysis in English Canada has been as limited as the constitutional discourse of the politicians. Canadians have not been exposed to different perspectives on the constitutional question. They have been ill-served by analysts who can't see the forest for the trees or those who consider a departure from federalism to be a crime of *lèse-majesté*.

This book presents an alternative vision. It begins with the premise that a constitutional crisis exists in this country because of Québec's dissatisfaction with its status within Confederation. This volume moves away from the Manichaean perspective that underlies much of the constitutional discussion, in which the "good" federalists are pitted against the "bad" advocates of a powerful Québec. It examines the nature of Québec's restiveness within Confederation and explains why a rearrangement of constitutional authority, vague and contradictory statements inserted into the text of the constitution, and institutional face-lifting will not satisfy Québec's requirements. We firmly believe that the constitutional crisis will persist whether or not a deal is struck in the summer of 1992 and irrespective of the outcome of the Québec referendum in the fall of the same year. As long as a sovereignist party remains a major political force in Québec; as long as tens of thousands of Québécois regularly take to the streets to affirm their identity and their desire to thrive in North America; as long, in other words, as the issue of Québec's empowerment is not confronted honestly, the crisis will continue to daunt Canadians.

Up to now, Québec's interlocutors have tried to contain, indeed ghettoize, the issues of language and culture, as if cultural survival and expansion can somehow be separated from the economic and social context. This approach, which underlies the definition of "distinct society," emphasizes language, culture and civil law. Yet, the evolution of Québec nationalism over the last thirty years has shown that cultural and socio-economic questions cannot be arbitrarily dissociated. They are in fact intimately linked and form the core of Québec's constitutional demands.

Renewed Federalism versus Sovereignty

If by chance some kind of arrangement is reached in 1992 among the various parties to the constitutional talks, it will only be a matter of time before the consensus breaks down. Indeed it is difficult to imagine how Québec's distinctiveness can be reconciled with the notion that all provinces are equal; how Québec's role in protecting and promoting its distinct identity can coexist with Ottawa's commitment to defend and strengthen Canada's linguistic minorities; how Québec's desire to limit the federal government's spending power can be harmonized with Ottawa's determination to act as the national government, even in areas of provincial responsibility, such as education, for example. Whatever arcane formulas are found to conceal these contradictions will soon be shown to be meaningless shells.

If the constitutional discussions break down, what then? That question has never really been faced in English Canada. Some observers have envisaged the Canadian army being called into action to protect the anglophones and the First Nations in Québec, to impose a Canadian corridor through the secessionist province, or to protect federal assets there. Others have advocated a policy of retaliation of the let-the-bastards-freeze-in-the-dark variety.

Even academics have lent a hand in conjuring up such cataclysmic scenarios. It is not inconceivable that Canada could become another Yugoslavia. No country has a monopoly on civility when hatred is given free reign. But instead of imagining Armageddons and thereby tacitly justifying them, academics should give voice to restraint and enlightened self-interest. As Canadians, we cannot in good faith turn our backs on the freely expressed will of the Québécois majority, if that majority chooses sovereignty. It is our conviction that Canada should not pursue policies of revenge and retaliation in the face of the right of a people to self-determination. In an era of globalization sovereign peoples should be able to arrive at mutually beneficial arrangements to regulate matters of common concern.

This book calmly examines constitutional options other than federalism, given Québec's irrepressible desire for empowerment, options that will benefit English Canada. In so doing, it hopes to make a fresh contribution to a constitutional discourse that has gone stale over the years.

Three Nationalisms in Search of a Future

We believe that the First Nations, the Québécois, and other Canadians can share half a continent and work together towards their mutual fulfillment. Three prerequisites are necessary to achieve this goal. First, the aboriginal peoples should enjoy a maximum degree of autonomy. They must have a real voice in broader questions affecting their well-being and this voice must find institutional expression at the highest levels of government. Second, if the Québécois choose sovereignty, Canadians should respect that choice. A number of studies have shown that sovereignty is an economically viable proposition. Whatever short-term difficulties this course might bring to Québec would undoubtedly also be felt by a majority of Canadians. It is therefore imperative that a mutually beneficial arrangement be worked out between Canada and Québec to minimize instability and disruption in the period following Québec's accession to sovereignty.

This kind of co-operation would pave the way for the creation of long-term co-ordinating mechanisms. The two states could manage broad areas of common interest, such as the environment, trade, and possibly monetary policy, to the mutual benefit of their populations. Such a course would certainly be preferable to a retreat into self-sufficiency or to an obtuse policy of retaliation. What guarantee do we have that Canadians and Québécois will reach a mutually advantageous arrangement when historically this goal has persistently eluded them? For one thing, the constitutional stumbling block, a major impediment to understanding, will have been lifted. Beyond that, there are no guarantees, except for the belief that women and men do not consciously act against their own best interests.

Clearly, the Québécois are far ahead of the Canadians in elaborating the mechanical and technical aspects of such an association. However, the contributors to this volume firmly believe that co-ordination and co-operation between the two states cannot simply be left to the market or to bureaucratic and institutional structures, as suggested by the much-cited European Community model. Over the years, both Canada and Québec have developed a tradition of social solidarity which is now being eroded by the market-driven model of economic development that has become the fashionable nostrum of many governments. It is important to protect this tradition if we wish to avoid the disintegration of the social fabric, so plainly evident in the contemporary society of the

United States. The management of our interdependency must be done in an open and transparent fashion through structures that are subject to public scrutiny and control.

Our vision is light-years away from the one being discussed at the negotiating table and in the media in 1992. It pleads for enlightened self-interest, for mutual respect of cultural diversity on this northern half of the continent, for public empowerment and social justice. It deals with substance and structure, not semantics and cosmetics.

The Building Blocks of Association

Although the thrust of this book is about Québec sovereignty, not all the authors share the same perspective on this issue. They all believe, however, that a fundamental restructuring of Canada that takes into account the three national aspirations is inevitable. Association is presented here not as an abstract notion, but in its economic, social, legal and human dimensions. Throughout, our aim has been to examine the full range of issues Québec, Canada and our aboriginal peoples will have to address in the event they decide to negotiate a new political and economic relationship. The first issue to consider is what association means.

Countries can be associated in a variety of ways and with varying degrees of closeness. Clearly, factors such as markets, culture, history, law and other institutional considerations affect any new power-sharing arrangements. So the first question that this book addresses is conceptual in nature: the need to find the right balance between the sovereign aspirations of two national communities and the minimum kinds of institutional arrangements needed to attain social stability along with high levels of economic well-being for the two parties involved.

At a time of globalization, it is imperative for countries everywhere to learn to manage their interdependence. In the 1990s, the challenge is for nation states to pool their sovereignty and find new techniques to promote co-operation between states. If they do not, sovereignty becomes a prison that forces countries to become inward- rather than outward-looking.

There are many ways to broaden the concept of association and by implication sovereignty. The European Community offers one model. The Canada-U.S. Free Trade Agreement offers another. Association can also be addressed on a sector-by-sector basis; that is, specific arrangements might be negotiated to maintain a common approach to investment and financial institutions. Thus, the first challenge to Québec and Canada is to look at the kinds of association compatible with their different notions of sovereignty and with their different views of economic association.

The first section of this book examines the context of the current crisis and the different policy choices open to the players. In his essay, Daniel Drache explores the political and economic costs of Québec independence without association. Since the relationship between English Canada and Québec is increasingly troubled, English Canada has to prepare itself to take seriously the sovereignty option. Drache then examines what models of association Canada and Québec might want to explore. Roberto Perin explains why the dynamic pushing Québec towards independence is a tangle of political, social, economic and cultural issues. It is a fundamental mistake for English-Canadian commentators to think that the Québec question simply requires a good regional development program or the strengthening of bilingualism. If there is to be an end to the deep antagonism between English Canada and Québec, Canada will have to accept that Québec's "difference" has real and immediate political consequences. Confronting this difference is the only way to defuse the most dangerous and unstable aspects of this situation.

David Bell develops the argument that Canada and Québec have to find alternative ways to realize their national aspirations. Francophones do not want to become second-class citizens any more than anglophones. Each needs a strong national government. Each community wants to be understood. The question for English Canadians is to find new spokespeople to address these concerns. Bell examines the process and dynamics of prenegotiation — what it will take to get to the negotiating table. He shows that the present constitutional crisis is the result of crude deal making among Canada's political élites who have debased the idea of national unity. Building national consensus requires a win-win kind of politics. This is possible only if the prenegotiation process provides a proper framework.

The Mechanics of Power Sharing

The second broad issue addressed in this book is the institutional one. Serious students of Canadian federalism have only recently begun to look at the kinds of institutional arrangements that a sovereign Canada and an independent Québec might need. They will have to address a range of complex legal, technical and institutional matters. For instance, Canada and Québec would have to work out new arrangements with respect to citizenship, the role of the Supreme Court, the Charter of Rights and Freedoms, and the composition of the Senate as well as the House of Commons.

In addition, association has to be premised on a commitment to economic union that guarantees the free flow of goods, services, labour and capital. While the goal is association, negotiations on economic association offer an ideal opportunity for recasting state-market relations. What kind of vision does the current group of politicians bring to such an undertaking? Miriam Smith develops the important point that at the moment there is a common economic agenda underlying both Québec and English-Canadian concerns. Indeed there are striking similarities between the Mulroney-Clark constitutional proposals and the Bourassa-Parizeau vision of power sharing. Both are dominated by a neo-liberal vision of state-market relations.

Reg Whitaker and Philip Resnick take a very tough look at the politics of reassociation. Whitaker rejects the idea that Canada without Québec would disintegrate. His essay refutes the argument that Canada could not survive Québec's departure. On the other hand, Resnick argues that the costs of Québec sovereignty are great and the danger of an emotional backlash, too likely. Reassociation, he believes, would not occur under such conditions. Resnick argues that Canada and Québec would be better off if Québec stayed within a reformed federal system. He advocates a range of other options, including confederal arrangements and asymmetrical federalism, which Ottawa's current proposals wilfully ignore.

The Question of First Nations' Entitlement

The third area to be addressed is the question of aboriginal rights. While many conceive the current crisis as a deeply rooted conflict between Western regional alienation and Québec nationalism, Canada's First Nations are also at the table with their own national aspirations. Any resolution of the present constitutional crisis has to include the recognition of the inherent right of Canada's aboriginal peoples to self-determination. This issue raises many difficult questions for Québec, Ottawa and the provincial premiers. Mary Ellen Turpel and Kent McNeil argue that in the event that Québec declares its independence, legally and morally Québec (and Canada) have fiduciary responsibilities to the aboriginal people. If Canada and Québec are to act in accordance with international law, neither can set aside the rights of Canada's First Nations. This is not a matter that can be dealt with perfunctorily. It raises basic questions of human and political rights. Turpel and McNeil contend that Quebec's and Canada's relations with its First Nations will prove decisive in the international recognition and acceptance of any new Québec state.

The Economic Partnership

Economic issues are addressed next. Economic policy is one of the central questions in any future relationship between Québec and Canada. At the top of the list is the need to negotiate currency and central banking arrangements, a division of the national debt, an exchange rate mechanism, and an appropriate trade as well as tax policy. The range of issues is at once complex, technical and inevitably political.

Indeed, Harold Chorney shows that there are a variety of ways to divide the debt and that no method is unbiased. In their essay, Arthur Donner and Fred Lazar reveal how monetary policy could be shared between Québec and Canada, provided the structure of the central bank is changed. Lazar then analyses the advantages of a common trade policy. Québec and Canada face an unprecedented balance of payments crisis, the result of high interest rates and a high Canadian dollar. In dollar terms, Canada's government deficit is small by comparison. If Canada and Québec ever hope to get off this treadmill, they need an industrial strategy to strengthen the competitiveness of Canadian and Québec industry. This will require a fundamental change in trade policy and particularly in our dealings with Washington. Free trade has not guaranteed Canada and Québec either secure or enhanced access to the United States market. Thus the challenge is for both to formulate a common trade strategy sufficiently strong to eliminate the structural weaknesses of their respective economies.

Our Common Future

The final area of great concern to Canada and Québec is the pressing need to address transnational issues and policies. The protection of the environment, the preservation of minority language rights, the future of the military are some of the issues that transcend national boundaries. Developing a new relationship requires both governments to address these complex social, legal, economic and strategic questions.

In the area of the environment, the issue of regulation is particularly complex because it is the responsibility of many government departments. What are the appropriate kinds of policies and intergovernmental mechanisms needed to ensure that Canada and Québec protect the environment with strong, effective measures? Barbara Rutherford's essay outlines the magnitude of the problem and proposes a variety of measures. In the area of minority language rights, there is an enormous potential for bitter wrangling. Ken McRoberts suggests a plan of action that guarantees minority language rights of francophones in Canada and anglophones in Quebec. Finally, Douglas Bland analyses some options relating to defence co-operation.

Empowering English Canada: A Final Word

The final section of the book is addressed to English Canada. Canada was built on Québec, and it is difficult to imagine its existence without Québec. Yet what does the future hold for this new country? Michael Mandel explores the increasingly anachronistic, but powerful, appeal of constitutional politics. As he reminds us, the legalization of political discourse is nothing less than "politics by another means." He examines the link between the legalized form of politics and its conservative substance. If English Canada is to establish a new arrangement with Québec, it needs to disempower the undemocratic judges who increasingly decide public policy as well as find new, effective instruments for the expression of popular power.

Barbara Cameron also addresses the question of constitutional renewal, but from a very different perspective. She shows that two competing views of Canada's constitutional arrangements now exist. On one side, there is the élite conception and on the other, that of the popular sector as articulated by such broadly based organizations as the Action Canada Network, the National Action Committee on the Status of Women, and the Council of Canadians. She makes the important case that real constitutional renewal for English Canada requires much more than simply amending the current constitution. English Canada needs its own constitution to close the gap between the sociological reality of Canada and the existing structure of Canadian federalism. The only way to escape the current constitutional torpor is to have a constitution that addresses the concerns of democratically minded Canadians. English Canadians see themselves as a national community, but they do not have common national political institutions. It is this absence that Cameron examines.

In conclusion, the signs are everywhere that Canada's political leaders are too timid to negotiate a new constitution acceptable to all Canadians. They will continue to be driven by the short-term political needs of deal making. This is what they do best, even when it is not in our best interests. It is imperative to look beyond the constitutional deal on offer in 1992 in order to see the issues that will become tomorrow's headlines.

The legacy of the Conquest was largely Québec's problem. Now it has become Canada's as well, and English Canadians have become increasingly frustrated with Québec, the so-called "spoiled child" of Confederation. It is time to address this old antagonism and leave behind the excesses of provincialism and the neo-conservative politics of the last decade. The drive for empowerment will stop only when Québec has all the power it needs to protect its collective identity.

I
Getting to the Table

Negotiating with Québec: A New Division of Powers or Secession?

Daniel Drache

The unthinkable may come to pass. The persistent increase in support in Québec for the goal of sovereignty or other options that could lead to Québec's separation from Canada is remarkable. Should the popularity of this option continue to increase, in a very short time Canadians will have to consider new kinds of institutional arrangements for power sharing.

Public Opinion Support for the Sovereignty Option 1960-1991

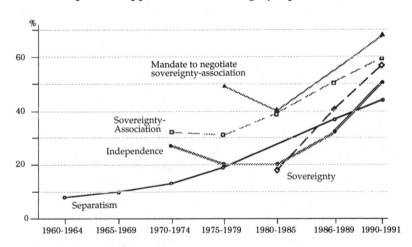

Note: The chart is based on the results derived from 153 public opinion polls. The figures are the average by period and by option.
Source: E. Cloutier, J. Guay, and D. Latouche, *Le Virage. L'évolution de l'opinion publique au Québec depuis 1960*, Montréal: Québec/Amérique, 1992, p. 45. This chart is reproduced by permission of Editions Québec/Amérique.

For the moment, it is unclear exactly what those negotiations will entail. Yet one thing is certain. They will be difficult, because none of the options will be conflict free or cost free. Ignorance, indifference or any sort of prejudice can only make matters worse.[1] If the people of Canada are to avoid bitter and ugly confrontation, English Canadians, Québécois and aboriginal peoples will have to look long and hard at the real choices on offer.

In a world of trading blocs and increased capital mobility, power sharing and sovereignty can no longer be conceived in narrowly traditional terms. The nation state is now more open than ever to the international economy and hence extremely vulnerable to the uncertainties of global markets.[2] Despite these new pressures, it remains the crucial instrument for stabilizing what is left of national economies and for protecting people from the intensely volatile business cycle. Thus, irrespective of the constitutional crisis, Québec and Canada would have had to rethink in a fundamental way the economics of political union. They would have had to redefine the kind of state and society people both need and want. They would have had to decide how they intended to build strong industries, upgrade their work-forces and strengthen their respective international performances.

This requires that Canadians and Québécois have a strong, effective state authority to maintain their respective autonomy against the politically erosive forces of continentalization and global markets.[3]

Paradoxically, in negotiating the Free Trade Agreement with the United States, Ottawa has ceded enormous control of the direction of the economy in the name of enhancing market access. Many Canadians believe that this step is counterproductive and dangerous to the long-term future of Canada.

Despite our willingness to reassess the nature of our relationship with the United States, English Canadians appear unable to rethink the structure of Canadian federalism. Canada's political élites cannot agree on the substantive content of a plan for improving the institutional design of federal-provincial power sharing. Nor can they agree on what measures are needed to modify the division of powers between Ottawa and

Québec. More by default than design, Canada's two national communities are at the point of no return.[4]

For the past thirty years Québec has struggled to find a new place within the federal system.[5] Initially, the response to its grievances seemed positive: Volume 1 of the Royal Commission on Bilingualism and Biculturalism, published in 1967, and the report of the Pepin-Robarts commission, published in 1979, gave important support to Québec as a distinct society and recognized its claim for special status.[6] But since then, the mood has changed dramatically. The public discourse has shifted to individual rights and multiculturalism as the defining elements of Canadian federalism.

The latter development has had far-reaching consequences. Québec is perceived as a spoiler that demands more power and blocks the federal government's efforts to establish "national and universal" programs. Any further devolution of powers to Québec threatens to dilute the central government's capacity to act for the common good.[7] Paradoxically, this is happening at a time when Québec has rapidly developed social, cultural and economic institutions to promote its distinctive character. In the current negotiations, the irony is that Québec is the only player with the clout to challenge the federal constitutional agenda. But it has experienced much difficulty in getting its agenda heard, let alone taken with the seriousness it deserves. One of the reasons is that the other provincial premiers, although they openly challenge Québec's claims to a new political status, exploit Québec's demands to advance their own narrow interests. This has created a constitutional stalemate. Provincialism has clearly become more important than Québec nationalism. The question is whether, in the final analysis, Québec's drive for recognition will be embedded in the constitution or whether Québec will take the next step and embrace full sovereignty.

Québécois have long demonstrated a strong preference for the first option. Recent public opinion polls show that a significant bloc wants to remain in Canada. But the polls also indicate that Québécois want to be part of Canada only if their language, culture and economy can be protected. This requires special powers for the Québec government.[8]

Special Status or Sovereignty: What Will Québec Accept?

It has never been clear to English Canadians just how much power Québec needs or is entitled to.[9] Federalists have never had the courage to answer this question unequivocally and honestly. They have never been able to bend their minds to accept the simple truth: there are no fixed limits nor easy ways to cap Québec's drive for more power inside Canadian federalism. Québec needs all the power it can obtain to protect its language and culture and to develop its economy. François Vaillancourt has provided a lucid explanation of this phenomenon. He shows that the drive for empowerment cannot be static for one essential reason: francophones are much less mobile than anglophones. Francophones are much less likely to leave Québec than anglophones and even the better-educated francophones have very few employment opportunities outside Québec.[10]

Given these factors, no Québec government can accept for very long any significant restrictions on the scale and scope of its activities. Québec governments will always face pressure from francophones because of their restricted mobility. State intervention will always matter and there will be constant pressure on the state to expand its authority. This is why language policy is such a central element to any Québec government policy. Inevitably, the need to safeguard Québec's culture and language quickly spills over into other areas and becomes the economic glue of Québec-based nationalism.

The demand by Québécois that their provincial government take account of these economic consequences of language differences pushes the province towards a single goal: to have full jurisdictional authority over its own social, economic, cultural and development policy. None of these objectives are easy to obtain. Yet Québec governments continue to see the advantage in managing the development of both their human resources and financial capital in an unfettered way. With these powers, Québec society has a fighting chance to survive the pressures of North American integration. Without them, Québec's future is dim indeed.

With respect to human capital, Québec wants unrestricted responsibility for immigration, education, training, health, working conditions, language, labour policy and culture. In the area of capital, Québec seeks full control of both domestic and foreign savings, as well as a greater say in the regulation of its financial institutions and its taxation policies. These new responsibilities would permit it to oversee related jurisdictions equally important to it, such as the environment, agriculture, mining, forestry and fisheries. In the area of general economic policy, the same internal dynamic is at work. Québec will eventually attempt — not by stealth, but by force of circumstance — to gain wider jurisdictional responsibility for law and order, customs, treaties, justice, and monetary and fiscal policy.

In many of these areas, Québec already has acquired significant authority. Indeed, it has been broadening its sphere of activity persistently for over thirty years. But despite these many positive changes, the results have been mixed and the recurring federal-provincial disputes costly. A divided jurisdiction is a perennial breeding ground for all kinds of jurisdictional conflicts that produce policy incoherence rather than encouraging strong, effective legislation.

In the past, the worst effects of these turf wars were mitigated by an aggressive Québec state. It found ways to maximize its bargaining leverage against Ottawa. The ad hoc political reforms of the Quiet Revolution are a case in point. Keynesian demand policies permitted Québec governments to quickly master the technique of "reform by the cucumber principle." This meant that Québec sliced off a little more federal authority for itself each time it needed more power. It worked so long as the changes were not written into the constitution. But Québécois now see that there is something intrinsically wrong with this system of brokerage politics that can never give them what they really need: exclusive jurisdiction in areas that really matter. English Canadians also consider crude deal making counterproductive, but for very different reasons. Reducing the power of the federal government any further has little appeal at a time when all public opinion polls underline that Canadians want a strong, not a weak, national authority. A new division of powers would be a fresh start. It would permit both Québec and Canada to develop policies better suited to the needs of their respective populations.

In practical terms, a new division of power amounts to a massive change in Canada's political system. Federal spending in areas of Québec's exclusive jurisdiction would have to end and, in other areas, be rethought completely. Rethinking the constitutional division of power in this way goes to the heart of the matter. Canada's élites would have to accept that the old ways of running the country no longer suffice and that Québec has to have a status commensurate with its responsibilities for developing its culture, language, economy and nationality.

In theory, this vision makes a great deal of sense. In practical terms, it is not in any way part of Ottawa's constitutional agenda. Canada's political élite are trying to cut a deal on the old way of "doing" politics. The easiest way to meet Québec's demands for more power is to slice federal authority ever more thinly. Canada's power brokers are intent on offering Québec symbolic reform rather than substantive change. Québec will get additional exclusive powers; it will be recognized as a distinct society; and a way will be found symbolically at least to return its lost veto over language and cultural issues.

So far, Bourassa has played his cards with brio and daring. By not being physically at the table, he has persuaded his counterparts to give him Meech Two — an upgraded version of Meech One. If it passes, Bourassa now believes that it is possible to "build a dynamic Québec without destroying Canada." He has stipulated that new federal proposals must contain the substance of the Meech Lake Accord, which recognized Québec as a distinct society; provide for a new federal division of powers; and not reduce in any fundamental way Québec's existing powers.[11]

The problem with these kinds of compromises is that they are not a plan of action inspiring confidence. Piecemeal reform does not satisfy, in any permanent sense, Québec's drive for empowerment. Is it not time to face reality? State authority cannot be artificially delimited, but rather needs to be strengthened, especially in this era of globalization of markets and interdependence. This is what Québec wants and needs, but will not obtain within the present process. It will not acquire the exclusive authority it is seeking.[12] It cannot expect the federal government to develop either better policies to suit Québec's needs or a new constitution when Ottawa's median voter is a unilingual anglophone.[13] Sooner or later, English Canadians will have to confront the fact that Canadian federalism has limits and that, however flexible it is and has been, it has reached its breaking point.[14] What, then, is the alternative?

The first alternative for pragmatically minded Québécois is a powerful Québec unconstrained by constitutional arrangements appropriate to another age. If the first option fails to materialize, then a majority of Québécois will likely want to enter the next century as members of a sovereign nation state. Sociologists now estimate that approximately 40 percent of Québécois are hardcore indépendantistes. (See Graph 1.) Despite all the predictions about their pending demise, they have not abandoned their dream. Indépendantistes remain the alternative political force in Québec. So long as they see that Québec is not treated with the respect it deserves, they will always be an inch closer to achieving their goal. If English Canada hands Québec another humiliating provocation, this will sweep them into power. But this too comes with its own costs and uncertainties.[15]

Sovereignists are further ahead in working out the structures and institutions of power sharing than their English-Canadian counterparts. They have been thinking about the unthinkable for the past twenty years. In the event of Québec's independence, the question English Canadians must face is: Can there be a basis for a new form of association? After all, we are bound to each other by markets, history and social custom. Canada and Québec share a common economic space. We have economies that are highly integrated. We bear joint responsibility for aboriginal rights, the environment and social policy, and have a common trade policy. We also share the continent with the United States. Assuming that any act of reassociation will be limited by Canada's and Québec's distinct market structures, by law, by subjective factors and by a multitude of other institutional influences, it is possible to believe that there is a range of options.[16] In reality, there are only two: either Québec and Canada can choose not to have any formal political association and each can decide to go its separate way, or they can find new ways to manage their interdependence and to pool what remains of their sovereignty.

Much has been written about the first of these two post-independence scenarios and a great deal of it is not well informed, accurate or well intentioned.[17] It is meant to send a chilling message to Québécois: if they choose sovereignty, they will lose everything from peanut butter to toilet paper.[18] Much less is known about the second option. This is a mistake. English Canada needs to be better informed to see what is possible and indeed desirable. While each choice is a distinct possibility, there is a world of difference between the two.

Autarky or Interdependence?

Consider the first option. If Québec chooses to be sovereign, English Canada may reject the idea of what one writer has called "squaring politics and principles."[19] It may decide that a new relationship would give Québec too much control over future decision making. In those circumstances, Québec and Canada can pretend that the other does not exist. This would amount to a retreat into a form of autarky or economic self-sufficiency. It would require a giant effort on the part of Québécois and Canadians to disassemble the dense network of commercial, personal, social and community ties.

In these circumstances, Canada and Québec would effectively be cutting the bonds of a common history and shared experience. There would be minimal co-operation and co-ordination between governments. Without this co-operation, they would not be able to manage their interlinked economies either efficiently or coherently. Many of the economic difficulties that have plagued Canada's economic union would intensify. Each party would eventually resort to erecting non-tariff barriers to protect its markets and strategic interests.[20] There would be less government co-ordination in such key areas as investment, taxation and labour-market policy.

This beggar-thy-neighbour policy is the worst-case scenario. It is premised on Canada's punishing Québec for the breakup of the country. It makes for bad economics and, even worse, it makes no long-term political sense.

Cutting Québec's links to Canada's markets would increase the costs of disassociation. Companies would be faced with a high degree of uncertainty and instability. In such an atmosphere, many of the key economic decisions made outside of

Canada and Québec would have a negative impact on local economies. Many U.S. corporations operating in Canada would be reluctant to spend new monies on research and development or expand production facilities. In such circumstances, Québec has at least one critical advantage. It has the highest degree of local control of its corporate structure of any Canadian province. Almost 70 percent of corporate revenues come from locally controlled firms.[21] Even then, Québec's economy would not escape unscathed from a trade war. But neither would Canada's industries. Everyone's livelihood would be disrupted by the erection of obstacles to integration. In the end only the United States would benefit. It would emerge as the dominant player, with Canada and Québec being forced to adopt U.S. tax, spending or other regulatory policies.

The second option is association. It assumes that sovereignty has to be pooled in a time of global markets and growing economic interdependency. This means that Québec and Canada have to negotiate a new way to reassociate and manage what they share in common. The most likely model assumes a two-tier federalism. Québec would be a nation state with full powers. Its National Assembly would have full taxation and legislative authority; the Québec Supreme Court would be Québec's final court; and it would have its own constitution.[22] But in other key jurisdictions, powers would be shared with Canada. There would be a common market; a new union would be premised on a commitment to building a strong economic association. There would have to be a number of powerful intergovernmental institutions to co-ordinate the union and to address a range of critical cross-border issues such as the environment, aboriginal entitlement, foreign investment and Canada-Québec-U.S. trade, all of which transcend the national jurisdictions of Québec and Canada.

On a range of issues such as fiscal policy, the environment, social policy and trade, the two levels of government have many common interests. If Canada and Québec expect to maximize the benefits of economic union, there will have to be more, not less, co-operation and co-ordination between governments than now exists. The need for governments to harmonize their efforts extends not only to economic questions but equally to a range of complex social issues that transcend narrow jurisdictional boundaries. These too would have to be managed more coherently. A new kind of power-sharing arrangement is premised on three conditions: first, each party has a stake in seeing that the process succeeds; second, the parties share enough in common to have a decision-making process that is effective and efficient; third, they have a sufficiently high level of economic integration to make policy coordination more attractive than non-cooperation.[23] Without the third element, the process would probably break down. With it, Québec and Canada stand at least an even chance of forging a new relationship. Still, Québec and Canada would also need to create a political forum where political decisions can be taken and policies co-ordinated with respect to stability, equity and growth.[24] There are at least six major socio-economic priorities to address:

- Stabilization. Monetary and spending decisions are crucial for ensuring the stabilization of the economy. If Canada and Québec share a common currency and one central bank, and recognize each other's investors and depositors as residents, financial stability is ensured. But, should standards diverge and policies conflict, a single financial area would be in jeopardy. Much attention has to be given the kinds of new institutional arrangements that would accommodate the twin goals of sovereignty and association. What would be the minimum necessary institutional mechanisms to ensure stable power-sharing arrangements?
- Distribution. With governments spending less, steps are needed to safeguard existing programs. Will the new arrangements continue to equalize opportunities for Canadians and Québécois? How can existing distributive mechanisms (unemployment insurance, the Canada Assistance Plan, regional development, satisfaction of the First Nations' claims to the land and resources) be strengthened in both communities?
- Equity. Policies are needed to deal with the challenge as well as the threat of the globalization of markets and the internationalization of production. How will common social standards be maintained and improved? How will Canada and Québec deal with the new strains and frictions of negotiations

to reach a new arrangement? What new policies are needed to protect Canadians from the uncertainty of global markets?

- Growth. A critical component of Québec's and Canada's cultural identity is social solidarity. To maintain this social solidarity requires a high level of economic activity. The new association will have to find ways to enhance growth prospects. What kinds of measures and initiatives will be needed to increase Canada's and Québec's leverage in negotiating with the United States and other trading blocs?

- Harmonization of regulatory norms. In an increasingly interdependent world, Canada and Québec have to develop tough and effective measures to protect the environment. The public expects strong leadership from the national government but, under present arrangements, environmental issues fall under provincial jurisdiction. The Canada Environmental Act is intended to set new, tougher environmental standards. Québec's geographic location makes it particularly vulnerable to air and water flows down the St. Lawrence that carry toxins and other dangerous pollutants. How can co-ordination be improved on environmental issues? What new statutory authority do Québec and Canada require in order to legislate tougher and more comprehensive environmental standards?

- Competitiveness. New competitive pressures are forcing all countries to produce more with less. There is pressure to compete on costs. This necessarily involves a smaller workforce, fewer producers and leaner industries. The successful countries will be those that mobilize their resources, retrain their work-forces and restructure their industries by strategic planning. They will also understand that the management of markets and investment decisions is too important to be left to the private sector. Markets have to be regulated and the behaviour of multinational corporations has to be subject to effective public scrutiny. How will these kinds of regulatory norms be established in new power-sharing arrangements between Canada and Québec?

The Politics of Spite versus the Politics of Solidarity[25]

There is nothing at the present time that helps us predict whether, when the crunch comes, English Canada and Québec will choose autarky or interdependence. The most recent poll by the Centre de Recherches en Opinion Publique (CROP) confirmed that even Québécois who are in favour of sovereignty want to continue their association with Canada. If Québec were to separate, it found, 45 percent think that Québec would be defended by the Canadian army, 44 percent believe that Québec would use the Canadian dollar, and an equal number think that Québec citizens would remain Canadian citizens.[26] This confirms that, culturally and politically, the glue for continued association is there for Québécois. But it may not be anywhere near as strong in English Canada.

Elite opinion in English Canada will matter in any future negotiations with a sovereign Québec. The federal government has already built strong ties with many of the largest and most powerful Québec firms. It has pursued a strategy of reinforcing its links with the business community there. In particular, it has used procurement contracts to guarantee it the frontline political support of such Québec giants as Bombardier, Marconi Canada, Pratt and Whitney Canada, CAE Electronic Systems, Bendix, Matrox Electronic Systems, Heroux Inc., Canadair, Bell Canada and Photo Lambert Ltd. These top ten suppliers to the federal government accounted for nearly $850 million in 1987/88 or, 54 percent of all federal procurement contracts in that province.[27] That Ottawa has consciously decided to work with a small but powerful group of companies explains why corporate Canada favours renewed federalism. But it does not predict what corporate Canada would do faced with long and painful negotiations. Would it prefer economic stability over the politics of spite? Business does not want its profits endangered nor the incomes of Canadians and Québécois threatened. Thus it has to keep its bottom line open and flexible. Behind its emotional rhetoric, would it see that economic union is preferable to no federal arrangements at all?

The role of the media will also be critical in shaping the future of Québec-Canada relations. If the media think that there is sufficient public support for economic association with Québec, then they will accept to build on this foundation. If not, and if the press is vicious and partisan, it could poison any possibility for the future success of negotiations.

Regional discontent is another factor that threatens to derail the whole process, should provincial politicians decide to roll the dice for their immediate electoral advantage. But is any premier prepared to go to the wall against Québec? Ontario and Alberta indeed have radically opposed views. It costs Alberta little to play hardball with Québec. But to refuse outright any future association with Québec would be a luxury that Ontario's already battered industries could ill afford.

If the process is an open one, a political consensus could be reached. Canadians pride themselves on their pragmatism, their sense of fair play and their willingness to compromise in politics. But as David Bell argues in this volume, Canada's federal governments have also recently developed in their dealing with Québec a taste for confrontation, political blackmail and, in extreme circumstances, armed intervention. Time will supply answers to these and other disturbing questions about the ability of Canada's political culture to accommodate change. In the meantime, we have to find new ways to reconceptualize power sharing between Québec and Canada in order to find ways to strengthen rather than undermine social solidarity.

The now defunct Economic Council of Canada, in a careful assessment of Canada's constitutional options, suggested a starting point. In an era when economic activity increasingly transcends national boundaries, economic well-being depends on reducing barriers between states. Any attempt to reverse this trend immediately creates huge problems and inflicts heavy costs on governments, on businesses and on people. The Council found that it would be a fundamental mistake for every province to try to provide its own social and regulatory programs. The duplication of programs and services imposes an intolerable burden on the Canadian taxpayer. Canadians need a blueprint that will tell them how they have to adapt their existing institutions to meet future needs: which will have to be scrapped and which new ones created.

Devising new power-sharing arrangements between Québec and Canada could be a powerful force for constructive change. This process is premised on the idea of not only maintaining existing east-west linkages but strengthening and deepening them. Despite the harmful effects of free trade, there is a solid base to build on. For the moment at least, "in all provinces, the local market remains by far the most important."[28] In 1984, roughly two-thirds of gross output in each province was sold in local markets. Significantly, the Economic Council of Canada found that in all provinces, interprovincial trade (19.3 percent) was more important than international trade (17.5 percent) as a proportion of gross output (the broadest measure for assessing the relative weight of domestic and foreign markets). It further estimated that interprovincial trade accounted for about 2 million direct jobs.

Yet the allure of increasing external trade is never a sufficient basis for economic union. The flow of goods and services Canada-wide also reveals important and increasingly sharp differences between the provinces. First, export markets have become more central for almost all provinces. This has brought new pressures and strains on Confederation. Second, Québec and Ontario remain bound to each other by interprovincial trade even if the United States is now a larger market for both Québec and Ontario manufacturers. Combined trade between the two amounted to about $23 billion. In dollar and volume terms, each is about equally dependent on the other, but Québec is more dependent on the Ontario market than Ontario manufacturers are on the Québec market. Ontario has a very small trade surplus (less than 1 percent) in manufacturing with Québec.[29]

These economic linkages serve as an important corrective to the idea that Canada lives by exports alone, even if in recent times exports have continued to grow faster than interprovincial trade. What should never be forgotten is that interprovincial trade is of critical importance to local manufacturers. The volume of interprovincial trade, at nearly 18 percent of GDP, is in fact much higher in Canada than within the European Community, at 13 percent, or the European Free Trade Area, at 4 percent. Given this fundamental difference, how can it best be used to advantage?

What is apparent is that a way has to be found to make the political and the economic sectors work together rather than against each other. To date, economists have not shed a great deal of light on how this could happen. Rather, Canada's economics profession has in large part focused narrowly on costing the breakup of Canada — thinly disguised as an exercise in deterrence. They have adopted a Solomon's sword approach in discussing the division of the national debt, the future of the army and other similar economic issues. As Harold Chorney details in his contribution to this volume, the methodology is as simple as it is unreliable. Common assets and liabilities are calculated and divided proportionately between Canada and Québec. But when dealing with complex social and legal arrangements, social and political questions can never be reduced to a simple spread-sheet method. Clearly, a more substantive and comprehensive approach is in order. Any kind of new power sharing between Québec and Canada has to start from a different set of premises for designing a new relationship. Very different visions of policy co-ordination, market power and sovereignty have to be reconciled. Here too there is a range of models to choose from.

The simplest form of economic union takes its inspiration from a regime of free trade. This option does not require very much institutional innovation for either Canada or Québec. Essentially, Canada and Québec would have to negotiate a comprehensive agreement to manage their economic association. They would need to take measures to create a common market. Parliament would co-ordinate the union. This option holds out the promise of safeguarding the independence of the parties while promoting greater interdependency and access to each other's markets. The current free trade agreement is a case in point. It is premised on a comprehensive negotiated agreement that lays out the norms and rules of economic association. Among other things, the agreement creates new regulatory norms for governments; establishes a new relationship between the private and public; and empowers business by making it easier to invest and close up shop with minimal government restrictions.[30]

The chronic weakness of the free trade model is that it leaves everything to the market and has little sophisticated understanding of harmonizing and co-ordinating the policies of the contracting parties, namely the two governments involved. It has no provision for intergovernmental co-ordination or even for a powerful group of administrators to implement, monitor and enforce the agreement. Finally, it underestimates the problem of adjustment. Instead, it requires a huge leap of faith to implement and a blind faith in the efficiency and self-organizing capability of markets.

A second concept of economic association is patterned after the European Community (EC) notion of supranationality. On the surface, this is a powerfully suggestive and attractive model for Québec and Canada. They already have a high level of economic integration; they share common institutions and have acquired much experience — both bad and good — in intergovernmental co-operation. Premier Bourassa believes that the EC has much to teach us in this regard. It could serve as a model for a new political superstructure, one that offers a clear alternative to Canada's system of executive-style federalism.

But it is not clear that Bourassa's concept of economic union, with Québec as the *"état français dans le marché commun canadien,"* has very much in common with the political dynamic behind European integration.[31] This model requires that the governments involved create a powerful set of institutions to co-ordinate and harmonize all aspects of community policy, such as banking, the environment, energy and social policy. It needs a powerful bureaucracy with real power to override narrow national interest and a supreme court whose decisions have a higher authority than national courts. It requires the adoption of a common currency and a central bank, as well as an elected parliament. These institutions do more than balance the opposing needs of supranationality and respect for national sovereignty. Their principal task is to co-ordinate a complex set of governmental, private-sector and local institutions towards a common goal of political and economic integration.

A final proposal is something much more simple. It does not require something as ambitious as the EC model or so crudely inadequate as the free trade option. Given Canada's recent disaster in attempting to negotiate a comprehensive agreement with the United States, there is much to be said in favour of a sector approach. It minimizes the need for concessions between two asymmetrical partners. Power sharing could be decided on a case-by-case basis or in sector-by-sector negotiations. This would be the least disruptive scenario. Rather than running the risk of a great deal of dislocation by reconstructing Canadian federalism anew, this model minimizes the need for wholesale change. Québec and Canada would attempt to minimize regulatory and supervisory conflict and duplication by finding ways to use existing structures. They would still need common institutions like a reformed bank. They would adopt the principle of mutual recognition of each other's regulatory norms and, wherever possible, continue to share existing institutional arrangements. For instance, in the case of financial markets, Québec's central bank would establish a working relationship with the Canadian payments clearing system in order to minimize costs and avoid harmful delays. The major challenge here would be to find a way to reconcile Canada's and Québec's needs within a common financial market. But if Canada and Québec adopted markedly different regulatory standards, a system of mutual recognition would break down.[32]

Negotiating with a sovereign Québec does not require a leap of faith as much as a view of what can be. No one model can supply all the answers. At a minimum, Canada and Québec need to have an economic union that minimizes trade and other barriers between the two. It also has to provide for the necessary institutional arrangements for intergovernmental co-ordination in order to find ways to pool their sovereignty. Finally, it has to see the virtues of a sector-by-sector approach to minimize the costs and disruption of new power-sharing arrangements. New political institutions will also be required to ensure full accountability.

In the past few years, English Canadians have either avoided the issue of the relationship between Canada and a sovereign Québec or invented scenarios of confrontation and violence. The aim today for Canadians, Québécois and aboriginal peoples is to find ways to be innovative, practical and lucid in inventing a new relationship. This will not only require each community to re-examine many of its preconceived ideas about the other communities, but also its ideas about what is possible and indeed necessary for political empowerment. All parties will be forced to make concessions and take risks. When a country has a full-blown constitutional crisis, it does not have the luxury of accepting inaction and drift as the best or indeed the only strategy.

Answering the Québec Question: Two Centuries of Equivocation

Roberto Perin

There is an alarming inability in English Canada to come to grips with the Québec question.[1] For the past thirty years, constitutional discussions have met with impatience, weariness and rejection. Generally, people have failed to understand the nature of Québec's demands and how these relate to the process of constitutional reform. Accusations that Québec wants to be above the law or is demanding more than its fair share, and depictions of Québec as the spoiled brat of Confederation, are still heard today, as they were more than a century ago. The failure to understand the nature of the Québec question has deep roots. Consequently, it is important to turn to the past, not to dredge up old animosities or awaken new ones, but to get a full appreciation of this complex and vital issue. The historical record contextualizes a problem. It goes beyond a random snapshot of reality and provides breadth and depth. History helps us to appreciate the thread that ties Québec's present demands to a history of struggle for survival and affirmation.

The Origins of the Québec Question

The Treaty of Paris, which officially ceded Québec to the British in 1763, made no concessions to the cultural uniqueness of the *Canadiens*, as they were then called. The exigencies of in-

The author wishes to thank Matteo Sanfilippo who provided critical insights into this paper.

ternational politics, specifically the threat that Britain perceived to her security from the American and French revolutions, altered this policy somewhat. But the hope that Québec would be made "thoroughly British" never really faded. The British and American immigrants who came to the colony in the aftermath of the Conquest were the embodiment of this hope. They fiercely resisted recognition of the *Canadiens'* linguistic, legal, religious and political rights, claiming that Québec was their own country and that its bountiful resources belonged to them. Although the British minority never constituted more than one-quarter of the population, they clearly believed that they alone were fit to govern. At the very beginning of the nineteenth century, an editorial described *Canadien* political leaders as "petty politicians; who are as much fitted to direct the measures of a commercial and enterprising people, as a church beadle is to be Chancellor of the Exchequer."[2] (The depiction of Québec as a priest-ridden society has a long history!) Not all British Quebecers shared these views. Some were more conciliatory. But in the highly charged and politically polarized atmosphere created by the Constitutional Act of 1791, they were the exception rather than the rule. In any event, the outcome of the Uprisings of 1837–8 left no doubt as to who was the boss in Québec.

The political élite in both of Britain's parties firmly believed that Québec, being the sole British entry point into North America, could never be left in the hands of a "foreign" (that is indigenous) majority. And yet these "foreigners" had formally been deemed British subjects since 1763. After crushing the Uprisings, London resolved that it would never again allow the *Canadiens* to threaten its interests in North America. Union with Upper Canada, the option long advanced by the anti-*Canadien* British merchants of Québec, became official policy: the *Canadiens* would be turned into a minority and eventually assimilated. This policy was elegantly given intellectual justification by Lord Durham. He magnanimously sought to "elevate" the backward, priest-ridden peasants of Québec to a thoroughly British character to help them compete with their more enterprising neighbours.

But the Union did not produce the expected results. Because English-Canadian members of the Assembly were politically divided between Tories and Reformers, their French-Canadian colleagues managed to secure a degree of political power. In the heady days of the 1850s, they even managed on a few occasions to impose their will on a majority of English-Canadian members. But one swallow does not make a summer. The real motor of political change was located in the prosperous farming communities of south-western Ontario, which found a dynamic representative in George Brown.

The Goal to Assimilate French Canadians

Brown, who was the leader of the Reform Party, associated the French Canadians with everything that was wrong with the Union: corruption, Church domination, ignorance, stagnation. He wanted desperately to change the constitution. When Confederation, of which Brown can justly be considered the chief architect, was finally approved, he exulted: "French Canadianism [is] entirely extinguished."[3] Brown's idea was to contain "French Canadianism" to the province of Québec; in other words, to ghettoize and tribalize the French Canadians. This would allow the British element to get on with the business of building and running a continental nation. Although Brown later suggested that the settlement of the West would be accomplished by the French and the English working together, his terms for French-Canadian immigration to the Prairies were clear.[4] Once they left Québec, French Canadians could not claim such privileges as Catholic schools and the public use of their language. Otherwise, what would be the point of Confederation? French Canadianism, which the new constitution so successfully contained, would again wreak havoc on the nation.

In the fifty years after Confederation, Brown's plan was fully realized. Canada outside Québec became thoroughly British, both internally and internationally. The linguistic and religious rights of French-Canadian minorities were suppressed in most provinces, while overseas, Canadians professed their British personality in the Boer War and through the heavy human sacrifice of the First World War. The French Canadians came to enjoy only a shadow of the political power which they so proudly flaunted in the 1850s.

It is true that throughout the post-Confederation period, French-Canadian political leaders were prominent in the af-

fairs of state and French Canadians were an essential component of any government in Ottawa. But it is equally true that
their political representation did not carry the weight that
George-Étienne Cartier had imagined in an earlier period.
John A. Macdonald, much praised by political historians for
his tolerance and pragmatism, when confronted with the unanimity of English-Canadian opinion over Riel's hanging ignored the representations of his Québec ministers and
dismissed the powerful French-Canadian reaction as a "brush
fire."[5] Wilfrid Laurier, for his part, condescendingly rejected
French-Canadian opposition to Canada's participation in the
Boer War. "The Province of Québec," he averred, "has no
opinions, but only sentiments."[6] To paraphrase Macdonald,
then, French Canadians were treated generously, as a nation,
when they were needed to cobble together political alliances,
but increasingly, as a faction when English Canadians expressed their political will about Canada's British character. If
French Canadians governed, they did so on the majority's
terms.

Confederation did create an institutional political structure,
the province of Québec, that French Canadians theoretically —
at least — controlled. Never one to minimize events in which
he was a leading participant, Cartier presented this achievement as if it were the triumph of Papineau's struggles for
national sovereignty. His newspaper, *La Minerve*, heralded the
triumph of Confederation in these terms:

> The new constitution recognizes the French Canadians
> as a distinct and separate nationality. We constitute a
> state within a state. We enjoy the full exercise of our rights
> and the formal recognition of our national independence
> … We have in the hands of our administrators all that is
> most dear and precious to us, and we must profit from
> our own good fortune.[7]

The Limits of Political Power

The British North America Act neither implicitly nor explicitly
recognized the existence of a separate and distinct nationality
within the Canadian federation. Linguistic and religious rights
were limited and, taken together, they did not necessarily des-

ignate a particular national group. There were, for example, Catholics who were not French Canadian. Québec, for its part, was given no more powers than any other province. Its special needs were expected to be met through the general provisions of article 92 of the constitution, which enumerated the items under provincial jurisdiction. In other words, its distinctiveness was hidden in clauses that applied equally to all the provinces. In short, *La Minerve* may have told French Canadians what they wanted to hear, but its interpretation of the BNA Act was not reflected in the text.

In addition, as a principal author of the constitution, Cartier well knew that there were real constraints on the powers of the Québec legislature, that is on the will of the French-Canadian majority. Both formal and informal, these were designed to safeguard the interests of the Anglo-Protestant élite. Since the crushing of the Uprisings just thirty years earlier, French Canadians understood that in order to exercise political power, they had to promote the economic prerogatives of this élite. Leaving nothing to chance, the business class insisted on specific constitutional guarantees. It matters little whether some of these safeguards were in fact exercised. What is significant here is that Cartier not only knew about them, but probably framed them himself.

What were these guarantees? Under the BNA Act, Ottawa had the consitutional authority to disallow or reserve provincial legislation considered to be against the national interest. The lieutenant-governor, appointed to all intents and purposes by the prime minister, was supposed to be Ottawa's watchdog in the provincial capital. So was the Québec Upper House, whose members were named by the lieutenant-governor. The Legislative Council had the power to veto bills passed by the Assembly and informally was expected to safeguard the interests of the Anglo-Protestant minority. The right initially exercised by legislators to run concurrently for seats in the Provincial Assembly and the House of Commons ensured that federal parties exercised a tutelage over their provincial junior partners. In effect, the first Québec cabinets were the creatures of Cartier, the political boss of the federal Conservative Party.

Specific guarantees were entrenched in the constitution to protect the rights of the Québec English-speaking minority. The boundaries of the counties where they formed a majority could not be altered, except by amendment to the BNA Act. Anglo-Protestants had their educational rights guaranteed in the constitution — and as if this was not enough, they provoked a political crisis to secure institutional autonomy and lavish funding for their schools. In this regard, leading French-Canadian politicians danced to the minority's tune to the point of short-changing the majority's schools.

Consequently, while the constitution explicitly and implicitly recognized the minority's rights, nowhere did it acknowledge the cultural distinctiveness of the only French-Canadian province, nor the idea that Canada was made up of two dominant cultures.

Little wonder, then, that the writings of French-Canadian nationalists betrayed a suspicion of the state. In a very influential essay written just prior to the Quiet Revolution, historian Michel Brunet deplored the fact that, unlike other North Americans, French Canadians had rejected the state as an instrument for the promotion of their collective well-being. According to Brunet, a deeply rooted anti-statist bias inherent in French Canadian thought was responsible for this behaviour.[8] And yet in a state so hemmed in by Anglo-Protestant power, was it not necessary to look to other, parallel structures to secure the autonomous development of French Canadian society and culture?

The Church as a Vehicle of French-Canadian Power

The one institution that French Canadians controlled, the Church, offered several advantages in this respect. Whatever opinion they may have had about its role elsewhere, the political and economic élite in Britain and Canada valued its socially and politically stabilizing influence in Québec. As a result, it could pursue unhindered its development in the province. In addition, as an international institution, the Church had the financial and human resources to meet the new challenges confronting French-Canadian culture in the Union period. Since the elements of this culture — a distinct religion, language and legal system — had a weak institutional expression prior to the Uprisings of 1837–38, they were sustained by the political struggle for popular sovereignty. Papineau's defeat placed French-Canadian culture in grave danger, which was compounded by the subsequent expansion of English-Canadian demographic and economic power. In this crucial context, French-Canadian culture had to develop a solid institutional base or disappear. The Catholic Church met this challenge admirably.[9]

From the 1840s to the Second World War, establishments spanning a wide range of social activities were founded under the aegis of the Church. Educational and social-welfare institutions readily come to mind here. In many countries, these relied heavily or depended directly upon the state. In Québec, they were largely self-supporting and staffed by male and especially female religious communities. In many jurisdictions, Catholic institutions were private, and supplemented those of the state; in Québec, Catholic institutions were the public ones. The Church was also heavily involved in the promotion of popular forms of economic life: co-operatives, credit unions, farmers' and workers' unions, professional associations. Without its strategic human, moral, intellectual and even financial support, one might well wonder where such strong associations as the Mouvement Desjardins, the Confédération des syndicats nationaux, the Centrale des enseignants du Québec, or the Union des producteurs agricoles would be. In a number of other countries, these organizations would from their inception have had close connections with political parties and, consequently, an indirect relation to the state. In Québec they developed independently of political and state institutions. In the century after the Union, French-Canadian society evolved largely outside state structures through an institution that was entirely under French-Canadian control. Contemporary observers may lament the obsession of Catholic ultramontane theoreticians with the dangers of state intervention, but these thinkers knew what Cartier would not publicly admit: the state masked the power of the Anglo-Protestant élite. The distinct society that we know today was primarily the creation, not of the state, but of the Church. To their credit, the ultramontane thinkers provided intellectual justification for a movement that led to the consolidation and expansion of French-Canadian culture.

Although the constitution did not recognize the existence of a separate and distinct French-Canadian nationality, it did provide Québec with enough autonomy to carry out this process of consolidation and expansion. The BNA Act was, after all, the product of a largely rural, politically decentralized society. But in the twentieth century, the constitution became increasingly inadequate to respond to the mood of an industrial and urban Canada. The economic crisis of the 1930s shockingly revealed these inadequacies.

During the twenties and thirties, emerging social forces began to demand greater state involvement in the socio-economic life of Canada. The League for Social Reconstruction and the Co-operative Commonwealth Federation (CCF) were in the forefront of this struggle in English Canada. Basically, they advocated a constitutional revolution by demanding that Ottawa actively regulate the more inequitable aspects of the market economy and generously provide for the more vulnerable members of society. But these social democrats did not seem to be aware that their program challenged the very bases of French Canada's autonomy. By calling for social welfare to be placed under federal jurisdiction, they opened the door to Ottawa's intervention in the finance and administration of Church-run establishments. In other words, English Canadians would exert control over autonomous French-Canadian institutions. Furthermore, the regulation of the economy and the nationalization of some of its sectors would undoubtedly lead to the enormous expansion of the state apparatus in Ottawa where French Canadians, despite boisterous public campaigns to increase their numbers, were badly underrepresented and at times excluded.

The truth is that the social democrats of this era were no more attuned to the contemporary realities of Québec than were the progressives of the last century. They persisted in seeing French Canadians as a minority group defined by such "private" elements as language and religion, rather than as a national community possessing a wide range of institutions that gave it a fully public character. Minority rights and a certain degree of bilingualism, while acknowledged by some, were clearly peripheral to the social-democratic outlook. At the founding convention of the CCF, the most Frank Scott could say about minority rights was: "There is no reason why we might not come out with a bilingual currency in this country."[10] The fact that he couched his modest proposal in the negative undoubtedly reflected the degree to which his audience was prepared to accept it. Meanwhile, the CCF repeated the organizational errors made earlier by the trade union movement in Québec. Organizers, promotional literature, and meetings were in English only. Constituency organizations were firmly in English-Canadian hands and requests to create French-Canadian structures were firmly rejected.[11]

While some members of the League for Social Reconstruction lived and worked in Montréal, their understanding of the Québec of the 1930s was lamentable. Their perspective never transcended the Anglo-Protestant culture from which they came. The *Canadian Forum*, for example, presented Québec as corrupt, Church-ridden, authoritarian, anti-modern, parochial and xenophobic. Fascism was often on the lips of English-Canadian commentators as they described Québec nationalist movements.[12] Events in Québec, such as the rise of new political forces, popular outbursts of nationalism, expressions of anti-semitism, and anti-communism, were invariably likened to those in Europe, while those occurring in the rest of the continent were not. These views received confirmation from American social scientists working at McGill University in the 1930s. Sociologists Everett Hughes and Horace Miner depicted Québec as a folk society characterized by the parish and the family. In the absence of a lay social leadership, they affirmed, the clergy assumed the direction of Quebec society. The resulting domination of traditional values ensured that French Canadians would have a great deal of difficulty adapting to the exigencies of the modern world.[13]

But, although he spoke French, Everett Hughes remained cut off from the milieu he was studying. He did not establish meaningful links with French-Canadian academics, nor was he able to recruit French-Canadian students to conduct field research. Is it surprising, then, that his findings should be so out of touch with reality?

Despite these perceptions, Québec was not standing still. The 1921 census indicated that more than half of its inhabitants were city-dwellers and that the non-agricultural work-force slightly outnumbered the agricultural one. These shifts placed enormous strains on Québec's Church-dominated institutions.

The nationalist movement was slowly coming to terms with these changes. At the end of the nineteenth century, Jules-Paul Tardivel had added the concept of territoriality to French-Canadian nationalism. French Canadians, he intimated, could not inhabit a cosmic space for long. They would soon need a territory to define their reality. He failed, however, to define the geography of the new "Laurentian" state. Later, thinkers such as Errol Bouchette, Olivar Asselin, and especially Lionel Groulx increasingly spoke of the state, that is the government of this territory, as the agent for promoting French-Canadian interests. This vision harkened back to the ideal enunciated in *La Minerve*'s Confederation editorial, but it was also an abandonment of the tacit understanding reached in 1867 between the French-Canadian politicians and the Anglo-Protestant élite.

This intellectual ferment culminated in the 1930s in the *programme de restauration sociale* and the founding of a new political party, the Action libérale nationale (ALN). Like their English-Canadian counterparts, French Canadian progressives were coming to terms with the realities of large-scale industrialization and urbanization. They called for state intervention, including nationalization, to regulate monopoly capitalism and social welfare measures to assist the weakest segments of the population. As Joseph Levitt and Gregory Baum have pointed out, the similarities between the ALN and the CCF were striking.[14] But the difference was that English-Canadian progressives looked to Ottawa as their national government, while their French-Canadian colleagues turned to Québec. What resulted was a *dialogue de sourds* whose repercussions are very much with us today. The fact that the progressive movements in Québec and Canada are still divided along cultural lines is a direct legacy of the 1930s. The ultimate responsibility for their tragic inability to work together must rest with the English Canadians. They made no attempt to conciliate the need for state intervention with the autonomy of French-Canadian society. While French-Canadian intellectuals were perhaps no more mindful of the needs of English-Canadian society, at least their platform did not threaten the foundations of that society. Whereas George Brown had sought to ghettoize French Canada, now in the name of social equity, English-Canadian social democrats were not even prepared to tolerate a ghetto. They called for centralization and uniformity.

A National Government for Whom?

In any event, English-Canadian social democrats and nationalists would soon see the triumph of their program. The Report of the Royal Commission on Dominion-Provincial Relations[15] became their charter. Ottawa's unlimited power to spend as the instrument to ensure uniform levels of social services throughout the country became their doctrine. At last, English-Canadian progressives thought, the federal government would behave as national governments should. Released in 1939, the report justified massive federal involvement in areas traditionally regarded as provincial responsibilities. In the name of Keynes, the constitutional revolution was about to begin. The exigencies of war made it easier to implement a decisive and massive policy of centralization, which extended to economic planning, taxation and social policy. In the post-war era, Ottawa expanded its involvement to the fields of culture and the arts, higher education and research, housing, health and social security.

If French Canadians had any doubts about whose interests the "national" government in Ottawa promoted, the second conscription crisis soon disabused them. As well, Québec workers affiliated to Catholic unions also discovered during this period that the Ottawa bureaucracy systematically discriminated against them in favour of the international unions.[16] Once again, French Canadians confronted their relative political unimportance in Ottawa as they had during the Riel, Boer War and first conscription crises. However, the era of Keynes now posed an even greater threat to their collective social identity.

Clearly, the parallel institutional power structure with the Church at its core could not long survive the onslaught of large-scale industrialization and the changes this process brought to the role of government. Since the 1920s, Québec governments had made timid moves to respond to the new realities.[17] But the old order had a staunch ally in Maurice Duplessis. In the name of fiscal responsibility, the premier was determined to protect the role of the Church, as well as the historic pact between Québec governments and St. James Street. Even his government, however, reoriented its spending priorities in the post-war era in a direction that would be faithfully followed by successive Québec administrations during the Quiet Revolution.[18] This was not enough to meet the challenges of the Keynesian era. Duplessis finally succumbed to French-Canadian nationalist and business pressures: he created a Royal Commission on Constitutional Problems in 1953, and the following year, repatriated the power to collect provincial taxes, which had been ceded to Ottawa during the war.

Québec's discontent with the constitutional structure is certainly not a recent phenomenon. Objections to centralization were expressed by governments in the late 1930s and 40s. But the first articulated response to the Rowell-Sirois Commission came in 1956 when Québec's royal commission finally released its report.[19] The Tremblay commission, as it was familiarly known, gave official voice to the nationalism of Lionel Groulx. It proposed a binational vision of Canada rooted in territoriality. In this perspective, the national government of French Canadians resided in Québec City. This government should not only have the power to legislate in the areas of culture and social policy, where French Canada's distinctiveness was most apparent, but it should have the financial resources to implement these policies. The Tremblay commission insisted that Ottawa withdraw from the fields of jurisdiction it had occupied since the war, including unemployment insurance, pensions, and family allowances. The report demanded that the province be made responsible for manpower training and that it exercise primacy in the area of direct taxation. If this list of powers has a familiar ring, it might be well to recall that the Tremblay Commission enumerated them four years before the Quiet Revolution and thirty-five years before the Meech Lake Accord.

As the Quiet Revolution of the sixties swept away the old order that Duplessis sought vainly to protect, the constitutional question became more acute than ever. The century-old parallel institutional structure was rapidly dismantled, as the Church dramatically withdrew from its prominent role in the public sphere. Social scientists have approvingly, if incorrectly, referred to this process as the "modernization" of Québec, as if the province was not modern before 1960. But if the Church's achievements were to endure, one aspect of Québec's national existence still had to be confronted: the complex question of French Canadians' significant economic inferiority. Another body would have to take over from the Church and create an institutional structure to come to terms with this question. The government of Québec could fulfil this task, but only if it agreed to become the national government of French Canadians. This it reluctantly did under the relentless pressure of nationalist forces. The process was facilitated by the decline of St. James Street as the economic centre of Canada. The objectives of Papineau, reiterated in *La Minerve*'s editorial, finally became a reality.

"*Maîtres chez nous,*" the 1962 campaign slogan of the Québec Liberal Party, signalled the government's commitment to economic nationalism. The members of the professional-managerial-business class, who finally had access to the patronage of an activist and rapidly expanding government, most directly reaped the benefits of this policy. As the Tremblay commission had foreseen, though, the national government of the French Canadians had to recover the powers lost to Ottawa since the beginning of the war and to secure the financial resources to carry out its program. This led to a series of constitutional and fiscal confrontations with Ottawa.

Québec's Demands

This sudden explosion of demands stunned English Canadians. The question they so often asked during the Quiet Revolution — "What does Québec want?" — was a measure of their disorientation. The fact that the government of Québec came to constitutional negotiations not only with a clear strategy, but with sophisticated and complex legislative proposals of their own, clearly unnerved senior federal civil servants who had enjoyed until then a monopoly of knowledge and technique. Discussions over the pension plan are a case in point.

In the first five or six years of the Quiet Revolution, an honest effort was made to accommodate Québec's demands. The opting out formula allowed the province to develop its own pension and medicare plans with federal compensation. In this heady context, Québec rapidly developed social, cultural and economic institutions to promote its distinctive character.

French Canadians had also been agitating for the public use of French since the beginning of the century. In response to their demands, the Pearson government had instituted a Royal Commission on Bilingualism and Biculturalism in 1963. Its co-chair, André Laurendeau, was a sophisticated and cosmopolitan disciple of Groulx. His constitutional perspective broadly reflected the principles of the Tremblay report. He believed that bilingualism alone could not satisfy French-Canadian aspirations, but would have to be accompanied by constitutional reform recognizing the territorial base of Canada's binationalism and granting Québec special status. He was vigorously opposed by another commissioner, the old social democrat Frank Scott.[20] It is possible that Laurendeau's untimely death in 1968 spared the commission an embarrassing open split. It certainly curtailed any plan for the devolution of power to Québec.

One Ethnic Group Among Many

The Trudeau years significantly altered the contours of the constitutional question, particularly with regard to the work of the Royal Commission on Bilingualism and Biculturalism. Trudeau's rise to power, first as Minister of Justice, then as prime minister, brought the process of accommodation to an abrupt halt. Intellectually, Trudeau opposed the vision of a binational Canada based on territory, and consequently he rejected any constitutional arrangement giving special powers to Québec. In the interest of Canadian unity, French Canadians would have to regard Ottawa as their national government. This objective entailed some sweeping changes in Ottawa. In the first place, the symbols of that government would have to be less British and more truly Canadian. This process, already well underway before Trudeau's accession to power, was speeded up and culminated in the patriation of the Canadian constitution. Second, there would have to be more French Canadians in the federal bureaucracy and in the government. They would have to be given positions of responsibility reflecting their talents and training. Although at the end of Trudeau's mandate French Canadians were still under-represented in the civil service, especially in its upper echelons, their appointment to high-profile political positions camouflaged this fact. Finally, Ottawa would actively promote bilingualism both in the civil service and in the country as a whole. Francophones had to be served in their language if the government's claim to represent their interests were to be taken seriously. Trudeau maintained support in Québec throughout his years of office because he succeeded in convincing Québécois that he had achieved these objectives.

Seizing on the demands of the members of the Royal Commission representing the immigrant communities, Trudeau destroyed the link between language and culture that was the foundation of the French Canadian nationalist position. The doctrine of multiculturalism asserted that there were no official cultures in Canada, just two official languages.

No cultural group could therefore lay claim to a government or to public institutions. In this way, Trudeau swept aside the historic vehicles through which the French-Canadian nationality found expression. The intimation of this doctrine was that French Canadians were no different from any other ethnic group. And yet for over a century, French Canadians had struggled to create and maintain a public culture, something to which immigrant communities could never aspire.

Ideas, however, were not sufficient to reverse the course on which Québec had embarked. For the first time since the Uprisings of 1837–38, parties advocating the independence of Québec emerged during the Quiet Revolution. Although insignificant at first, they created a certain political and psychological momentum. The notion of territoriality took root in the public mind as French Canadians in ever greater numbers began to call themselves Québécois. This expression replaced the old elements of identity — which were considered too restrictive — with concepts regarded as more modern and pluralistic. Thus, religion and ethnicity gave way to language and the state. In any event, the popularity of parties committed to Québec's independence increased with each election. Practically, Trudeau had to adopt a carrot-and-stick approach in response to these developments. Spying, sabotage, and military intervention were liberally used to subvert the independence movement. But these actions did not arrest Québécois' concern with their collective future. In the 1970s, the Trudeau government worked out a number of agreements with Québec in the areas of immigration and manpower training. These showed that behind the theoretical intractability lay a practical willingness to compromise, as long as none of these accords were etched in constitutional stone. *Verba volant; scripta manent.*

The coming to power in 1976 of the Parti Québécois, which was committed to a referendum on sovereignty, changed the stakes. Trudeau solemnly promised Québec constitutional reform on the eve of the 1980 referendum. But it was to be his brand of reform, not theirs. The BNA Act would be patriated and modernized by the addition of a Charter of Rights which not only guaranteed fundamental freedoms, but entrenched minority rights. Elsewhere in this volume, Michael Mandel shows how the Charter was used to subvert Québec's claims.

These claims have been on the table for well over thirty years. Québec is the only player in Confederation with the political clout to challenge federal prerogatives. It has effectively been the vehicle for constitutional change in Canada in recent years. Yet each time it states its case, other interests come forward with their list of demands. The provinces, the regions, minorities, immigrant communities have all insisted that Québec is only one among many. They have alternately reduced Québec to a province, a region, an ethnic group like the others. This perspective has found powerful support in Canada's constitutions, which have scrupulously avoided recognizing Québec's national status. Yet two hundred years of history have affirmed it.

The Québécois perceived the failure of the Meech Lake Accord as a final and unmistakable rejection of their national existence by Canadians. Recently, however, new efforts have been made to reach an accommodation. Will it finally recognize the Québécois as a nation? Or will this reality again be concealed in clauses intended to apply to provinces, regions, ethnic groups? In this regard, it is distressing that Ovide Mercredi, the Chief of the Assembly of First Nations, in a statement to the Québec National Assembly's Committee to Examine Matters Relating to the Accession of Québec to Sovereignty, denied Québec's right to self-determination. In his view, only nations, which are ethnically homogeneous entities, can aspire to such a right. French Canada meets this criterion; Québec, an ethnically diverse society, does not. Mercredi chooses to forget that historically the notion of self-determination found concrete expression within the borders of the state. No state invoking the right of self-determination, including revolutionary France which conceived the principle, was ethnically homogeneous. For his own reasons, Mercredi prefers to relegate this issue to the ideal world. He also ignores the evolution of Québec nationalism over the last thirty years. He affirms that his is a new perspective on the question. Sadly, however, it is a very old perspective. It is not by denying the national existence of the Québécois that the just cause of the First Nations is advanced. Native leaders should remember that without Québec's challenges to the constitutional order, their demands would have lacked a forum. They should also consider carefully the history of Québec's relations with English Canada and be wary of the good intentions expressed by the latter in their regard.

As for English Canadians, when will they unambiguously address the Québec question? When will they give it a generous reply?

Getting to the Table: The Prenegotiation of Deconfederation

David Bell

Canadian political culture is rich in concepts of negotiation, compromise and pragmatism, but these have historically been linked to a notion of élite accommodation. Negotiations concerning the constitution of the Canadian state were typically carried out by élites, behind closed doors and with little public involvement or even awareness. A strong element in the backlash that led to the failure of the Meech Lake proposals was the rejection of closed decision making and the pattern of élite accommodation that had characterized all previous constitutional deliberations.

One interpretation of Canadian élite accommodation links it to the theory of consociational democracy.[1] Elites in societies that are badly fractured along ethnic or religious lines keep their respective masses apart and living in "solitudes" in order to minimize the opportunity for mass-based conflict, while the élites, who are committed to unity and harmony, work out compromises that they then "sell" to their supporters. This interpretation paints a highly favourable picture of élite accommodation as a crucial instrument of national unity. Whatever their origins and functions over the course of Canadian history, élite accommodation and consociationalism have fallen on hard times in recent years. A substantial portion of the Canadian public opposed the Meech Lake agreement not because of the substance of its provisions but because they rejected the closed decision-making process by which it was reached. The January 1991 Maclean's-Decima poll[2] posed the following question:

If a new constitutional proposal to replace the Meech Lake accord were introduced after a process involving extensive consultation and public input — including public meetings in every province — would you personally be much more likely to support the proposal, somewhat more likely to support it, no more or less likely to support it, somewhat less likely to support it or much less likely to support it?

The results showed that nearly half the respondents would have been more supportive.

However distasteful or unpopular the closed process may be, it became clear by mid-1992 that public consultation will have little further role to play before Ottawa presents its final constitutional package to Québec. The negotiation of sovereignty and reassociation will of necessity be carried on by élites, behind closed doors.[3]

How is this going to work? Negotiation with a sovereign Québec conjures up the image of parties sitting at a table and talking to one another. Nevertheless, before getting to the table, these parties must first go through a process of "prenegotiation" that may be lengthy, complex and unsuccessful. If it fails, the parties will not even get to the table. If it succeeds, the prenegotiation phase may have a formative impact on what happens at the table. Since one possible consequence of failed prenegotiation is violence, we are well advised to understand its dynamics. This point applies with special force to the current Canadian crisis. Sabre rattling needs to be avoided at all costs.

Prenegotiation

Prenegotiation begins when at least one party considers negotiation as a policy option *and* communicates its intention to the other parties.[4] How does this definition apply to the prospect of deconfederation in Canada? Clearly, the federal government has not yet communicated to Québec that it is prepared to sit down and negotiate terms of sovereignty and possible reassociation. On the contrary, during 1992 the federal government desperately attempted to work out new terms of agreement that will allow some version of the present federal arrangements to continue. By contrast, the current Liberal Québec government has been highly ambivalent. Through the Allaire report, published in 1991, it has indicated terms that it might find acceptable for continuing to participate in a modified Canadian federalism. One could argue that the Allaire proposals amount to a dismantling of Confederation and the setting up some sort of asymmetrical federalism. But it is important to recognize the distinction between reforming the existing system and rejecting it entirely. The Bourassa government has not yet crossed that delicate threshold. Or has it?

Following the report of the Bélanger-Campeau commission, published in 1991, and under pressure from both the Parti Québécois and nationalists within the Liberal Party, the Bourassa government introduced Bill 150 into the Québec National Assembly, and it quickly passed into law. The law begins with a lengthy preamble that refers to the passage of the 1982 Constitution Act "despite the opposition of the National Assembly," cites the failure of the Meech Lake Accord, and states axiomatically that "it is necessary to redefine the political and constitutional status of Québec."

Article 1, chapter 1 of the law declares that "the Government of Québec shall hold a referendum on the sovereignty of Québec between 8 June and 22 June 1992 or between 12 October and 26 October 1992." If the outcome of the vote is in favour of sovereignty, the law states that these results "constitute a proposal that Québec acquire the status of a sovereign state one year to the day from the holding of the referendum." The law is very explicit about the implications of the term *sovereignty*, which it defines as "a position of exclusive jurisdiction, through its democratic institutions, to make laws and levy taxes in its territory and to act on the international scene for the making of agreements and treaties of any kind with other independent states and participating in various international organizations."[5]

The law also established two special committees (with Robert Bourassa and Jacques Parizeau as members of both). One of these special committees is mandated to review proposals for constitutional reform from the federal government. If (and only if) these proposals are deemed sufficiently attractive to merit serious consideration by the Québec electorate, and provided that these proposals are already binding on the federal government and the other provinces, the National Assembly may agree to hold the referendum on the question of remaining in Canada under the terms of the new proposals instead of on the issue of sovereignty. This would, however, require an amendment to Bill 150. In effect, therefore, Québec has declared that it *is* prepared to enter negotiations over sovereignty (depending on the referendum outcome) if suitable terms for remaining in Canada fail to materialize. In a feat of equivocation reminiscent of Mackenzie King, Bourassa seems to be saying "sovereignty if necessary but not necessarily sovereignty." In his statement in the National Assembly on March 19, 1992, Bourassa indicated a strong preference for keeping Québec in Canada, which he described as a "rare privileged country": he declared that his government's preference is "the path of renewed federalism." However, he insisted that the "pride and dignity of the Québec people are not negotiable."[6] Even in this, his strongest pro-federalist statement to that point, Bourassa equivocated, leaving open the alternative course of independence. To be sure, Bourassa's pronouncements amount to a tough bargaining posture, designed in part to keep a knife to the throat of the rest of Canada in order to force acceptable concessions.

The fact is that two processes are occurring simultaneously. The obvious and visible process involves the negotiation of proposed reforms to the existing federal arrangements. Less visible in English Canada is the embryonic process of pre-negotiating deconfederation and reassociation. It began with Law 150.

The Role of Culture and Language

Negotiation is quintessentially a linguistic act. It involves the use of language to cajole, persuade, threaten, induce, drive, blackmail, intimidate and flatter. These are the familiar verbal weapons employed at the bargaining table and in everyday life. The object of negotiation is almost always to arrive at a written agreement of terms and conditions: some kind of formal resolution, a declaration, a treaty, a collective agreement and so on. Each of these outcomes involves careful use of *language*, a term that acquires special meaning in labour negotiations — for example, when the parties speak of putting "new language" in the collective agreement.

The political talk that takes place during negotiation — the *speech* — must be understood in relation to the underlying political culture: the available symbols and widely shared meanings that constitute the *language* of political interaction.

Canadian political culture is marked by ambivalence and duality with regard to the handling of domestic tensions, particularly Anglo-French relations.[7] At times the language of intolerance and assimilation has dominated political discourse. French have cursed *"les maudits Anglais,"* who have reacted angrily to having "French forced down their throats." Partisans on both sides have defaced honoured symbols, burned each other's flags and booed the singing of the national anthem in the other's language. But there is also a strong tradition of tolerance and compromise stretching back more than two centuries and given popular expression most recently in the poster/billboard campaign proclaiming *"Mon Canada comprend le Québec."* Federal politicians have invoked this tradition many times in attempts to cool down the angry talk about separation. In September 1991, Constitutional Affairs Minister Joe Clark set these sentiments in historical perspective: "The Prime Minister is talking about compromise because he remembers what happened in 1864 and 1867. He knows what's happened in this country through our history; we have to call upon people to be prepared to compromise, to try to respect other people's point of view."[8] Similar sentiments were expressed by the Leader of the Opposition, Jean Chrétien: "Let us all demonstrate over the next few months thoughtfulness, reason, generosity, a willingness to accommodate and a skill to negotiate."[9]

The NDP has long asserted that Québec would have the right to self-determination, including sovereignty, if the decision were reached democratically. Finally, the January 1991 Maclean's-Decima poll discovered that a majority of Canadians (51 percent) would simply "let Québec go" if it opted for independence. Nearly as many (47 percent) indicated that the rest of Canada "should do everything it can to convince them to stay."[10] But note the emphasis on talk ("convince") rather than military action ("send in the troops"). In fact, the possible use of force to prevent Québec from separating was not even discussed in the questionnaire. This, too, is apparently unthinkable. And yet we have already experienced, in this century, instances where the troops *have* been sent in to quell uprisings in Québec: during the conscription crises in both World Wars, and during the 1970 October Crisis. It is not difficult to imagine a scenario in which things fall apart and we experience a bloody (and possibly protracted) sovereignty crisis in the near future. How can this be avoided?

A great deal will depend on how we "frame" Québec's departure — the symbols and cultural themes we invoke in our talk about the impending transformation of our society. When politicians and others talk about a conflict in general terms, their remarks serve to "frame" the issue in relation to themes and symbols that exist in the traditions and political culture of the society. Students of negotiation have pointed out that negotiation itself is set in a discursive "frame" of language. Talk about the process (process frames) and the issue at stake (substantive frames) have an important and in some instances predetermining impact on the negotiation.[11] This is especially true in the case of prenegotiation.

The Frame for Negotiating with Québec

How might Canadians "frame" a negotiation over Québec sovereignty? Will we set it in the cultural tradition of bitterness, hostility and resentment that has at times poisoned Anglo-French relations? Or will we invoke the tradition of moderation, tolerance and compromise? The answer to this question is very important. The frame could facilitate or virtually preclude a successful and harmonious outcome. Much will depend on the retrospective perceptions of the efforts that have been going on to reform the existing institutions. Notice the instant association of the phrase "Meech Lake" with negative phrases of "death" and "failure."[12] One easy technique for discrediting the current efforts at "renewed federalism" is to invoke the ghost of Meech Lake. (The media in Québec trashed the Beaudoin-Dobbie report, dubbing it "Meech Two.") The same may be true of subsequent negotiations between Québec and Canada if the current efforts at reform do not succeed. Resentment against Québec may overtake a rea-

soned judgement about mutual interests and future association. But the fact of globalization is forcing countries to find
new ways to associate and to manage politically their interdependence. The Allaire report calls for what amounts to political autonomy for Québec, while insisting on strengthening
economic ties with the rest of Canada, eliminating provincial
barriers to trade and securing a true common market. It also
identifies the maintenance of stability as a key principle guiding the "transition process," in order to avoid economic set-
backs and loss of confidence. This suggests the value of
emphasizing economic considerations in looking ahead to
Québec sovereignty.

One of the most popular frames (in both French and English
media) of Canada's relationship with Québec involves the
metaphor of the family. This metaphor has two variants:
Québec as spouse (usually portrayed as the woman),[13] and
Québec as a difficult child. The first frame leads us to see the
prospect of separation in terms of divorce. It conjures up images involving revenge and bitter disputes (inflamed by pas-
sion) over dividing up the assets and custody of "the children"
(who might include Québec anglophones and natives, and
francophones outside of Québec, particularly in Acadie). The
metaphor of Québec as spouse silently reaffirms the myth of
two founding nations, presumes the rest of Canada is a singu-
lar, undifferentiated entity and ignores the existence of nine
distinct provinces.

The second variant of the family metaphor avoids some of
these biases. It sees Québec as one of the children, perhaps the
eldest child who is now going to leave home. This could yield
either a highly negative or a more positive frame. The negative
frame would view the child as a troublesome ingrate, who is
told to pack up, get out and not come back: The rest of the
family will be better off without you. A more positive version
of this frame would see the departure as an inevitable (but sad)
outcome of "growing up." We would all strive to keep the best
possible relationship with this new mature adult and perhaps
help out as much as we can.

Another type of frame sees the relationship in terms of a
partnership. It is analogous to the marriage frame but defines
the partnership much more in business terms. This frame
would lead to a careful assessment of assets and liabilities on

the dissolution of the partnership. We would focus on questions of who owned what and who owes what. It complements a favourite metaphor adopted by Robert Bourassa, who has often spoken about *fédéralisme rentable*. Once federalism no longer is profitable, it is time to dissolve the partnership and take up business on one's own. The business metaphor is also invoked implicitly when Québec is warned that there will be high costs to pay should Canada break up. The front page of *The Toronto Star* of September 23, 1991, carried a story by editor David Crane under the heading "Québec Split 'Costly.' " The opening sentence said, "Québec would suffer an immediate economic decline — its worst since the great depression of the 1930s — if it separated from the rest of Canada, a new report says." The report in question was one prepared by the Fraser Institute, called *Economic Consequences of Quebec Sovereignty*. It described in detail the alleged "transition costs" of separation, which will include higher interest rates, the flight of capital, a possible stock market crash, and a high public and foreign debt for the new country. In this scenario, the rest of Canada would also be plunged into recession "caused by the lack of confidence." It would be "extremely foolish" to break up Canada. Québec would find that its economic and social policies would be under attack if it attempted to negotiate free trade with the United States.

A similar theme underlies remarks by Prime Minister Brian Mulroney, reported the following day under the heading "Only Unity Can Guarantee Prosperity, Mulroney Says": "We are convinced that unity and prosperity go hand in hand, we can't have lasting prosperity without unity, or real unity without prosperity." [14]

In addition to "substantive frames" that characterize the general relationship and issues of contention between Québec and Canada, perceptions of negotiations are influenced by "process frames." The current process of negotiation has often been likened to a card game or game of chance. Recall Mulroney's boastful claim to have "rolled the dice" at precisely the right moment during the final stages of the attempt to ratify the Meech Lake agreement. Now consider this excerpt from a *Toronto Star* front-page story: "As Brian Mulroney steps up to the constitutional table again today, the big difference will be his cautious style. This time, instead of playing back-room games, he'll spread his cards flat on the table."[15]

Are metaphors like the card game important? Do they make a difference? Metaphors in general are indispensable. Indeed, we "live by" them.[16] But some metaphors are more harmful than others. They prevent us from thinking clearly about problems. Emotional figures deflect us from the possibility of working out positive relations that will serve our best interests.

Prenegotiation and Process: Clarifying the Options

In addition to framing the subsequent negotiation in general terms, the prenegotiation phase must also address a series of other specific aspects of the negotiation. What form might relations between an independent Québec and the rest of Canada take? One possibility is "sovereignty association." It is not impossible that the paradoxical conclusion that Philip Resnick has suggested in his contribution to this volume — namely that sovereignty and association would become mutually exclusive — may be correct. In his view, if Québec insists on declaring its sovereignty, the rest of Canada will be reluctant to discuss any terms of association beyond a loose trading arrangement. But even if there is a willingness to negotiate terms of association, what form will it take and how will the various assets be divided? This is the question posed by Daniel Drache in his chapter, and he has outlined a variety of possible scenarios and outcomes. A crucial aspect of the prenegotiation will involve clarifying these options and eventually simplifying them down to one or two choices that can be debated and then perhaps put before the public in a referendum or other vote.

Debating the Options

Once these options are formulated, how are they to be clarified? Where will they be debated, and by whom? This is not as straightforward as it might appear. For Québec, the National Assembly appears to be an appropriate setting within which to debate these matters. But the federal parliament in Ottawa does not represent the rest of Canada, because a substantial portion of its members are from Québec. Indeed, were it not for the support of Québec MPs, the Mulroney government elected in 1988 would have difficulty continuing in office. Mulroney himself is from Québec. Who, therefore, represents Canada, and in what institutional forum should its fate be debated? How do we arrange to debate and clarify options that can then be presented to the public of the other provinces? What is the role of the provincial premiers? Should any referendum be held across the rest of Canada as a whole, or should it be broken down by province? If this is done, should each provincial outcome determine the negotiating stance of the MPs or provincial leaders or other people chosen to negotiate on behalf of that province?

The Parties at the Table

This leads directly to the question of who represents whom and who should be parties to the negotiation. New terms of association between Québec and Canada will clearly call for new institutional arrangements, but as pointed out above, even the process of debating and deciding on these alternatives requires institutional reform. The Meech Lake process presumed that the only parties to constitutional negotiation are the eleven first ministers. Past practice and common sense suggest that the provincial governments would continue to have a major role. Each of them would be likely to approach the process as if it were a sovereign state debating the terms of future association (as occurred after the breakup of the Soviet Union). Clearly, aboriginal peoples would demand representation at any bargaining table. One could imagine anglophones and non-English and non-French speakers in Québec similarly insisting on representation (as indeed they did, unsuccessfully, in 1992). Demands for inclusion might come from a wide range of other groups representing women, ethnic minorities, gays, lesbians and all those whose heightened political activity has transformed recent Canadian politics. If their demands were to be heeded, Canada might find it necessary to establish a new constitutional assembly, perhaps on a functional basis, with representatives selected from a wide spectrum of groups. This new body might include some of the politicians who currently sit in the federal parliament. But it would have a role that would resemble that of a constituent assembly, and it might include individuals elected for the purpose of negotiating the terms of deconfederation who have no intention of continuing in political office afterwards. It would be an opportunity, in other words, for a much wider spectrum of Canadian citizens to take part in this crucial process. The role of political parties in this new body would need to be established.

The prenegotiation of deconfederation has begun. Whether it leads to negotiations to restructure Canada, collapses into angry and perhaps violent confrontation, or is eclipsed for the time being by the successful reform of existing constitutional arrangements will depend on the skill of current political leaders and the reactions of special-interest groups and the general public. If attempts to reform existing institutions succeed, Canada will survive until the next constitutional crisis. If they fail, we need to clear our heads, overcome our sadness and anger, and work constructively to ensure that the negotiation of new constitutional arrangements is handled rationally and without rancour. We must frame both the process and the substance appropriately. We must identify the core principles to guide our actions, including the crucial decision about who will become parties to the negotiation and what institutional arrangements will be made for debate and public consultation. Openness, legitimacy, good faith and, above all, a sense of responsibility must inform these critical months. Much hangs in the balance.

II
Reassociation: Strategy and Concepts

Québec-Canada Association: Divergent Paths to a Common Economic Agenda

Miriam Smith

Since the demise of the Meech Lake Accord, many studies have examined the possibility of Québec's independence and the range of options that would be available to both Québec and Canada to handle the economic and political consequences of a split. Two questions in particular have attracted attention. First, could Québec go it alone, without association with Canada? Second, is an association or economic union between Canada and an independent Québec workable? While most of the briefs to the 1991 Bélanger-Campeau commission favoured association, the idea that Québec could go it alone without Canadian co-operation is an integral element of the Québec bargaining position.[1]

There is a significant difference of opinion between the expert briefs to the Bélanger-Campeau commission and the commentary from English Canada on the likely success of these options. In the briefs to the Bélanger-Campeau commission, expert witnesses (and the Parti Québécois) argued that Québec could go it alone without association, using its own currency or the Canadian dollar. While there would be transition costs related to these options, Canada could do little in response. For example, there would be no way that Canada could prevent Québec from using the dollar.[2] With respect to trade, Québec would have some access to the Canadian market under GATT rules and the United States would be likely to negotiate a trade agreement with an independent Québec. These views minimize Québec's incentive to negotiate association with Canada.[3]

In contrast, English-Canadian commentators have stressed the costs to Québec of independence without association. If Québec used the Canadian dollar, it would surrender control over monetary policy to the Bank of Canada. The use of another country's currency has usually worked successfully over the long term for small, weak or imperially dominated economies, rather than for economies of the size and strength of Québec. In addition, the English-Canadian commentaries stress that using the Canadian dollar would create strong pressures towards further integration of policy, especially since the English-Canadian and Québec economies are already integrated.[4] More ominously, at least one English-Canadian commentator has argued that Québec could not use Canada's currency without Canadian co-operation.[5]

It is on the issue of economic association itself, however, that the greatest divergence of opinion occurs. The discussion on both sides draws its inspiration from the European Community (EC) model. The basic disagreement revolves around whether the EC is a model of political integration in which states are gradually *losing* their sovereignty or whether the EC is still an essentially intergovernmental arrangement in which states *retain* their sovereignty.

In one of the expert commentaries to the Bélanger-Campeau commission, Luc Bergeron argued that the EC provides a model for the way in which an association of sovereign states may come together for the purposes of economic association. His analysis stresses that the EC is an international treaty between independent nations, not a constitution that regulates relations between levels of government. The essentially intergovernmental rather than federal nature of the EC is confirmed by the fact that EC decisions are taken by the Council of Ministers, who are delegated by their national governments. Bergeron argues that regardless of the actual powers exercised at the EC level, the decision-making rules of the Community clearly indicate that decisions are made by the delegates of independent states. The democratic legitimacy of the EC stems from the fact that decisions are made by independent states whose governments are democratically elected. Even though states must abide by Community decisions, even those they oppose, the states themselves are at the heart of the EC decision-making process. Small states in the EC, in fact, have more ability to exercise their sovereignty than they would have if they remained outside the Community.[6]

While Bergeron's brief is the fullest exposition of this argument, his view is shared by the Parti Québécois, the Québec Liberal Party's Allaire report and even by Premier Bourassa himself, who suggested in the immediate aftermath of Meech that Québec might seek a new superstructural arrangement with English Canada.[7] In the view of Québécois, such an arrangement implies a relationship of equal and sovereign governments.[8] The political implication of this view is that an EC-style economic union between an independent Québec and English Canada would be feasible and would provide Québec with the benefits of both sovereignty and economic union.

In contrast, a number of English-Canadian commentaries on the EC have come to a quite different conclusion. These commentaries stress that it is very difficult to have economic union without political union. According to this view, the EC states have surrendered important aspects of sovereignty and, under the proposed political union, they will surrender even more (including such basic attributes of sovereignty as defence and security matters).

Unlike the Québec analysis of decision making within the Community, the English-Canadian analysis emphasizes the role of the European Commission rather than the importance of the Council of Ministers. The so-called Eurocrats of the Commission are explicitly mandated *not* to represent their home governments. In this view, the EC is essentially undemocratic. The European Parliament has very limited powers and thus the Community-wide electorate does not exercise any control over the Commission. The English-Canadian commentary leads to the view that not only are the European states surrendering their sovereignty, but they are surrendering their sovereignty to a supranational institution that is democratically inferior to current Canadian arrangements.[9] The political implication of this, of course, is that Québec will lose its newly acquired sovereignty if it enters into EC-style arrangements with English Canada.

Another twist to the English-Canadian view is the argument that Québec will actually have less power with a confederal arrangement than it has in the current federal system.[10] This is because the relationship between Canada and a sovereign Québec would be both bipolar and asymmetrical. The first consequence of this asymmetry would be expressed during the political transition. How willing would English Canada be to negotiate? For some, it is not clear what incentive a reconfigured Canada would have to renegotiate EC-style association with Québec after secession. Despite the fact that any political or economic instability that affects Québec will also affect English Canada, most English-Canadian analysts seem to think that other factors will outweigh this consideration. According to this view, there will be considerable resentment against Québec in a reconfigured Canada and neither politicians nor the public will be in any mood to compromise. In this perspective, it is not clear why Canada would agree to give Québec any control over monetary policy, commercial policy, trade policy or other aspects of policy that would be required for an economic union. If one of the advantages of Québec independence for English Canada is to end Québec's involvement in Canadian affairs and to allow English Canada to develop its own politics, policies and priorities, then it is unrealistic to expect English Canada to countenance further Québec involvement in Canadian affairs. This kind of sabre rattling is English Canada's current strategic response to the Bélanger-Campeau commission and to the confidence of the Parti Québécois that Québec can survive and prosper independent of English Canada.

The second problem with the asymmetry and bipolarity of the Québec-Canada relationship goes beyond the politics of the transition to decision making in a Québec-Canada association. The English-Canadian analysis suggests the difficulty of devising decision-making rules for two-party agreements when one partner is smaller than the other. If Québec were to be afforded an influence commensurate with either the weight of its GDP in Canada or with its population, it would be outvoted every time. This is the sense in which analysts like Doern, Soberman and Courchene argue that Québec would have less influence after independence than it has in current federal arrangements. And, even if Canada were to agree to a relationship of equals, a relationship of equals is a recipe for decision-making deadlock in a bipolar association. Thus, Ronald L. Watts points out that "where each constituent government (in a bipolar association) plays such an important role in the development of common policies, agreement has often been difficult to reach, particularly where any redistribution of resources has been involved." [11] The choice in asymmetrical arrangements is deadlock or domination.

In contrast to the bipolar Canadian situation, in the EC the smaller states have influence by making alliances with other small states. For some issues, unanimous decision-making rules apply. In a multiparty agreement, some countries will win and some countries will lose from issue to issue. Even the economic hegemony of the EC has some incentive to reconcile the smaller and less influential states. In a bipolar arrangement, however, there is much less room to manoeuvre. To those who point to the Canada-U.S. Free Trade Agreement (FTA) as an example of such a successful arrangement — and most of the authors in the volume edited by Watts and Brown feel that the FTA has been successful — the rejoinder is that the FTA does not entail the level of policy co-ordination that would be required for Québec-Canada economic union.

This is only one example of the two solitudes at work in this debate. There is a whole set of differences of opinion about a range of other issues, such as the allocation of assets and debt, the division of territory, the economic costs and benefits of Québec's membership in the Canadian federation and the likely economic costs and benefits to both Québec and English Canada of Québec's independence. [12]

This set of differences suggests that the negotiation of Québec's independence is going to be a difficult and dangerous process. The English-Canadian and Québec commentators cited above are some of the most influential figures in the debate, and they are likely to influence developments during a transition to Québec independence. The two sides have begun to stake out their positions for the battle to come. This process of strategic manoeuvring will in itself profoundly influence both the constitutional debate and the probability of association in the event of Québec's independence. As Peter Leslie has recently pointed out, the process of constitutional change cannot be separated from the outcome. [13]

A Common Assumption: The Underlying Neo-liberal Agenda

Despite the differences between the English-Canadian and Québec positions on economic association, the two sides share one fundamental assumption: that securing an economic union under neo-liberal state policies is an essential part of constitutional reform or post-independence association. There is a striking level of consensus on this point. The debate revolves around whether such arrangements will be centralizing or decentralizing within the Canadian federation, or whether they should be assured through an economic union between an independent Québec and Canada. Thus, the debate is about which powers should belong to which governments.

What is the goal of an economic union with free movement of people, goods, services and capital? Its goal is to reduce the scope for intervention, whether by the federal state or by the provinces.[14] This is the import of the 1991 federal constitutional proposals on economic union.[15] While these proposals are seen in Québec as centralizing, in reality they displace power from governments to markets. As such, they constitutionalize neo-liberalism by proscribing the activist state at both federal and provincial levels. The requirement for fiscal co-ordination between different levels of government removes the last vestiges of fiscal autonomy from the provinces, thus precluding distinctive fiscal strategies. And the enforcement of an economic union means that all kinds of development policies will be made unconstitutional. The rhetoric is deceptive — ensuring the free flow of goods, services, labour and capital. It sounds as if we are unblocking the arteries of the economy and allowing prosperity to flow, when in fact we are diminishing the scope for political choice by constitutionalizing economic policy.

The concern with the powers and scope of government intervention runs through nearly all of the English-Canadian commentaries on constitutional reform. Securing the economic union and the Canadian common market is the first and most important goal of constitutional change, according to the Business Council on National Issues (BCNI). Not surprisingly, the BCNI favours the development of a "sensible, cost-efficient, and accountable" federal system, one that avoids inefficiency and duplication and which reduces the cost and size of government.[16]

In this vein, the BCNI reacted positively to the federal government's 1991 proposals. According to the Council, the constitutional crisis is an opportunity to "modernize" our institutions of government, to eradicate duplication between different levels of government, and to strengthen the economic union (the proposed new section 121 of the constitution, as stated in the 1991 federal proposals). As always, the BCNI attempts to veil the impact of its agenda, arguing that "economic reforms, constitutional or otherwise, do not automatically carry with them a social cost."[17] The BCNI's main reservations about the proposed section 121 are that the federal government's implementation date (July 1, 1995) is too late and that exceptions for legislation promoting regional development or equalization should be narrowly defined.[18] Similarly, the BCNI supports the government's proposals for co-ordination and harmonization of macroeconomic policies. In a point made in most of the Québec briefs, the BCNI argues that macro policy has been conflictual and poorly co-ordinated in ways that have contributed to "a soaring national debt, high overall government debt levels, punitive real interest rates, overdependence on foreign borrowing, the misalignment of monetary and fiscal policies, [and] a heavy burden of taxation."[19] The Council favours the devolution of power to the provinces "where this makes sense," a position that is not far from Premier Bourassa's endorsement of the EC doctrine of subsidiarity (that powers should belong to the lowest levels of government unless there is a compelling reason why such powers be exercised by a higher level of government). The BCNI also supports limits on the federal spending power, mainly in the interests of restoring political accountability to government spending.[20]

The need for less government is presented in these analyses as the inevitable result of globalization. Globalization translates into the need to be competitive, and the need to be competitive in turn requires a paring down and decentralization of government.[21] There is no debate about or consideration of the alternative avenues that might be open to Canada or to the provinces to pursue distinctive strategies in the rapidly changing international political economy.

The same assumptions are found on the Québec side of the debate. The report of the Québec Liberal Party on Québec's constitutional options, the Allaire report, makes this crystal clear when it outlines the three goals of economic union: mobility of goods, labour and capital; customs and monetary union; and "restoring balance to Canadian public finances by reducing the size of the central state and imposing institutional limitations on its budgetary practices, including the establishment of specific targets to severely limit deficits and restrict its taxation power."[22]

Québec unions, which have often been the standard bearers of a social democratic and even socialist vision of a sovereign Québec, still support a strong role for the state in the economy. Both the Confédération des syndicats nationaux (CSN) and the Fédération des travailleurs et travailleuses du Québec (FTQ) argue that *concertation* and industrial policies will work best under sovereignty where Québécois, as a nation, will share a common culture and common objectives. However, like the BCNI and Québec business groups, the unions also stress the cost to Québec of Canadian monetary policies that contradict the efforts of the Québec state; they emphasize that federalism multiplies the costs and inefficiency of government in areas that are essential to Québec's development.[23] The CSN makes clear that its support for independence is not dependent on any particular political-economic vision of what a sovereign Québec will look like.[24] In other words, the CSN supports sovereignty, even as a neo-liberal and business-led endeavour.

Unlike the CSN, the Québec section of the Canadian Manufacturers' Association takes the position that its primary concern is the type of society that results from constitutional reform. Not surprisingly, its preference is for a political arrangement in which manufacturing competitiveness will be encouraged. Like the BCNI, it emphasizes the problems created by the federal system, such as interprovincial trade barriers, duplication and waste, and government debt.[25]

The celebrated Chambre de commerce brief, presented to the Commission after an extensive consultative process, contains a strong condemnation of the economic consequences of the current federal system and endorses a massive transfer of powers to Québec. Like the Allaire report, the Chambre supports constitutional measures that limit governments' ability to borrow. Like the BCNI, the Chambre finds the division of jurisdictions to be "a jumble of ineffectiveness, incoherence and waste."[26] And, while the Chambre supports the Canadian monetary union, it also calls for reforms to the Bank of Canada to make it more representative of the regions. The Chambre brief stresses the importance of retaining at least the current level of free movement of persons, goods and capital.[27] In contrast to the Chambre, the Conseil du patronat (Québec's employers' federation) takes a strongly federalist stance. That aside, the Conseil echoes most of the points made by the other Québec briefs, including the need to recast the division of powers and the paramount importance of preserving the Canadian economic space.[28] These points were also made by another important Québec business group — the Mouvement Desjardins.[29]

Thus, there is a substantial zone of agreement between Québec commentary (from business, unions and experts) and English-Canadian commentary (from experts and business groups). All agree that globalization necessitates competitiveness and that the current federal system stands in the way of a leaner system of government. All agree that governments must be reined in and made accountable for spending and that macroeconomic policies must be co-ordinated to ensure macro stability. The sole difference between the English-Canadian and Québec commentary is on the issue of sovereignty itself.

This zone of agreement between Québécois and English-Canadian commentators is perhaps to be expected given that the current drive for sovereignty in Québec is a largely neo-liberal project[30] and that the Tory government in Ottawa is resolutely committed to rolling back the state, albeit through incremental means. Furthermore, whether under sovereignty or under renewed federalism, the enforcers of the new Canadian economic order are the undemocratic and politically unpalatable mechanisms of intergovernmentalism.

The Canadian constitutional debate increasingly reflects the international capitalist revolution of the last decade. This revolution is putting new strains on the concept and practice of state sovereignty. Economic considerations dominate Canadian constitutional discussion as never before. In contrast to the European debate, however, there is very little discussion of the ways in which constitutional adjustment will affect the balance between states and markets in Canada. Rather, the debate — as always — has been about which levels of government will have which powers. Yet, under the guise of constitutional amendments or negotiations on association, the balance between states and markets could be shifted for good. It will be difficult if not impossible for future governments to undo what has been done, just as it is with the FTA.

My point here is that the assumption that solidifying the Canadian common market will be in the best interests of all Canadians *is* an assumption. Taking powers away from governments, turning them over to the market and arranging our constitution — with or without Québec — so that the hands of future governments of Canada are tied is another form of neo-liberalism by stealth. Devising constitutional arrangements that simply accept the bland assertions of the BCNI about what our response to globalization must be and then entrenching the twenty-first-century version of the night-watchman state (whether by constitutional amendment or by international treaty) is to put the political and constitutional seal on our future possibilities for political action. At the very least, we have to think about the ways that this round of constitutional reform will affect the balance between states and markets. A Social Charter will be empty rhetoric if federal and provincial states do not have the fiscal, institutional and political capacities to translate its words into reality.

Life after Separation

Reg Whitaker

What happens to Canada after Québec chooses sovereignty? Informed and reasonable speculation is required, given the momentous consequences. It is a commonly held tenet of the Ottawa national unity industry that if Québec departs, the "Rest of Canada" will break up and the parts will be eventually absorbed into the United States.[1]

This prediction is tainted at its source — it tends to come, after all, from those who have a strong stake in resisting sovereignty for Québec. In this sense, the "inevitable-breakup" argument is ideological and prescriptive. But does it in fact have an empirical ground? What is the likelihood that Canada without Québec would disintegrate? Obviously we are in a realm where there are no certainties, but we can at least assess the quality of the arguments to determine their degree of reliability.

The Cultural Disintegration Argument

English Canada, so the argument goes, has nothing to distinguish it from the United States, save the culturally and linguistically unique presence of Québec. Thus if Québec leaves, the rest of Canada will disintegrate shortly thereafter.[2]

There is, however, almost no empirical evidence that Canadians want to become American. Polls that ask Canadians to choose between remaining Canadian and opting for the United States have never shown much support for the second option. Nor has the alleged southward cultural pull found coherent political expression. There has never been a serious annexationist political movement in English Canada and there are no signs of any gathering force under the current crisis conditions. Even the halfway house of provincial separatism has never gained much support. During the late 1970s and early 1980s there was a flurry of interest surrounding Western separatist movements. But these were fringe phenomena that have now been superseded on the populist right by the Reform Party, which has gained far more support with an explicitly nationalist and anti-separatist platform. It is striking that separatist and/or annexationist movements have been unable to gather momentum even under the powerful north-south pull exerted by the Canada-U.S. Free Trade Agreement.

Of course, a whole new continentalist thrust could emerge under the stress of Québec's separation. But it would have to be based on elements already present, needing only to be activated. These elements, such as the penetration of Canada by American mass-marketed culture, are present in Québec and Europe and indeed throughout much of the Third World. Not even Japan can compete with the American cultural message. But it is a major leap from this observation to the conclusion that in the absence of Québec, English Canada would inevitably be sucked into the American political structure.

It is quite obvious that the cultural history of English Canada over the past thirty years has been one of growing maturity and self-confidence across a wide range of areas, from literature to pop music. The fact that these cultural achievements are rarely acknowledged in Québec is irritating to English Canadians, but beside the point. While it is true that American influences on English-Canadian culture, especially mass culture, are strong, Québec is also subjected to these influences and yet *its* sense of identity is not called into question. What *is* important is that English Canadians live and think within a common cultural framework, with regional variations, in which they recognize themselves as belonging to a distinctive community.

A sovereign Québec would do nothing to alter this. By and large, Québec has not influenced or shaped English-Canadian cultural identity in any significant way. Canada-with-Québec has been understood above all as a *political* community. Québec's departure undoubtedly would have considerable impact on English Canadians' political, but not cultural, self-image. As a cultural landscape, Canada has always been made up of two solitudes. If one of them departs, there is no reason for the other to commit suicide.

The Political Disintegration Argument

Canada, it is argued, could not remain a single political unit for very long. Ontario would have 49 to 50 percent of the Canadian population and the Western provinces would not tolerate increased central domination. The Atlantic region, finding itself cut off from the rest of Canada, would be no more than an East Pakistan. Canada would disintegrate politically, first into separate successor states. Then these would gradually, or perhaps quickly, be absorbed as states of the Union.

The first point to be made about this scenario is to concede that Canada after secession could not survive politically *without deep structural changes*. The premier of Ontario has dismissed the demand for a "triple-E" Senate (elected, equal and effective) as a non-starter in the current constitutional debate. But it is impossible to imagine a Canada without Québec simply continuing as a federation in which a single unit, Ontario, would control half the seats in the lower house, complemented by an unelected, ineffectual and unequal upper chamber. If Ontario-Firsters were to remain obdurate and continue to oppose constitutional innovation in the name of regional and provincial equity, then Canada would certainly break up. Clearly, Ontario is the linchpin for the future of Canada, given its geographical centrality and its demographic weight.

A few Ontarians have suggested that their province go it alone or establish some kind of one-on-one relationship with Québec (a return to the 1840s?). Yet it is hard to imagine that these voices would find deep resonance within the wider population. Ontarians have always been the most "nationalist" of Canadians, with the weakest sense of regional identity. To be sure, Canadians from outside Ontario have insisted that this nationalism tends to be a disguised form of Ontario-Firstism ("What's good for Ontario is good for Canada," as a former Ontario cabinet minister once blatantly asserted). Ontario arrogance is taking a bit of a beating under the combined impact of free trade and the great depression of the 1990s. But it is unlikely that Ontario would easily shift from a "greater Canada" vision to that of a "little Ontario," just because Québec

departed. Some major concessions with regard to representa-
tional structures will be required, however. In this regard, it is
significant that the premier's dismissal of the triple-E proposal
was not echoed by the Ontario legislative committee on the
constitution. It is more likely that if Québec departed, Ontario
would play the same conciliatory "statesmanlike" role towards the remaining provinces and regions as had previous
Ontario governments to Québec's demands for constitutional
change. Given Ontario's current economic weakness, it would
presumably make concessions in the interest of unity.

If Ontario opts for remaining part of a more equitably designed Canadian federation, what about the Western provinces? Despite the fact that Western alienation has real,
material roots, the notion of Prairie successor states going it
alone, or even in combination with one another, seems far-
fetched. British Columbia with its Pacific orientation clearly
would not be part of any united Western breakaway. Western
successor states might only be transition stages on the road to
absorption by the United States.

But statehood can hardly be an attractive political alternative to even the most alienated Westerner. If Albertans have
rightly complained about their lack of influence in Ottawa,
imagine the diminution of that voice were Alberta to become
a state of the Union. True, the U.S. Senate is based on equal
state representation, but this would mean that Alberta would
have two senators out of more than one hundred. Even combined with the states of Saskatchewan and Manitoba, the
northern Prairie representation in Washington would amount
to less than 6 percent of the Senate vote. On top of that, under
the U.S. constitution, Alberta as a state would automatically
lose control over the revenue from its energy resources. Even
from a narrow Alberta perspective, a revised Canadian federation, in which a chastened Ontario agreed to something like
a triple-E Senate to keep Canada without Québec together,
would be preferable.

In the era of continental free trade, there is actually less
argument in favour of political union with the United States
than before. The same logic that has emboldened Québec to
contemplate political sovereignty within a North American
free trade zone applies to Canada's contemplating life after

Québec's departure. There are few economic advantages to be gained by political union that are not already available through free trade between politically sovereign states. Conversely, the economic disadvantages imposed by free trade will not be alleviated by political union.

But what of political psychology? Would the loss of Québec constitute such a psychological blow to Canada's political self-esteem that it would suffer, in effect, a collective nervous breakdown? The Canadian motto is *a mari usque ad mare*. Abraham Rotstein has written of English-Canadian "mappism,"[3] an inability to conceptualize the country except as a geographical unity. Would the departure of Québec fatally rupture this vision of Canada by putting a hole in the middle of the map? Perhaps mappists could simply attach themselves to a new map with the same tenacity with which they clung to the old. After all, devotion to a geographical expression is not devotion to some transcendent ideal.

The more serious variant of this argument is that Atlantic Canada would be physically cut off from the rest of Canada — presuming that professors Bercuson and Cooper do not first reconquer the Eastern Townships for Greater Canada.[4] This need not make the Maritimes and Newfoundland into an East Pakistan. After all, Alaska is separated from the continental United States by a foreign land barrier about as great as that separating New Brunswick from the Ontario border. No one has thought to describe Alaska as a North Pakistan. The main point is that the political repercussions of the physical separation are entirely dependent on the terms of Québec sovereignty. If Canada and Québec were to enter into a customs union within a broader North American free trade area (with free movement of goods, capital and persons), the Atlantic provinces would be no more cut off from Ontario than they are now. Of course, a messy and mutually disadvantageous separation agreement would have more serious consequences.

Mappism apart, the political disintegration argument becomes weaker the closer one examines it. One of the more striking observations of the past few years in English Canada is the growing political cohesion in the face of the emerging nationalist/sovereignist consensus in Québec. It is notable how very little response there has been in English Canada to the decentralist option in the current constitutional debate. At the outset, conservative economists such as Tom Courchene and think-tanks such as the Fraser Institute saw an opportunity to exploit the sovereignist thrust in Québec to impose a neo-conservative "dismantle-the-national-state" agenda. Everyone could, by local option, choose to be Québec. The blue-chip Group of 22 (high-profile politicians, businessmen and bureaucrats, including Allan Blakeney, the former social-democratic premier of Saskatchewan) presented a scheme for general devolution of powers to the provinces.

This concept has won little public support. After close consultation with the Business Council on National Issues, the federal government's 1991 constitutional proposals failed to lift the devolutionary banner aloft. Indeed, these proposals aroused some antipathy in Québec for actually suggesting greater federal power to enforce an economic union. The regional conferences held under the auspices of the Beaudoin-Dobbie committee in early 1992 have made it clear that there is no grassroots support for radical decentralization from any region, save Québec. On the other side, there is strong support outside Québec for the maintenance of an effective national government, national standards in social programs, equalization payments, and preservation and promotion of Canadian culture. This reaction might have provided the opportunity for compromise around asymmetrical federalism. Refusing this opportunity, Beaudoin-Dobbie recommended devolution not to Québec alone, but to all the provinces. They placed the neo-conservative decentralist agenda back on the table again, despite the indifference and hostility to the idea from most Canadians outside Québec. Ironically, it was Québec that quickly shot down the Beaudoin-Dobbie proposals as not offering enough devolution.

Beneath the cool attitude of English Canadians to decentralization is a sharper sense of a Canadian national identity. As a number of observers have argued persuasively, the Charter of Rights has given expression to a more inclusive idea of national citizenship. This is, of course, not true for Québec. This emergent Canadian idea of citizenship is not dependent on Québec. In fact, it may actually be in contradiction with tendencies there. Québec's more collective-rights consciousness has clashed with the individual-rights emphasis in English Canada. This was seen during the controversy over Bill 178 (the "sign law") and Québec's use of the notwithstanding clause. There is no reason to believe that Québec's departure will somehow derail the evolution of this Canadian identity. If anything, it might accelerate it by removing a structural impediment.

Today, the most extraordinary evidence of the bankruptcy of radically decentralized provincialism is the rise of the Reform Party. This party resolutely focuses its right-wing populist agenda upon the national stage. It avoids participation in provincial politics even though in Alberta (and maybe elsewhere) it need only run for election to win office instantly. Reform is the only national party in English Canada that has publicly premised its constitutional policy on a two-track option: one based on Québec's staying and the other on its going. There is no reason to think that if Québec secedes Reform would suddenly revert to Alberta- or Western-based separatism. Nor has there ever been the faintest suggestion of annexationist sentiment among the Reform Party faithful. They have always focused on what their leader articulates as the New Canada.

To take the point further, Reformers would probably become even more firmly national in focus were Québec to leave. They would be likely to inherit the political support of the right-of-centre across English Canada from a Tory party utterly discredited and destroyed by the Mulroney national unity fiasco. The Liberals would doubtless lose heavily on the right if they retained Québécois-without-a-base Jean Chrétien as leader. Historically, their support in English Canada rested on their reputation as the party that could best accommodate Québec. Thus, politics in a Canada without Québec would probably be dominated by two parties: the right-wing Reform and the centre-left NDP. Neither one has strong provincialist roots; each stresses class and national issues. If adjustments to representative institutions were to be made in order to strengthen regional/provincial representation at the centre, a reconfigured Canada might be more nationally integrated, although more ideologically divided.

There is yet another reason that Canada without Québec might be more rather than less integrated. Elite accommodation and intergovernmental relations have been the only mechanisms used by the Canadian political system to respond to the Québec question. This tradition came to a somewhat catastrophic end with Meech Lake. One of the many ironies of the Canadian experience is that pressures for democratization from below in both national communities have driven both communities farther apart as each has sought to define itself in national-democratic terms. This has sharpened the contradictions between them at both the symbolic and substantive levels and has made it difficult to reconstitute élite accommodation to paper over these differences.

During the Meech Lake imbroglio, there was much debate over whether the negative English-Canadian reaction to the notion of a Québec round represented anti-Québec sentiment. Such sentiments were certainly present. But English Canada felt itself denied a voice. Its demand that the debate become a Canada round with a strong democratic component made sense. If federalism is to be renewed in the present crisis, this cannot simply be another Québec round. If the current talks do not speak to this emergent English-Canadian demand for new forms of collective expression, they will fail.

Political separation would assist English Canada's search for more representative and democratically accountable institutions than it has now. In the process, the English-Canadian sense of empowerment might actually increase. Canada might also be a less nasty place than is suggested by those who postulate an ugly revanchist reaction to the departure of Québec. The progressive and inclusionary aspect of English-Canadian nationalism exhibited in the 1988 movement in opposition to free trade did undoubtedly take a beating with the language controversies and the failure of Meech Lake. But sovereignty for Québec might well allow this nationalism to find a more generous and progressive expression than when it is trapped within the sterile and self-destructive us-versus-them situation of National Unity federalism.

English-Canadian responses to the aboriginal claims for self-government are important here. Joint recognition by Québec and Canada of the First Nations' inherent right to self-government is a necessary step towards a peaceful and mutually beneficial settlement. Both new nations would be based on the concepts of communitarian diversity and inclusive nationality. This conforms as well with the status of both Québec and Canada as open, multicultural states with immigration policies predicated on full citizenship rights for all newcomers. These elements are hedges against narrow nationalism.

Québec's sovereignty has the potential for allowing English Canadians to experiment with the need for democratic reform of representative institutions. The issue has become identified with the triple-E crusade from the West and Atlantic Canada. But the issues raised by this territorially based demand are far-reaching. The question of gender parity in a reformed and elected second chamber is an example of how political innovation is linked more generally to the drive for democratization. Yet when this reform becomes entangled with Québec's concerns over its own power in the Senate, the process of renewal comes to a halt and the democratic agenda is sacrificed in the interest of national unity. No one suggests that progressive reforms like this one would automatically succeed in a reconfigured Canada. But it is clear that such reforms are impeded in the present situation. The reason is not that Québec is the enemy of democracy, but that accommodating aboriginal, Québec, and Canadian aspirations is simply unmanageable. This has imposed a structural constraint on democratic reform, a constraint which could be removed with Québec's accession to sovereignty.

The Economic Disintegration Argument

It is alleged that Canada could not survive as a viable economic unit without Québec. Clearly, Québec sovereignty will not be cost-free for Canada. The price cannot be estimated with precision and reliability because of the general uncertainties surrounding secession. Such calculations can only be made for the short and medium run. The more important question is: Would the resulting adjustments prove unmanageable for an already fragile and challenged Canadian economy? It is hypocritical for the federal government to make this claim when its own macroeconomic policies have had disastrous consequences. The Canada-U.S. Free Trade Agreement (FTA) and the drive towards continental marketization have already done a great deal to weaken Canada's east-west links in favour of the dominant north-south pull. The era of globalization imposes its own logic on economic development, especially when governments insist upon reducing the role of the state and freeing market forces. Supporters of these trends are ill-placed to blame Québec sovereignists for situations they themselves created.

One can argue that the impact of Québec's secession on the Canadian economy is dependent on the precise form of the post-separation settlement. Three possible outcomes are analysed here.

In the first outcome, English Canada fails to negotiate a free trade or customs union. What happens when the hard-line school in English Canada gains the upper hand in negotiations? The Canadian economy will definitely suffer, in some regions more than others. Ontario will have the most to lose, as it trades more with Québec than any other province. The Atlantic provinces will be cut off in a real sense from the rest of Canada. The Western provinces will, however, feel the effects less than their eastern neighbours, since they do little significant business with Québec. Under this differential impact, one might indeed hypothesize that Québec's sovereignty would have an accelerating effect on Canadian economic disintegration.

In the second, English Canada and Québec succeed in negotiating a free trade or customs union within the wider context of North American free trade. Such an arrangement would reduce political friction between Canada and Québec in the sensitive post-separation period without the need for common political institutions. Under such an arrangement, it is difficult to see how economic disintegration would be accelerated, at least beyond the present rate under the FTA. Adjustment would definitely be a problem; Québec and Ottawa would each have to establish programs to deal with job loss and other aspects of economic dislocation.

In the third outcome, English Canada and Québec decide to set up intergovernmental co-ordinating mechanisms. Politically, this would be much more difficult to achieve in the immediate aftermath of separation. However, in the longer run such a regime might emerge out of a free trade arrangement. After all, economic co-operation usually leads to political co-ordination between states. If this were to happen, there might be greater economic integration in the northern half of the continent than is the case at present.

Two States for the Price of One?

Disintegration scenarios are not particularly credible. They are tainted by their ideological origins as anti-sovereignty arguments. Informed speculation (and we can offer no more than this) suggests that there can be reasonable confidence in Canada's holding together without Québec. This confidence is dependent on two variables: first, that the Canadian provinces, especially Ontario, show flexibility in recasting a federation without Québec; second, that motives of revenge and punishment do not gain the upper hand in negotiating with Québec. If Canadians decide to refuse a mutually advantageous post-separation settlement, the self-serving prophecies of doom will no doubt be fulfilled.

Given the real strengths of Canadian national identity, there are grounds for optimism. Canada will have to pull together, especially in the aftermath of separation. In negotiating with Québec, Canada will finally have the opportunity to express its own personality as a nation.

Dividing in Two:
A Test for Reason and Emotion

Philip Resnick

Certain obstacles exist to negotiating a new form of association between a sovereign Québec and a sovereign Canada. Given the current mood of opinion in Canada outside Québec and the political climate certain to accompany the breakup of Canada, any meaningful Canada-Québec association may be difficult to achieve. Getting through the transition period may turn out to be the greatest single obstacle to any happy marriage between sovereignty and association in the near future.

Support for Sovereignty in Québec

Before one can discuss association, one must first examine the degree of support that sovereignty is likely to garner in Québec. In places like the Baltics, Ukraine, Slovenia or Croatia in recent years, majorities of 80 to 90 percent in favour of independence were not uncommon, providing unequivocal evidence of popular support, at least within the dominant nationality. There is no reason to expect a figure anything as high in any future Québec referendum. The split among francophones at the time of the 1980 referendum on sovereignty-association was about 50–50, while Québec's population as a whole voted 60–40 against the Parti Québécois option. Polls in the immediate post-Meech period did suggest support for sovereignty in the 65 percent range, though the figure has fallen significantly since. Moreover, many who are supporting sovereignty at the current juncture are, in fact, supporting sovereignty-association, even as many of the professed supporters of renewed federalism along the lines laid out in the Québec Liberal Party's Allaire report have, in fact, got a form of sovereignty-association in mind.[1] Unlike the East European cases, therefore, it does not appear to me that Québec francophones in overwhelming numbers would be prepared to support a pure sovereignty option, the one that Jacques Parizeau and the PQ have in mind. Yet sovereignty with association, as Québécois should surely know by now, is not something that Québec can vote for itself; association would require the concomitant approval of English Canada. Any evidence that Québec opinion remained sharply divided would weaken Québec's hand in future negotiations with Canada.

Beyond ongoing divisions among francophones, two significant groups in Québec are almost certain to vote against sovereignty: (1) anglophones and, to a slightly lesser degree, allophones (non-French, non-English-speaking residents of Québec); (2) Québec's aboriginal peoples, who in the case of northern Québec make up a clear majority of the population, with an uninterrupted presence going back for centuries. The refusal of the Cree of northern Québec to go along with any sundering of the Canadian Confederation would have telling consequences, both political and moral, for opinion in the rest of Canada, and turn the question of a sovereign Québec's exact borders into a burning one right from the start. The unhappiness and possible flight of Québec anglophones and allophones in some numbers would simultaneously ensure that a rancorous atmosphere would surround any possible negotiations between Québec and an emerging (English-) Canadian state. (To be fair, the ill-treatment of francophone minorities outside Québec would similarly poison relations.)

Opinion in English Canada

Even assuming that divisions among Québec francophones can be overcome and aboriginal and minority anglophone concerns within Québec somehow resolved, the first priority of English Canada, clearly enough, would be to forge its own identity in a context in which Québec was doing the same. Looking at this process from the perspective of someone living in western Canada, I can see a looming incompatibility between the internal dynamics of English-Canadian nationalism in the aftermath of Québec's independence and the negotiation of any ongoing association with Québec. The sense of much

English-Canadian opinion, even as I write in early 1992, is that Québec has had something of a stranglehold over federal politics for close to thirty years. There would be very little inclination to show indulgence towards Québec in any post-independence negotiations — be it over the division of the national debt, the operation of the St. Lawrence Seaway, currency agreements or any other issue. (And this again assumes that the issue of Québec's boundaries has been resolved without recourse to force.) There is more than a little animosity among English Canadians towards the personalities both of Bourassa and Parizeau and towards what many interpret as a Florentine style of politics and negotiation on the part of Québec, in which short-term manoeuvres and deliberate ambiguity veil deeper, long-term objectives.

The pressure of public opinion within English Canada might be averse to concessions to Québec, even if, as in the economic field, these might be seen as serving English-Canadian interests as well. The price of maintaining the internal unity of English Canada, torn by its own regional cleavages, might well be a very hard line in the initial breakup period. This would make any kind of association with Québec other than some kind of loose trading relationship a non-starter. For if sovereignty for Québec speaks to the reality of national sentiment within that society, it follows that some of that same sentiment would be at work in an emerging English Canada. With Québec now seen as the "other," and in certain quarters, for example among Reform Party supporters, as the dark force that brought the crisis of Canada's dissolution down upon our heads, even a purely economic association would be very difficult to engineer. One should not underestimate the power of emotion in national breakups of the type we are contemplating: the desire to do injury or exact revenge may well outweigh any cost-benefit analysis of economic advantage on the English-Canadian side.

Of course, there would be no unanimity of opinion on this subject in English Canada, any more than there would be in Québec surrounding a putative vote for sovereignty. And there can be no gainsaying the strong economic links between Québec and the rest of Canada after 125 years of common statehood, or the interest, from the English-Canadian point of view, of maintaining a land route between the Atlantic provinces and the rest of Canada across Québec's territory. Nor are the dispositions of English-Canadian opinion with regard to Québec nationalism all negative. Many would be prepared to accept the implications of a clear Yes vote for sovereignty in a future Québec referendum, provided satisfactory terms for outstanding issues — from aboriginal and anglophone minority rights to the division of the debt — could be negotiated. Such English Canadians might view a Québec vote for sovereignty as a chance to disengage (English) Canada from Québec, freeing English Canadians to forge the type of nation we would want.[2]

Modalities of Association

The long shadow of the United States would also be there, throughout the meltdown of Canada, to introduce a sobering element into both English-Canadian and Québec opinion. The Canada-U.S. Free Trade Agreement has already proven itself an extremely divisive and increasingly unpopular option where many English Canadians are concerned. The desire to resist wholesale political absorption into the United States — the historical mainspring of English-Canadian nationalism — would be a force fostering an ongoing east-west connection, including some association with Québec.

Québec, for its part, despite a more pro-American tilt in a number of respects than the rest of Canada, would also have reason to think twice about severing all ties with English Canada. Québec depends on the English-Canadian market for its exports to a greater degree than English Canada depends on Québec. More important still would be Québec's relative weakness in any negotiations with the United States, for example over a Québec-U.S. free trade agreement. The Americans have already made it clear that there would be no automatic follow-through on the existing FTA where a sovereign Québec was concerned; nor are they particularly keen on what they see as the protectionism of "Québec Inc." — its corporatist alignment of business, labour and government.

Association with Canada is therefore something of a necessity for Québec, if its newly acquired sovereignty is to be more than a sham *vis-à-vis* the United States. And this is without opening up the Pandora's box of language and culture, which a Fortress Québec would now have to defend all by itself within North America.

This leads to the observation that sovereignty for both Québec and English Canada may yet turn out to be something less than the nineteenth-century model of the all-powerful nation state would suggest. *De facto*, there would be economic and geographical forces, not to speak of forces of political sentiment and cultural survival, militating for some minimal form of Canada-Québec association. This would include trade, and possibly currency; it might extend to forms of military co-operation, the harmonization of levels of immigration and some co-operation in the sphere of foreign policy (both Canada and Québec would stand to gain significantly from speaking with a single voice in the councils of the UN, NATO, the OECD, GATT, the IMF and the World Bank). None of this would come automatically or easily following Québec's independence. And the structures of any such Canada-Québec association would invariably have to favour the Canadian partner with about 75 percent of the population and close to 80 percent of the economic resources, in ways that the adherents of *souveraineté pure et dure* would find difficult to accept. But a partnership of equals between (English) Canada and Québec is a non-starter where majority English-Canadian opinion would be concerned. For unlike the European Community with its twelve members and, until recently, a roughly even balance among its members, any Canada-Québec arrangement would be asymmetrical from the start.

At the end of the day, therefore, one might end up with two ostensibly sovereign states in the northern part of North America, and with aboriginal peoples exercising a good deal of self-government over important parts of each. Yet these two sovereign states would share some common arrangements in a number of areas that touch on relations with the external world, such as trade, defence, foreign affairs, and in their relations with one another — the free flow of people and goods between them, a single currency, parallel protection for minority language rights. These, at the minimum, would entail bureaucratic co-ordination; but they might also have to extend to ministerial co-ordination, and with time, to some parliamentary/legislative co-ordination as well. In other words, one might see the emergence of some of the same structures which supporters of asymmetrical federalism or confederal-type arrangements have been postulating in our current constitutional debate.

A brief sketch of these two alternative options might be helpful to the reader. Asymmetrical federalism would entail a direct trade-off between increased powers for the National Assembly and government of Québec and a decreased role for MPs, senators and ministers from Québec at the federal level. If Québec — but not the other nine provinces — were to attain control over several of the areas of federal jurisdiction spelled out in the Allaire report — for example, culture, communications, housing, labour-market training and unemployment insurance — then two things would follow: (1) Québec would have to receive formal compensation — through tax points — to help it finance these activities, even while giving up any rights to federal transfer or equalization payments for them in the future. (2) Québec MPs, senators and ministers in Ottawa could no longer make decisions for the rest of Canada in areas over which Québec would now be exercising full control.

The federal parliament and government would *de facto* acquire a dual character. For matters in which Québec was still bound by federal jurisdiction, its legislators in Ottawa would have the same role as those from the rest of Canada. But in exclusively (English-) Canadian matters, only legislators from Canada outside Québec would make decisions. Bills coming before Parliament would have to be clearly designated as applying to Canada with or without Québec; the same would be true for agenda items coming to cabinet.[3]

For such an arrangement to function, the areas of exclusively Québec jurisdiction would have to be kept fairly limited. For in a parliamentary system it would prove unacceptable for a political party with a majority of seats in Canada including Québec, but only a minority of seats in Canada outside Québec, to exercise power over both, if Québec had opted out of a whole range of federal jurisdictions. The rest of Canada would demand the right to be governed by a majority of its own choosing. In other words, if Québec were to press for exclusive jurisdiction over (for the sake of argument) the twenty-two powers spelled out in the Allaire report, asymmetrical federalism of the type outlined above would become quite unworkable. We would instead have to move to a more confederal-type arrangement.

Under such a scheme, Canada outside Québec would continue to have provincial and territorial governments and legislatures with much the powers that they currently enjoy. There would be a government and a parliament for English Canada, with an elected House of Commons and a Senate in which the West, the North and the Atlantic provinces would outweigh Ontario by better than two to one. Québec would have no representation in the parliament of English Canada or in its government. In turn, Québec would acquire most of the powers that the Allaire report enumerated. But in five or six crucial areas — foreign policy, defence, international trade, currency and citizenship, and possibly the environment — there would be the understanding that we need an ongoing union. And we would have to develop the political structures, both a parliament and a government for our union, to accomplish this.[4]

If either of these alternatives is ever achieved, however, it will entail more democratic forms of constitution making than we have known until now. One clear result of the Meech process has been a profound antipathy within English-Canadian opinion to the top-down style of executive federalism that has dominated our constitutional process. Yet sovereignty in constitutional matters — as the Québécois were the first to show in the run-up to the referendum of 1980 — ultimately must reside not with parliaments or legislatures, but with the people. There is a new spirit of Rousseau or Jefferson abroad in our historically Tory, counter-revolutionary society that would ensure that the people of English Canada, no less than those of Québec, would have the final say on any associational model that might be devised. In much the same way, the people of English Canada would have to have the final say on the internal organization of any future (English-) Canadian state.

Bearing in mind these more participatory and democratic features of sovereignty in late-twentieth-century Canada, let me stress the obstacles that may make any associational outcome difficult, if not impossible, to realize in a post-independence scenario. The insistence on the Québec nation-alist side on achieving sovereignty first, before any association with Canada can be concluded, may satisfy a deep-felt desire, at least on the part of Québec's cultural élites, to undo the legacy of the Conquest. This very symbolic event, however, may trigger off sentiments of hurt and ultimately hostility in English Canada that may make the achievement of just such a new Canada-Québec association so much the more difficult. It may also induce a significant number of English Canadians to support closer integration with the United States, with whom we already share so much in the economic and cultural arenas, in preference to continuing integration with a politically es-tranged and culturally alien Québec. The disposition to favour a clean "surgical" break with Québec — undoubtedly accom-panied by territorial acrimony — may well gain the upper hand.

Renegotiating the Existing Arrangement

English Canada's refusal, for its part, to recognize that Québec is a nation in the sociological sense has until now made it much more difficult to envisage any restructuring of Canada along asymmetrical federal or confederal lines. Yet only such mea-sures would begin to address the aspirations to significant autonomy that go far beyond indépendantiste circles in Québec (one thinks of the two-to-one support for the Allaire report at the Québec Liberal Convention of March 1991), and offer the promise of any lasting solution to our national crisis. And paradoxically, this very toughness on the English-Cana-dian side may well drive Québec opinion into a harder sovereignist mould, thereby jeopardizing any future Canada-Québec association.

Quite clearly, any functioning association would require agreement on the minimal things we need to share, and this in an atmosphere of mutual trust. If trust is absent, all we will be able to fall back on is a Hobbesian motif for co-operation based on fear for our respective survival. Yet this would make for a very fragile association indeed, with numerous *arrières-pensées* and suspicions on both sides. One can hardly envisage the delegation of effective powers to some superstructural level under such circumstances. The best we could hope for is a Canadian version of the Commonwealth of Independent States, with Québec playing the role of Ukraine, suspicious of (English) Canada, and Canada playing Russia and no less suspicious of Québec. This is a far cry from the integrative model of association being pursued by the European Community.

This leads me to conclude in a manner that implicitly challenges the underlying premise of this volume. Not because I am seeking to be contrary, nor because I personally would be unwilling to see English Canada negotiate with a sovereign Québec — should that event arise. But we would be wise first to explore other options seriously — from asymmetrical federalism to confederal arrangements — options that the federal proposals inspired by *Shaping Canada's Future Together* and the Beaudoin-Dobbie report wilfully ignore and that the sovereignty option also sweeps to one side.

Everything I have been arguing suggests that it would prove much easier to renegotiate the existing Canada-Québec relationship in a fundamental fashion — and this is what I, for one, have in mind and what I think was being articulated in several of the constitutional conferences in 1992 — without our going the route of two separate nation states first. For in the end, any meaningful Canada-Québec association would have to mean something less than a fully sovereign Québec or a fully sovereign English Canada. Yet there may never be any such association if, emulating some of the nationalities of the former Soviet Union or Yugoslavia, we press the logic of nationalism — Québécois, English Canadian or aboriginal — to its more intransigent conclusions.

III
Aboriginal Rights:
Mega-Questions for
Canada and Québec

Does the Road to Québec Sovereignty Run through Aboriginal Territory?

Mary Ellen Turpel

The problem here is a denial of the past, or a narrowness of vision that sees the arrival and then spread of immigrants as the very purpose of history.

—Hugh Brody[1]

Québec's resources are permanent; we do not owe them to a political system, or to specific circumstances. They are a gift of nature, which has favoured us more than others in this respect by allowing us to play a more important economic role, thanks to our resources ...

—Government of Québec[2]

It is important to respect the aspirations of Québécois to self-determination, if they act in accordance with international law.[1]

At the same time, it is difficult to address in a totally dispassionate way the spectre of "Québec secession." Every time I begin to write about the international legal and Canadian constitutional dimensions of Québec separation or accession to full sovereignty from the perspective of aboriginal peoples'[3] status, one area of my so-called professional and personal

---

Meegwetch to Paul Joffe for our discussions about the issues discussed in this paper and for what he symbolizes for me in this struggle: a non-aboriginal Quebecer deeply committed to justice for aboriginal peoples. *Meegwetch* also to Paul for inspiring the title of this paper. Responsibility for the views expressed in this paper are strictly my own.

"expertise" as an aboriginal woman and law professor, I am confronted with my concern for the status and rights of those most marginalized in this discussion — the aboriginal peoples in Québec.

The claim by Québécois for full sovereignty, as it has been conceived by many secessionists,[4] appears to rest on the erasure of the political status of aboriginal peoples and the denial of their most fundamental rights to self-determination. These are two most critical points, seemingly resisted by the main political parties in Québec, and not taken seriously enough outside Québec by Canadian politicians, intellectuals or the academic community. I am cautious with terminology here because just writing the expression "Québec secession" poses a problem — it conjures up an image of a single territory and a homogeneous people setting up a new state. The point of this essay is to demonstrate that it is not this simple.

How can it be presumed that there can be an accession to sovereign status for Québec without considering the pivotal matter of the status and rights of the aboriginal peoples in this scenario? What does it mean to "consider" the status and rights of aboriginal peoples in a secessionist scenario? It is not a perfunctory matter, or an administrative decision considering how best to transfer a head of jurisdiction (Indians and lands reserved for the Indians)[5] from the federal authority to a newly independent Québec state. It is more complex than this, in both a legal and political sense.[6] The political success of the secessionist movement will ultimately be judged on its democratic process, its respect for fundamental human rights and, in the end, its political legitimacy in the eyes of the international community. I believe that the relations with aboriginal peoples could prove to be the key to assessing that legitimacy and could well influence the international recognition and acceptance of any new Québec state.

Who are the aboriginal peoples in Québec? Most people know something about the Crees in northern Québec because of their current opposition to the Great Whale hydro-electric project in the James Bay territory, or perhaps because of the *James Bay Northern Québec Agreement.*[7] However, it is not only the Crees whose homeland is captured in some sense by the provincial boundaries of Québec. There are also Inuit,

Naskapi, Mikmaq, Maliseet, Mohawk, Montagnais, Abenaki, Algonquin, Atikawekw and Huron whose homelands are at least partially within the geographical boundaries of the Province of Québec. I say "partially" because, using the Mikmaq as a case in point, the Mikmaq of Gaspé comprise one of the seven districts of the Mikmaq nation, Mikmakik, which extends into Nova Scotia, New Brunswick, Newfoundland and Prince Edward Island. A District Chief from this region sits on the Mikmaq Grand Council, the traditional governing body of the Mikmaq people situated in Cape Breton, Nova Scotia. The administrative boundary of the province of Québec for Mikmaqs in the Gaspé is an arbitrary boundary unrelated to their identity, both territorially and spiritually.

To note this is nothing new for aboriginal peoples given that all provincial boundaries are somewhat arbitrary from an aboriginal historical perspective. These provincial boundaries, internal to Canada, do not demarcate aboriginal homelands. Indeed, even certain international boundaries suffer likewise from a similar arbitrariness. I will use the Mohawks at Akwesasne as another case in point. Their community extends over two provincial boundaries (Ontario and Québec) and an international boundary with New York State. Their sense of division is compounded by the existence of three boundaries which in no way correspond to their own territorial, spiritual or political identity as Mohawks or members of the Iroquois Confederacy. What about "Québec secession" for these First Nations? While some aboriginal peoples in Québec do speak French, their cultural and linguistic identities are first and foremost shaped by their own First Nations culture, history and language.[8]

While the Province of Québec is undoubtedly no worse than any other province in terms of its history of a strained relationship with aboriginal peoples (although I would argue this is not an appropriate threshold for assessment), the recent confrontation with Mohawks at Oka in 1991 and the ongoing battle with the Crees over further hydro-electric development in the James Bay territory seem to have particularly embittered relationships between aboriginal peoples and the provincial government. Not surprisingly, when a future is laid out by the secessionists which envisages a fully sovereign state, claiming to exercise complete jurisdiction over peoples and resources within the current provincial boundaries, aboriginal peoples express concern. Given the recent political history of Québec, the impact of the change in political status of the province on aboriginal peoples' historic relationship with the Crown presents a chilling potential for a complete breakdown in the political relationship between aboriginal peoples and Québec.

Open discussion, dialogue and consideration of aboriginal peoples' status and rights need to begin immediately in Québec, but they also require an *informed basis*, founded on principles of equality of peoples, mutual respect and self-determination. There are basic human rights principles at issue in this debate and the legitimacy of the sovereignist movement may well stand or fall on how these principles are reconciled. The sovereignist movement cannot continue as a virtual steamroller ignoring or denying aboriginal peoples' status and rights and still hope to be successful. Thus far, the secessionists have not presented a framework for dialogue which embraces basic principles of respect for aboriginal peoples and their status and rights. Instead, aboriginal peoples have been offered vague assurances that they will be treated well by a new Québec state. When aboriginal peoples have articulated their concerns and set out some basic principles upon which to begin a dialogue with Québécois, they have been unjustifiably attacked and diminished. It seems that, on the part of the Québec sovereignists, there is no genuine commitment to understanding the aboriginal perspective on full sovereignty for Québec.

Self-determination: The Competing Claims

The explosive political atmosphere encircling the debate over full sovereignty and aboriginal peoples was revealed when the National Chief of the Assembly of First Nations, Ovide Mercredi, appeared in 1992 before the Québec National Assembly's Committee to Examine Matters Relating to the Accession of Québec to Sovereignty.[9] The National Chief, appearing with Chiefs and Elders from a number of the First Nations in Québec, told the Committee:

There can be no legitimate secession by any people in Québec if the right to self-determination of First Nations are denied, suppressed or ignored in order to achieve independence. Our rights do not take a back seat to yours ... Only through openness, of the mind and of the heart, can questions of such vital importance to your people and ours be reconciled. The alternative, which we do not favour, is confrontation ...

The response to this, and other submissions, both by the Québec media and some members of the Committee, was one of outrage. It was as if the sovereignists were wilfully blinded to the principles articulated by aboriginal peoples in support of their rights. This is particularly frustrating given that, at many levels, the principles that aboriginal peoples advance for the basis of a political relationship with Canada or a sovereign Québec are not very different from Québec's position (self-determination, territory, identity). At least in some cases, I believe the aboriginal position could prove stronger legally and politically. Since the Lesage era in the 1960s, French Canadians have argued that they want to be masters of their own house (*maîtres chez nous*). Aboriginal peoples have asserted an equally powerful concept — self-determination or self-government.

Sovereignists seem to see threats only when aboriginal peoples articulate their own perspectives. The worrisome point in this fury over the National Chief's appearance before the Committee on Sovereignty is that he is a committed moderate. There were no threats of violence, only pleas for dialogue and for measures to prevent a confrontation over the competing positions. As Chief Mercredi stated: "I, as National Chief, welcome constructive dialogue between First Nations and Quebecers on constitutional issues. We should build partnerships in support of our respective rights and not construct hierarchies of your rights over ours." Nevertheless, there seems to be a powerful drive towards castigating aboriginal peoples for advocating aboriginal and treaty rights. For example, the National Chief was chastised by Claude Masson of *La Presse* for speaking "exaggerated, insulting and outrageous words" and said that the aboriginal leadership "must behave like reasonable and responsible human beings and not like warriors or criminals with a right of life and death over every-body else."[10] This utter misrepresentation of the basic princi-ples advanced by the National Chief, a leader who has worked hard to build alliances and open dialogue with Québec, demonstrates how wide the gulf is growing between sovereignists and aboriginal peoples. The era of disciplining aboriginal peoples for being different is over. Political support for the aspirations of Québécois will not be won in Canada or around the world with this type of denigration.

There has been an obvious strategic decision in the Québec independence movement to view aboriginal issues as business for a later date — after the accession to full sovereignty. The executive of the Parti Québécois has recently adopted a reso-lution to this effect. There seems to be little priority placed on dealing with aboriginal peoples' status and rights before ac-cession.[11] In response to aboriginal suggestions that the situa-tion is critical in Québec, there is a "why only pick on us" sentiment in the secessionist movement's response to aborigi-nal peoples, which is ill informed. Aboriginal peoples have been vigorously advancing their right to self-determination, territory and cultural rights at all levels in Canada and inter-nationally. The *Delgamuukw* action in British Columbia is a case in point. This case, which is now before the British Co-lumbia Court of Appeal, is an assertion of Gitksan and Wet'suewet'en political and territorial sovereignty against the federal and provincial Crown.

The movement for adequate recognition of aboriginal and treaty rights is not confined to Québec. With or without the prospect of Québec's secession, the rights will be advanced in that province, too. But in light of the sovereignist agenda, it is seen as critical here because the movement for full sovereignty calls into question aboriginal peoples' status and rights in a most immediate and far-reaching way — there will be a deci-sion made about the future of all peoples in Québec, in a referendum to be held by October 26, 1992. Issues relating to that referendum — self-determination, territory and identity — are brought directly to the fore by the sovereignist agenda which, once engaged through Bill 150, is a veritable jugger-naut. Aboriginal peoples cannot be expected to ignore what is coming at them full force.

Moreover, these issues deserve more than just passing consideration in the context of the discussions in this text of negotiating with a sovereign Québec. From a human rights perspective, could there legitimately be a fully sovereign Québec without according equal consideration to the aspirations and choices of aboriginal peoples? To simply begin the discussion by sketching the contours of negotiations with a sovereign Québec may be putting the cart before the horse. For aboriginal peoples, Québécois and Canadians there is a great deal at stake. Either one legitimizes *a priori* the reduction of First Nations peoples to the status of ethnic minorities with no right of self-determination, or one recognizes that there would be several other potential sovereign entities with which a Québec state would have to negotiate.

Negotiating with a sovereign Québec could only mean, for aboriginal peoples, a political relationship based on negotiating international treaties between emerging independent peoples. Existing treaties involving Canada, aboriginal peoples and Québec, such as the *James Bay Northern Québec Agreement*, would not have continuing validity, and Québec would not be able to claim the benefits of such treaties. If full sovereignty is declared by Québec, this would amount to a unilateral breach of that agreement. The *James Bay Northern Québec Agreement* was not only explicitly negotiated and ratified in a federal context, but also contained perpetual federal and provincial obligations that cannot be altered without the aboriginal parties' consent. A unilateral declaration of independence would be a clear breach of that agreement and Québec could not claim the benefits of the agreement while not respecting its negotiated terms.

Aboriginal peoples are not simply a head of jurisdiction, as seems to have been presumed by many Québécois and others outside the province. The first peoples in Canada are political entities — "peoples" in the international legal sense. This means that as peoples (with distinct languages, cultures, territories, populations and governments), aboriginal peoples have full rights of self-determination. For the purposes of discussions over sovereignty, aboriginal peoples must be seen to enjoy the status of peoples with a right to self-determination. This position is supported by both Canadian and international law. The International Bill of Rights (an instrument which I presume a fully sovereign Québec would want to respect in order to gain entry into the international community) recognizes the right of *all* peoples to self-determination. By this it is meant that peoples should freely determine their political status and that this should not be determined for them by a state, or an external actor.

Aboriginal peoples are independent political entities with distinct languages, cultures, histories, territories, spiritualities and governments. As such, they can choose or determine their future relationship with Canada or a sovereign Québec. This should not be determined for them by other peoples or governments. At present, the position of many sovereignists does not embrace self-determination for aboriginal peoples. It presumes that aboriginal peoples are not peoples or are too insignificant and dispersed to be independent political actors.[12] As academics and intellectuals, we should not promote recognition for a fully sovereign Québec if it means that aboriginal peoples' competing rights of self-determination will be compromised.

We need to recognize that when the political discourse shifts to Québec's secession, it moves from the familiar realm of federalist considerations of distinct society and the recognition and protection of distinct identities to the less certain context of political and territorial sovereignty. With this shift, there is a different grid structuring the debate, one with far broader implications. Once basic concepts of control over territory and peoples are put so squarely on the agenda by people in Québec, the struggles in which aboriginal peoples are engaged across Canada come sharply into focus. The basic presumption which operates in the minds of many sovereignists is that they either have, or will automatically acquire, sovereignty *over* aboriginal peoples in Québec. Flowing from this sovereignty, some Québécois believe that the French-Canadian majority in Québec can decide what it wants to do with aboriginal peoples. But what is the source of their sovereignty over aboriginal peoples and territories? Is it the right of the French-Canadian nation in Québec to self-determination?

It would seem clear that the French-Canadian people are faced with the competing rights to self-determination of aboriginal peoples. Moreover, the right to self-determination is not a right of the province of Québec.[13] In international law, provinces do not enjoy a right of self-determination, peoples do. Consequently, other peoples who may have competing claims, especially to territory, cannot be ignored. Sovereignists in Québec have, in effect, constructed their claim on the basis of the province of Québec as the entity which will exercise the right of self-determination. However, this would unjustly efface the competing and legitimate rights of aboriginal peoples.

As this short discussion illustrates, the competing self-determination claims by French Canadians and aboriginal peoples need to be carefully examined before we can deal with referenda or territory in an equitable and mutually respectful manner. Indeed, these three issues — self-determination, referendum and territorial claims — are critically interwoven in the current Canadian context. No single issue can stand alone without the others being considered. An independent Québec state would not meet with international recognition if aboriginal peoples were not treated as peoples, with full enjoyment of human rights, including the right of self-determination. Self-determination for aboriginal peoples may well require that they be involved as full, equal, and independent participants in the decision about the accession of Québec to full sovereignty. I emphasize "independent" because aboriginal peoples must be dealt with as "peoples," not "minorities" subject to the political will of the province. As distinct political entities, aboriginal peoples must participate in that process through their leadership and not be presumed to be "represented" by members of the Québec National Assembly or the federal parliament.

The federal government also has obligations to recognize aboriginal peoples' rights to self-determination. If there are to be negotiations with Québec on secession, then aboriginal peoples cannot be treated as a head of jurisdiction along with monetary issues or other items. Aboriginal peoples must each decide their relationship with a new Québec state. As United States President Woodrow Wilson stated in 1917, " ... no right exists anywhere to hand peoples about from sovereignty to sovereignty as if they were property."[14] Aboriginal peoples cannot be handed from one sovereign (the federal Crown) to another (an independent Québec state) as if they were property. Yet this seems to be the presumption operating in Bill 150, the Allaire report, and the Bélanger-Campeau commission report, where aboriginal peoples are viewed as minorities, authority over which can be simply transferred to a sovereign Québec.

The persistence of this mindset of viewing aboriginal peoples as minorities or of an inferior status to French or English newcomers goes to the very problem Hugh Brody identifies in the quotation set out at the beginning of this essay: there is a narrowness of vision here which sees the arrival and spread of immigrants (whether they be French, English or otherwise) as the very purpose of history, including Canadian history. It is this vision which selects immigrant political objectives as superior to and more compelling than those of aboriginal peoples. Aboriginal perspectives and political aspirations are treated as secondary within the immigrant vision. Yet the immigrant vision has been vigorously challenged. Even some voices in Québec have challenged it, although they seem to fall on deaf ears. For example, Professor Daniel Turp (Université de Montréal), a leading sovereignist academic frequently cited by the Parti Québécois, acknowledged, when he appeared before the Committee on Accession, that "in my opinion [aboriginal peoples] constitute peoples who are self-identified as peoples ... this would confer on them a right to self-determination at the same level as Québec ... the same rules apply to aboriginal peoples as to Québécois."[15] This aspect of his opinion has been largely ignored by sovereignists who instead emphasise the right of the French in Québec to self-determination.

We know that the Canadian constitution is premised on a privileged reading of history, or the immigrant vision of (only) two founding nations, and that it has marginalized or excluded aboriginal visions. Aboriginal peoples, Québécois and other Canadians should strive to establish a more honourable and collaborative process. This entails fundamental changes to existing political processes and constitutional structures. Moreover, in the context of secession, it requires a full airing of opinions on aboriginal peoples' status and rights.

Territory

In 1992, David Cliche, the Parti Québécois "native policy" adviser and a member of the executive of the Parti Québécois, argued that, upon secession, Québec will naturally take the territory within the current provincial boundaries. This position was endorsed by the leader of the Parti Québécois, Jacques Parizeau. What it ignores is that aboriginal peoples have no say in the matter. The decisions over the control of aboriginal territories should be made by aboriginal peoples, not Québec or the federal government. Cliche opposes this view and suggests that the sovereignists would offer the aboriginal people the best deal they could ever get. But this promise misses the point, because self-determination for aboriginal peoples is not about the prospects of a good deal some time in the future. It is about peoples deciding freely their political and territorial status now and not being forced into political arrangements without that independent collective decision.

The gulf in our respective understandings of the situation is a broad one. I believe that from an international legal perspective, and in terms of the political legitimacy of the sovereignist movement, only aboriginal peoples can decide their future status. This cannot be usurped by the sovereignists, just as French Canadians want to decide their future without this being unilaterally usurped by the federal government.

Much of the sovereignist argument on territorial claims has rested on a doctrine of international law called *uti possidetis juris*, which is offered to support the claim that they will enter independence with the territory they had before. In this case, the secessionists say the territory they had before is Québec within the current provincial boundaries. They sometimes call this the principle of "territorial integrity." This doctrine is said to displace the ordinary principle of occupation as a basis for territorial sovereignty. The international law on whether *uti possidetis* is compelling is dubious at best, with the leading scholars in the field wondering whether the doctrine is even a norm of international law.[16] Even the International Court of Justice has cautioned that this doctrine is problematic as it conflicts with a significant principle in international law — self-determination.[17] The sovereignist claim to take the territory within the current provincial boundaries is weak, internationally, especially given that much land in the province is subject to aboriginal claims which have yet to be resolved, and which are tied in to aboriginal self-determination. The secessionists will have to present other arguments that can satisfy international legal standards if they hope to be recognized as a legitimate state with the existing provincial boundaries as their territorial base.

Control over aboriginal peoples' territories has been essential for the prosperity of Québec. This certainly has been the experience following the boundary extensions of 1898 and 1912. It is clear that the secessionist position is rooted in a realization that these territories are of continued significance. Issues of control over territory are fundamental to the secessionists because mass development projects like James Bay II (Great Whale) are part of their economic plan. Aboriginal peoples have legitimate concerns about the territorial consequences of full sovereignty. Would this mean that a new Québec state can unilaterally make development decisions? James Bay may be but a glimpse of what aboriginal peoples could face with Québec secession and full claims to jurisdiction over their territories. It has been an enormous struggle, albeit increasingly successful, for the Crees to gain support for their opposition to further James Bay hydro-electric development. As Grand Chief Coon-Come reflects:

> Bourassa's dream [of hydro-electric development] has become our nightmare. It has contaminated our fish with mercury. It has destroyed the spawning grounds. It has destroyed the nesting grounds of the waterfowl. It has displaced and dislocated our people and broken the fabric of our society. And we have decided, knowing the behaviour of the animals, that we will not be like the fox who, when he sees danger, crawls back to his hole. We have come out to stop the destruction of our land.[18]

In this quotation notice that the Grand Chief says "our" when he refers to the land and to the fish. This contradicts the view of the government of Québec (excerpted at the outset of this essay) that the land and resources of the province are a gift of nature to the people of Québec, in which regard they are more favoured than others.

The territorial claims of the secessionists to the current provincial boundaries are legally and politically insecure. The territory was not given to Québécois as a gift of nature. It was a gift of the federal government in 1898 and 1912 — a gift made without the consent of the owners, aboriginal peoples. French Canadians will have to support their territorial claim to the lands within the existing provincial boundaries with something other than erroneous theories about gifts of nature or *uti possidetis*.[19] No one can presume these are theirs to take when the original occupants of the land, aboriginal peoples, assert their rights. Voting in a referendum in support of this position is not enough either, legally or politically.

Referendum: The Who/Whom

In 1902, Lenin posited the critical question in politics as "who/whom": who rules whom, who decides for whom? Bill 150 provides for a referendum sometime between October 12 and 26, 1992. The who/whom question is pivotal. Bill 150 states that if the results of the referendum are in favour of secession, they will "constitute a proposal" that Québec acquire the status of a sovereign state one year to the day from the holding of the referendum. What question will be put to voters, who will vote, and the weighing of the results are all unclear at this point. For aboriginal peoples in Québec, the ambiguity of the referendum is threatening because if a vote is registered in favour of sovereignty, it could legitimize the appropriation of aboriginal territories and the assumption of authority over them. They would be the "whom" ruled by the "who" in a simple majority referendum.

Is a simple 50-plus-1 majority enough in these circumstances? If it was, this could mean that aboriginal peoples' self-determination rights would be overridden, as aboriginal peoples may simply be outvoted by larger populations in non-aboriginal regions of Québec. This kind of a referendum could not be held up internationally as supporting accession to sovereignty because of its implications for aboriginal peoples. Referendums are numbers games and aboriginal peoples would be set up for exclusion unless double majorities or separate referendums are employed. Aboriginal peoples will have to insist on double majorities, or independent (traditional) means for expressing their views on accession to full sovereignty. They cannot be lumped into a general referendum if the result is to be accepted for any purposes as a legitimate mandate for statehood.

While concerns about the status and rights of aboriginal peoples are grave, it is nevertheless important to stress that this is a great opportunity for the sovereignists to lead the way on self-determination. There is a natural alliance which could be struck between aboriginal peoples and the secessionists whereby aboriginal self-determination could be respected as a priority. This requires an immediate dialogue with aboriginal peoples within a framework of respect for the equally compelling right of aboriginal peoples to self-determination. This dialogue cannot be informed by the "trust us, we'll give you a good deal later" attitude which seems so popular among sovereignists.

Such an alliance would be a historic event and could lead to interesting and innovative political arrangements with Canada and a new Québec state. However, the basic principles for such an alliance, such as aboriginal self-determination, must be discussed and openly embraced by the sovereignist movement. This requires a reconsideration of elements of its vision of a new Québec state. Particularly, the territorial integrity position would have to be revised to embrace at least the principle of shared and co-managed resources. Currently, there is no indication that this is happening and the responsibility is really on the sovereignist side to demonstrate a willingness to respect the right of aboriginal self-determination.

As the title of this essay would suggest, the road, to full sovereignty for Québec runs through aboriginal territory. There is no detour, no other path. There is only one road, and it must be a course of justice and respect for aboriginal peoples. The secessionists will be well advised to look carefully at the map of this road now that they have chosen the path of statehood. Should Québécois fail to deal with aboriginal self-determination, their movement stands to lose a great deal of legitimacy and support both in Canada and the international community.

Aboriginal Nations and Québec's Boundaries: Canada Couldn't Give What It Didn't Have

Kent McNeil

The issue of Québec's boundaries has recently attracted considerable attention in the press, particularly during the current round of constitutional discussions. The question being asked is this: If Québec decides to separate from the rest of Canada, will it be entitled to retain its present boundaries, or will adjustments have to be made? This article deals with Québec's northern boundary, which has been changed twice since Confederation.[1] First in 1898, concurrent statutes of Canada and Québec drew the northern boundary of the province along the Eastmain River to Patamisk Lake, and due east from there to the Hamilton River.[2] Then in 1912, Canada and Québec extended the northern boundary to its present location along Hudson Strait and Ungava Bay (see Map 1).[3]

Authority to make these changes has generally been assumed to be contained in the Constitution Act, 1871, which, among other things, provided:

The Parliament of Canada may from time to time, with the consent of the Legislature of any Province of the said

I would like to thank Robin MacKay for his invaluable help and research for this article, and Michael Posluns, Peter Usher and Martin Weinstein for their very helpful suggestions for source materials. Brian Slattery read a draft and provided many useful comments, for which I am most grateful. Of course, responsibility for the ideas expressed rests on me.

Map 1

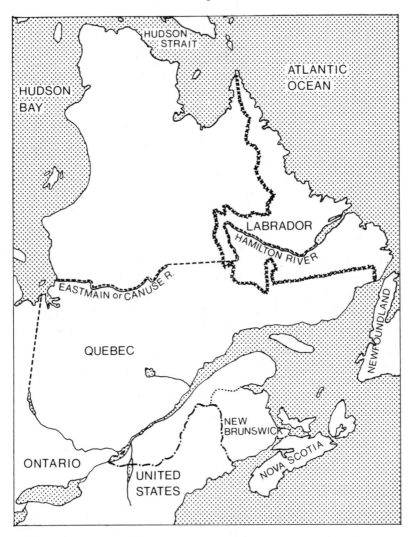

Boundaries of Québec:

———— As set by the Quebec Boundary Acts of 1898

xxxx   As determined by the Privy Council in *Re Labrador Boundary*
        [1927] 2 D.L.R. 401.

Maps 1 and 2 have been reproduced with the publisher's permission
from Kent McNeil, *Native Rights and the Boundaries of Rupert's Land and
the North-Western Territory* (Saskatoon: University of Saskatchewan
Native Law Centre, 1982).

Dominion, increase, diminish, or otherwise alter the limits of such Province ... [4]

The purpose of this article is to challenge this assumption on the ground that it is rooted in an unacceptable colonial view of Canadian history which disregards the existence of aboriginal nations in the region under consideration.[5]

While the discussion in this article focuses on Québec, it is important to realize that the colonial assumptions being challenged relate to other parts of Canada as well.[6] In British Columbia, for example, it has been assumed that the British Crown was able to acquire sovereignty over the aboriginal nations living there by so-called discovery and settlement, without an actual conquest of those nations and without their consent.[7] The arguments presented in this article regarding the Hudson's Bay Company Charter, by which the Crown appears to have asserted sovereignty over what is now regarded as northern Québec, apply equally to other parts of Canada which were supposedly within the Charter's limits, such as northern Ontario, most of the Prairie provinces, and the eastern part of the Northwest Territories.[8] The problem is therefore a general one: the claims of France and Britain, and hence of Canada, to sovereignty over the aboriginal nations and their territories rest on shaky foundations.[9] But before examining the nature of the problem in northern Québec, the main aspects of the current debate over that province's northern boundary from the colonial British and French perspectives need to be understood.

The Evolution of Québec's Boundaries

Those who suggest that Québec's northern boundary should be re-examined in the event of separation argue that the territories included in Québec in 1898 and 1912 were not part of that province historically, and were added on the understanding that Québec would remain in Canada. Québec received those territories not as a sovereign state but as a province, and so is not necessarily entitled to retain them if the Québécois opt to leave the Canadian federation.

From the colonial perspective of the European powers, however, the historical extent of Québec's territory has never been

Map 2

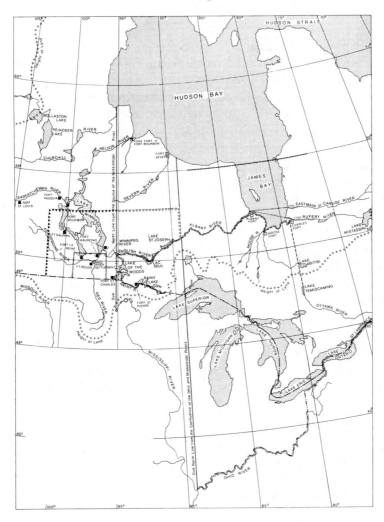

MAP 5 — LEGEND

.... Southern boundary of Rupert's Land proposed by Hudson's Bay Company, 1700-1

•••••••••••••• Southern boundary of Rupert's Land proposed by France, 1700-1

—••—••—•• Southern boundary of Quebec set by *Quebec Act,* 1774

—•—•—•—• Boundary between Canada and the United States since 1818

⁄⁄⁄⁄⁄⁄⁄⁄⁄⁄ Boundary of Manitoba set by *Manitoba Act,* 1870

▼▼▼▼▼▼▼ Boundary of Manitoba set by statute in 1881

▽▽▽▽▽▽▽ 1881 boundary of Manitoba in north-east according to *Ontario Boundaries Case,* 1884

— — — — — North-eastern boundary of Ontario according to Ontario Boundaries Arbitration, 1878, and *Canada (Ontario Boundary) Act, 1889*

—I—I—I—I— North-western boundary of Ontario according to *Ontario Boundaries Case,* 1884, and *Canada (Ontario Boundary) Act, 1889*

■ French forts west of Lake Superior
□ English forts on Hudson Bay

authoritatively determined. The reason for this is that France and Britain were colonial rivals in North America until the cession of New France to Britain in 1763. Britain's claims to the north went back to voyages of so-called discovery into Hudson Bay, and the royal charter which created the Hudson's Bay Company in 1670. The charter purported to grant to the Company a vast territory called Rupert's Land, comprising all the lands draining into Hudson Bay and Hudson Strait.[10] France, however, disputed the extent of Britain's claims. A couple of wars and two peace treaties failed to resolve the issue, with the result that the boundary between Rupert's Land and the colony of New France was never settled.[11]

For this reason, it is not clear that the 1898 statutes involved an *extension* of Québec's boundaries, particularly as in 1701 the Hudson's Bay Company had been prepared to accept the Eastmain (then the Canuse) River as the boundary between Rupert's Land and New France (see Map 2).[12] The uncertainty is apparent from the debate in the Canadian House of Commons on the 1898 Act, during which some members of Parliament from Québec argued that the statute merely described the existing northern boundary of the province, while some members from English Canada argued that it extended the boundary north from its former location at the height of land between the Hudson and St. Lawrence watersheds.[13] As the Act itself "declared" the boundary to be along the line described therein, in contrast to the 1912 Act which "increased" the limits of the province, the view of the Québec members was not explicitly rejected.[14]

Be that as it may, the territory covered by the 1912 Acts was clearly added to the province, given that those statutes expressly increased the limits beyond those declared in 1898.[15] However, before concluding that Québec should not be allowed to retain that territory if it separates, the historical location of some of Québec's other boundaries from the perspective of the European powers should be taken into account.[16] Going back to New France, the claims of the French to the west extended far beyond the present boundary between Québec and Ontario to include the area around the Great Lakes and part of the Prairie region.[17] After New France was ceded to Britain, a new Province of Québec was carved out of the ceded territory by the Royal Proclamation of 1763.[18] As the boundaries established by the Proclamation left many French settlements outside the province, one reason for enacting the Québec Act in 1774 was to extend the limits to encompass the excluded French population.[19] Québec was accordingly redefined by the Act to include all of what later became Upper Canada, as well as the region south and west of the Great Lakes to the Ohio and Mississippi rivers. These territories were later taken away from the province, partly when Britain gave up its claims to the region south of the Great Lakes to the newly created United States in 1783, and then by the division of Québec into Lower and Upper Canada in 1791. So French Canada was in fact reduced from the territory claimed by the King of France prior to 1763 to the truncated province of Lower Canada, which entered Confederation as Québec in 1867. Leaving aside the claims of the aboriginal nations, Québec might thus assert with justice that the northern territory it received in 1912 was meagre compensation for what it had lost. To those who would like to see a sovereign Québec reduced to its 1867 boundaries, Québec might well ask why it should not be entitled, as a matter of historical right, to the portion of Canada embraced by the 1774 boundaries or the boundaries of New France.

Aboriginal Nations and Québec's Boundaries

The Constitution Act, 1871 authorized the Canadian Parliament to alter provincial boundaries *within* Canada, not to add territory to a province from *outside* the Dominion.[20] The validity of any extensions of the boundaries of Québec (and other provinces) after 1871, therefore, depends on whether the territories involved were part of Canada at the time. The governments of Canada and Québec obviously thought that the territories which were purportedly included in Québec in 1898 and 1912 were part of Canada. This belief was based on the order in council by which the British Crown transferred Rupert's Land to Canada in 1870.[21] The assumption was that, regardless of where the boundary between Québec and Rupert's Land was located at the time, all the territory in the Hudson watershed between Québec and Hudson Strait became part of Canada in 1870.[22]

That assumption would be valid if Rupert's Land did in fact include the whole of the Hudson watershed in 1870. However, that view of the extent of Rupert's Land was authoritatively rejected by the Privy Council in 1884 in the *Ontario Boundaries* case.[23] The decision in that case, which involved a dispute between Ontario and Manitoba over the location of the boundary between those two provinces,[24] depended in part on the terms of the Québec Act. That Act defined the boundary of the province of Québec in part as following the Ohio River westward to the banks of the Mississippi, and from there northward to the southern boundary of the Hudson's Bay Company territory, otherwise known as Rupert's Land.[25] The Privy Council decided that the northern boundary of Québec in that region in 1774, and hence of Ontario after Confederation, was the English River, which is a considerable distance north of the height of land between the Mississippi and Hudson watersheds (see Map 2). So the Privy Council obviously rejected the Hudson watershed definition of the Hudson's Bay Company's territory. Their Lordships' reasons for doing so are, I think, best summed up in the following comment by the Lord Chancellor during the arguments of counsel before the Privy Council:

I do not think one would be disposed to dispute the proposition that, so far as the Crown of England could give it, it [the Royal Charter of 1670] gave to the Hudson's Bay Company a right, if they were able to make themselves masters of the country, to the territory up to the sources of the rivers; but they did not make themselves masters of the whole of that country, for some other nation had come in the meantime.[26]

The nation referred to was France, which had established settlements within the Hudson watershed south of the English River between 1670 and 1763, thereby defeating any claims to the region by the Company.[27] The case therefore reveals that, in the opinion of the British Empire's highest court, the King of England could not establish a firm claim to such a vast region simply by sending a few ships into Hudson Bay and issuing a royal charter.[28]

In the *Ontario Boundaries* case, no one appears to have considered that the aboriginal peoples were nations with territorial rights which also had to be taken into account in determining the extent of Rupert's Land. This is not surprising, as attitudes to the aboriginal peoples during the latter part of the nineteenth century were notoriously ethnocentric, if not outright racist.[29] There can be little doubt that attitudes of this kind underlay the unquestioned assumption in the case that the presence of aboriginal peoples was irrelevant to European claims to sovereignty.[30]

Ethnocentric attitudes which deny aboriginal peoples the status of nations are unacceptable today. In *Simon* v. *R.*, Dickson C.J.C. quoted from a 1928 decision of Patterson J.:

> ... the Indians were never regarded as an independent power. A civilized nation first discovering a country of uncivilized people or savages held such country as its own until such time as by treaty it was transferred to some other civilized nation. The savages' rights of sovereignty even of ownership were never recognized.[31]

Speaking for the Supreme Court of Canada, Dickson said:

> It should be noted that the language used by Patterson J., illustrated in this passage, reflects the biases and prejudices of another era in our history. Such language is no longer acceptable in Canadian law and indeed is inconsistent with a growing sensitivity to native rights in Canada.[32]

In *A.G. of Quebec* v. *Sioui*,[33] the Supreme Court unanimously found that the aboriginal peoples were independent nations during the period of colonization of North America. Lamer J. said:

> ... we can conclude from the historical documents that both Great Britain and France felt that the Indian nations had sufficient independence and played a large enough role in North America for it to be good policy to maintain relations with them very close to those maintained between sovereign nations.
>
> The mother countries did everything in their power to secure the alliance of each Indian nation and to encourage

nations allied with the enemy to change sides. When these efforts met with success, they were incorporated in treaties of alliance or neutrality. This clearly indicates that the Indian nations were regarded in their relations with the European nations which occupied North America as independent nations.[34]

The Hudson's Bay Company Charter therefore must be re-evaluated in light of these decisions. The starting point is the *Ontario Boundaries* case, which decided that territory effectively occupied by other nations could not be part of Rupert's Land. *Simon* and *Sioui* tell us that the old ethnocentric view that aboriginal peoples do not qualify as nations is no longer acceptable. So territory within the Hudson watershed which was occupied and controlled by aboriginal nations has to be excluded from Rupert's Land.[35]

Further support for the view that aboriginal nationhood must be taken into account in assessing European claims can be found in the United States, where the Supreme Court has considered the impact on aboriginal peoples of the royal charters by which the Stuart kings attempted to partition North America. In *Johnson* v. *McIntosh*, Marshall C.J. said that "[t]hese various patents cannot be considered as nullities; nor can they be limited to a mere grant of the powers of government."[36] In that case, Marshall was concerned, among other things, with upholding the validity of property rights derived from Crown patents.[37] However, when he returned to the issue of the charters in *Worcester* v. *Georgia*, he acknowledged that they could only give what the Crown had as the first European power to "discover" that part of North America, namely an exclusive right to acquire lands from the aboriginal nations by purchase.[38] Although some of these charters purported to grant the soil from the Atlantic to the Pacific, Marshall remarked that in fact

[t]his soil was occupied by numerous and warlike nations equally willing and able to defend their possessions. The extravagant and absurd idea, that the feeble settlements made on the sea coast, or the companies under whom they were made, acquired legitimate power by them to

govern the people, or occupied the lands from sea to sea, did not enter the mind of any man.[39]

In the Supreme Court's view, as expressed by Marshall, "these grants asserted a title against Europeans only, and were considered as blank paper so far as the rights of the natives were concerned."[40]

The view that the British Crown could not acquire sovereignty over a territory occupied by a non-European nation simply by issuing a royal charter was confirmed by the Privy Council in *Staples* v. *R.*,[41] an 1899 decision involving the validity of orders in council made for Matabeleland (Southern Rhodesia) under the Foreign Jurisdiction Act, 1890.[42] Staples's counsel, Mr. Rawlinson, contended that the Act was inapplicable because Matabeleland was a British dominion, as the Crown had granted a royal charter to the British South Africa Company, authorizing it, among other things, to hold lands there. The Privy Council did not agree with him. The following exchange reveals what the Lord Chancellor thought about the effect of charters:

> Lord Chancellor: ... Have you ever heard of sovereignty being insisted upon by reason of such a grant? It is new to me that such a thing was ever heard of.
> Rawlinson: I ask you to look at the terms of the grant.
> Lord Chancellor: The terms of the grant cannot do what you assume it can do, namely give jurisdiction of sovereignty over a place Her Majesty has no authority in.[43]

Later, the Lord Chancellor said that sovereignty could be acquired by settlers taking possession, and recognition of that act by the Crown, but in this case neither had occurred, and so Matabeleland had not become a dominion of the Crown.[44]

The cases just discussed undermine further the assumption that the British Crown acquired sovereignty over the whole of the Hudson watershed by discovery and the issuance of the Royal Charter of 1670.[45] So the better view is that the charter did not effectively grant the whole of the watershed to the Hudson's Bay Company, but merely authorized the Company to acquire sovereignty for the Crown and lands for itself by going out and taking control of the territory.[46] To the extent that the territory was occupied and controlled by aboriginal nations, the Company would have had to assert and enforce jurisdiction over those nations and their lands before it could be in control. In order to determine what areas the Company acquired sovereignty over on behalf of the Crown, the historical record therefore has to be examined to see what areas the Company actually controlled.[47]

Returning to the portion of the Hudson watershed to the east of Hudson Bay, there can be no doubt that in 1670 it was occupied and controlled by aboriginal nations, namely the Cree, Innu (Naskapi-Montagnais) and Inuit.[48] The Hudson's Bay Company built fur-trading posts on the coasts of Hudson and James bays, but did not penetrate far into the eastern interior until around the end of the eighteenth century, when some of the main rivers were explored, and a few inland posts, such as Neoskweskau (1793) on the Eastmain River and Nichicun House (1816) on Nitchequon Lake, were built.[49] Beyond the limits of the posts, the Company's jurisdiction may have extended over its own employees, who included a few aboriginal persons, but virtually no attempt was made to govern the aboriginal nations generally or to control the territories occupied by them.[50] The governor of the Company, Sir George Simpson, admitted this before the Select Committee of the British House of Commons on the Hudson's Bay Company in 1857:

> [Mr. Grogan] What privileges or rights do the native Indians possess strictly applicable to themselves? — [Simpson] They are perfectly at liberty to do what they please; we never restrain Indians.
>
> [Grogan] Is there any difference between their position and that of the half-breeds? — [Simpson] None at all. They hunt and fish, and live as they please. They look to us for their supplies, and we study their comfort and convenience as much as possible; we assist each other.
>
> [Lord Stanley] You exercise no authority whatever over the Indian tribes? — [Simpson] None at all.
>
> [Stanley] If any tribe were pleased to live as the tribes did live before the country opened up to Europeans; that

is to say, not using any article of European manufacture or trade, it would be in their power to do so? — [Simpson] Perfectly so; we exercise no control over them.

[Mr. Bell] Do you mean that, possessing the right of soil over the whole of Rupert's Land, you do not consider that you possess any jurisdiction over the inhabitants of that soil? — [Simpson] No, I am not aware that we do. We exercise none, whatever right we possess under our charter.

[Bell] Then is it the case that you do not consider that the Indians are under your jurisdiction when any crimes are committed by the Indians upon the Whites? — [Simpson] They are under our jurisdiction when crimes are committed upon the Whites, but not when committed upon each other; we do not meddle with their wars.[51]

As the aboriginal nations were in actual control of most of the area east of Hudson Bay, the territory the Company acquired there was in fact very limited.

In 1869, the Hudson's Bay Company surrendered all its rights to the lands and territories within Rupert's Land back to the British Crown, subject to certain conditions.[52] The surrender was accepted by the Crown on June 22, 1870, and Rupert's Land was admitted into Canada along with the adjacent North-Western Territory as of July 15, 1870, by an Imperial order in council.[53] However, the boundaries of the transferred territories were not defined.[54] Nonetheless, the Company could surrender no more than it actually had, which we have seen would be limited to the territory it controlled. Moreover, the Crown did not purport by the 1870 order to admit territories from outside its dominions into Canada. The territory which Canada received on the east side of Hudson Bay by the Rupert's Land transfer would therefore be limited to the trading posts and any other territory effectively controlled by the Company.[55] Territories which were occupied and controlled by the aboriginal nations would not have been included.[56]

Between 1870 and the enactment of the statutes of 1898 and 1912 which defined and extended Québec's northern boundary, Canada could not have acquired more territory east of the bay without Imperial involvement,[57] because that would have required an extraterritorial act of state, which Canada did not have the authority to carry out, as it lacked control over its foreign affairs.[58] Moreover, to the extent that those statutes purported to include territory in Québec which was not already part of Canada, they would be *ultra vires* for the same reason.

This constitutional impediment would have prevented Canada from acquiring additional territory even if it had been able to establish effective control beyond the areas controlled by the Hudson's Bay Company. But apparently that control was absent as well, at least up to the 1890s, and probably well into the twentieth century in much of the North. After the enactment of the Canada (Ontario Boundary) Act, 1889,[59] which set Ontario's northern boundary along the English and Albany rivers (see Map 2), the Canadian government did not seem to be certain whether the boundary between Ontario and Québec which ran due north from Lake Timiskaming intersected the shores of James Bay.[60] As for the interior on the eastern side of the bay, the knowledge was even less complete, according to a report by A. M. Burgess, Deputy Minister of the Interior for Canada: " ... next to nothing is known about the Eastmain but, this much is certain, like every other river, it has several branches and before it could be adopted as a boundary [for Québec on the north] it would be necessary to determine which of these branches is the Eastmain River."[61]

Between 1892 and 1894, explorations were conducted to determine the course of the Eastmain, which was then adopted as the northern boundary of Québec in 1898.[62] But given the rudimentary nature of basic geographic information, it seems quite obvious that Canada was not at that time in control of these regions or of the aboriginal nations living there.[63]

Further north, the absence of Canadian jurisdiction was even more evident. After discussing Canada's lack of presence throughout the North, including the regions around Hudson Bay and Hudson Strait, Diamond Jenness, in his book *Eskimo Administration: II. Canada*, concluded that "down to the very end of the nineteenth century ... Canada completely neglected her Arctic, and gave no thought at any time to the condition of its Eskimo inhabitants."[64] Canada's first attempt to exercise jurisdiction in those regions came in 1903, when it sent an expedition aboard the *Neptune* to assert Canadian sovereignty in the eastern Arctic and to establish a Northwest Mounted Police post at Fullerton Harbour on the northwest coast of Hudson Bay.[65] However, the main purpose of this and subsequent efforts to establish a Canadian presence was to forestall foreign challenges to Canada's weak claims. Canada had little interest in and exercised scant control over the aboriginal nations of the Arctic prior to World War II.[66]

After Canada obtained the capacity in the period from 1919 to 1926 to conduct foreign affairs,[67] as a matter of constitutional law it probably could have extended Canadian jurisdiction beyond the areas which the Hudson's Bay Company actually controlled prior to 1870. East of Hudson Bay, this extension of jurisdiction probably took place gradually as first the police presence and then government services such as health and education were expanded.[68] A historical investigation to determine the extent to which this has occurred cannot be undertaken here. Suffice it to say that, insofar as this has happened, it could have serious international implications, as the twentieth-century trend in international law, especially after World War II, has been in favour of decolonization and the right of peoples to self-determination. The world community might well view Canada's actions as an unacceptable example of twentieth-century colonialism.

As for Québec, any territory which the Hudson's Bay Company effectively controlled prior to 1870 and which was transferred to Canada in that year would have become part of Québec by the statutes of 1898 and 1912.[69] To the extent that those statutes purported to include additional territory, they would be *ultra vires* and therefore invalid. That invalidity would not have been retroactively corrected by Canada's acquisition of control over its foreign affairs.[70] Consequently, any subsequent extension of Canadian sovereignty over the aboriginal nations and their territories could not have extended the province's boundaries over those territories. So from a constitutional perspective, Québec presently consists of the territory included in the province in 1867 and any mainland territory within the Hudson watershed east and north of the Ontario-Québec boundary which the Hudson's Bay Company effectively controlled at the time of the transfer of Rupert's Land to Canada in 1870. Of course this conclusion has serious implications for the James Bay and Northern Québec and Northeastern Québec agreements, signed with the Cree, Inuit and Innu (Naskapi) in 1975 and 1978 to permit hydro-electric development in the Hudson watershed, but an examination of that matter is beyond the scope of the present article.

Aboriginal nations have generally been ignored in the constitutional history of Canada. Actions by France and Britain relating to the territory now called Canada have been accorded legal significance, while actions — and indeed the very existence — of the aboriginal nations have not. A 1670 charter issued by an English king to his cousin and seventeen associates, purporting to grant them a vast region which was virtually unexplored by Europeans, has been taken seriously, while the presence of numerous aboriginal nations in the same territory has been disregarded. Territories were transferred from France to Britain and Britain to Canada, and boundaries were drawn and redrawn, without consultation and without the consent of the aboriginal nations living there.

Now one might say that this is all in the past, and history cannot be remade. It is true that we cannot change what actually happened, but the significance we assign to historical events can and does change as those events are re-evaluated. In particular, the *legal* significance of past events is often open to reinterpretation. When the Privy Council decided in 1884 that Rupert's Land did not include the whole of the Hudson watershed, that overturned an assumption which the Hudson's Bay Company had held for over 200 years. To give a more recent example, in 1985 the Supreme Court of Canada decided that an 1890 Manitoba statute eliminating the protection accorded to French language rights in the province was constitutionally invalid, even though the statute had been relied on for so long.[71] The decision did not change the historical fact that the statute had been passed, but it did undercut the legal significance which had formerly been assigned to that event.

Colonial assumptions about the legal significance of events such as the issuance of the Hudson's Bay Company Charter and the 1870 transfer of Rupert's Land to Canada are still being relied on to deny the rights of aboriginal nations in Canada today. These assumptions persist, despite the fact that they have been seriously undermined by judicial decisions. The current debate over Québec's northern boundary is a case in point. Canadian and Québécois politicians alike express dismay when aboriginal people question the legitimacy of the claims of Canada and Québec to jurisdiction east of Hudson Bay, but the basis for those claims is rarely explained. This is hardly surprising, as the politicians are probably embarrassed by the colonial assumptions on which those claims rest. However, for the aboriginal peoples to be able to take their rightful place as self-governing nations within Canada, this country's colonial past must be acknowledged, and colonial attitudes must be abandoned.

No doubt some readers will be sceptical of the conclusion reached in this article that the only territory Canada was able to include in Québec in 1898 and 1912 was territory actually controlled by the Hudson's Bay Company in 1870. But if they have arguments for rejecting that conclusion that do not rely on unacceptable colonial assumptions, I would like to hear them. Others may say that, regardless of legitimacy or legality, the fact is that Canada and Québec have exercised jurisdiction over all the territory included in Québec, so the question is academic. However, I doubt whether many Canadians would be satisfied with a "might makes right" justification. Canadian society is supposed to be governed by the rule of law — indeed, during the events at Oka in 1990, both Canada and Québec invoked the rule of law as a reason for using armed force against the Mohawks.[72] Moreover, the international community might take a dim view of twentieth-century colonial expansion by Canada and Québec at the expense of the aboriginal nations.

Rather than trying to rely on indefensible justifications, it would be better for Canada and Québec to accept the weakness of their claims as a compelling reason for negotiating a new relationship with the aboriginal nations. This will have to take place, whether Québec decides to remain in Canada or go its own way. If Québec decides to separate, the matter will become urgent.[73] The terms of separation will have to be negotiated not only with Canada, but also with the aboriginal nations living in the territory Québec claims. The Québécois cannot assert a right to self-determination for themselves and at the same time deny that right to the aboriginal nations, especially where Québec's own claims to jurisdiction rest on shaky foundations such as the 1912 boundary extension.[74] The aboriginal nations may decide to align themselves with Canada, or go with Québec, or set off on their own. If the country disintegrates, the choice must be up to them.

IV
The New Economic
Landscape

The Case for a Single Currency and a Reformed Central Bank

Arthur Donner and Fred Lazar

If Québec secedes, a new set of economic arrangements will have to be negotiated. Should Québec and Canada adopt different currencies? Should each have its own central bank and pursue its own monetary and other macroeconomic policies? If each country is to have its own currency, should one be fixed in value relative to the other, or should the exchange rate between the two currencies fluctuate freely? Should the two countries adopt a single currency and central bank, with the bank more politically accountable?

This essay examines the practicality of each of the four options available to Québec and Canada for negotiating a currency and central banking arrangement. At one extreme, there is the dual-currency, flexible-exchange-rate option. Both countries would have their own currency, central bank and separate, independent monetary policies. The exchange rate between the two currencies would be determined in the international currency markets and would reflect the markets' evaluation of the policies pursued by the two countries and the relative strengths of the two economies.

At the other extreme there is a modest variation of the present arrangement involving a single currency and single central bank. Both Québec and Canada would have the same currency

The authors would like to thank all of the participants at the "Negotiating with a Sovereign Québec" conference, and in particular professors Chorney, Drache and Perin, for their valuable comments on and suggestions for improving this paper.

and share the same central bank to conduct monetary and exchange-rate policies. Obviously, representation on the central bank would have to change.

The two intermediate options entail separate currencies and central banks, but different arrangements for fixing, and maintaining within narrow bands, the value of one currency relative to the other. In one case, Québec alone would select the target exchange rate for its currency relative to that of Canada and the Québec central bank would have the sole responsibility for keeping the exchange rate within the target range.[1] The Canadian currency would serve as the *numéraire*. In the other option, both countries would select the target range and share the commitment to the system of a fixed exchange rate between them. The two central banks would co-ordinate their policies to keep the exchange rate within the target band.[2]

In our view, the best option for Québec and Canada is a common currency and single central bank, an arrangement quite similar to the present one. This option will necessitate a high degree of macroeconomic policy co-ordination between the two countries and thus impose constraints on their policy-making sovereignty. Developments in the European Community (EC) and the reality of the limited policy-making discretion available to small countries in an increasingly interdependent world economy, with more highly integrated capital markets, shift the balance towards this option. Of course, this does not imply that the present institutional structure for the Bank of Canada should be maintained. Nor does it mean that monetary policy should always have low inflation rates as its principal objective — a rigid approach that, under John Crow, the governor of the Bank of Canada, has given us the first made-in-Canada recession with painfully excessive double-digit unemployment rates.

The Pros and Cons of the Dual-Currency, Flexible-Exchange-Rate Option

Let us first consider the most extreme option: the dual currency, flexible-exchange-rate case. This option might offer the following advantages. The exchange rate between the currencies of Canada and Québec would be added to the adjustment

TABLE 9.1 Unemployment Rates, Provinces 1971, 1981 and 1991 %			
	1971	1981	1991
Newfoundland	8.4	13.9	18.4
Nova Scotia	7.0	10.1	12.0
New Brunswick	6.1	11.5	12.7
Quebec	7.3	10.3	11.9
Ontario	5.4	6.6	9.6
Manitoba	5.7	5.9	8.8
Saskatchewan	3.5	4.6	7.4
Alberta	5.7	3.8	8.2
British Columbia	7.2	6.7	9.9

Source: Statistics Canada, *Labour Force* (Catalogue 72-001)

mechanisms available to each country to manage economic disturbances. Moreover, each central bank would have autonomy in conducting its monetary policy and each country would have greater latitude in its taxation and expenditure policies.

How significant is exchange-rate flexibility in facilitating economic adjustments to various types of demand and supply shocks?

Exchange-rate realignments might accelerate the process, and diminish the asymmetric burdens of regional adjustments to economic and other types of shocks. (We have seen how a single-currency area in Canada with the subsequent uniform monetary policy for all its regions has compounded macroeconomic management problems.) But the feasibility of changing exchange rate parities to improve the effectiveness of the adjustment process has been questioned.[3] Furthermore, short-term movements in exchange rates are influenced increasingly by capital flows rather than by trade flows. The dominant influence of capital flows on exchange rates, and the tendency for exchange-rate movements to develop a psychological momentum towards overshooting equilibrium positions, are more likely to compound the adjustment problems.

The economic literature on optimal currency areas suggests that regions whose economies are subject to similar demand and/or supply shocks, have comparable wage- and price-setting structures, and/or have comparable trade patterns with other countries are good candidates for forming a single currency area.[4] Even regions that do not share any of the above similarities might still be candidates for a single currency area. What is required are alternative adjustment mechanisms to realignments in nominal exchange rates between Québec and Canada.[5] Thus, it is possible that exchange rate flexibility between Québec and Canada would do little to facilitate their separate adjustments to economic disturbances.

From the standpoint of policy autonomy, a separate currency whose external value is allowed to fluctuate freely would offer both the central bank and the central government greater scope in formulating and implementing their respective economic policies. The other three options, on the other hand, would circumscribe the policy sovereignty of both countries. For example, if Québec were to opt for pegging the value of its currency to that of Canada, the government of Québec and its central bank would have the responsibility for adopting the fiscal and monetary policies necessary to maintain the fixed exchange rate. As a result, Canada would be free to pursue an independent macropolicy course, at least relative to Québec, and thus effectively set the policy direction for Québec. Of course, Québec would have the right and the ability to revalue its currency and so maintain some degree of policy autonomy. But if the commitment to a fixed exchange rate were not credible, speculators regularly would test the government of Québec and unsettle the financial markets. This would present serious problems for any sovereignist government and would erode a major benefit of a stable exchange rate, the elimination of the exchange-rate risks for trade and capital flows.

On the other hand, Canada and Québec could co-operate to support the fixed exchange rate between the two countries' currencies. In this case, both countries would forgo some policy-making autonomy since they would have to engage in joint decision making on monetary policy and co-ordinate their fiscal policies in order to keep the exchange rate within a very narrow band.

A report prepared for the European Council under the supervision of Jacques Delors, with the assistance of the governors of the central banks of the European Community, set out the goal of a monetary union and a common currency for Europe and the process for achieving this goal.[6] Well before the attainment of this goal (that is, while each country still retained its own currency and central bank, but was committed to fixed parities with the currencies of all the other members of the EC), the Delors report advocated that each member of the EC would have to accept upper limits on its budget deficit. In addition, no government could resort to monetizing its budgetary deficit — printing money, via borrowing from the central bank, to finance some or all of the deficit recorded in a given year. In effect, for the commitment to fixed exchange rates to be credible to the financial markets, each member of the EC would have to sacrifice a considerable degree of sovereignty over its ability to conduct independent fiscal and monetary policies.

If this were the model adopted for the currency and central banking arrangements between Canada and Québec, periodic adjustments to the exchange rate between their currencies could be made, but only with the concurrence of the central banks in both countries. Otherwise, the financial markets would not believe that either government was willing to accept the policy-making discipline required by a fixed-exchange-rate regime. Once again, speculators could easily test the commitment to a fixed exchange rate and destabilize the currency market.

In the single-currency case, policy harmonization is much more extensive than in either of the preceding two cases. As noted in the Delors report, a single currency and central bank requires the co-ordination of the member countries' short- and medium-term economic policies and the complete liberalization of capital flows between the members. While all three of the options require some harmonization of the regulation of the financial systems of Québec and Canada, the single-currency option necessitates the highest degree of harmonization.

Despite the fact that these other options constrain the policy-making autonomy of Québec and possibly Canada, the additional loss of sovereignty in these cases is not significant compared to the loss of autonomy that small, open economies face even in a flexible-exchange-rate, multiple-currency regime. As barriers to international capital flows continue to decline, the scope for autonomy for such countries diminishes further.

The Bank of Canada has had limited economic independence, particularly in stimulating the economy — although it has been able to produce the first made-in-Canada recession. But even if the Bank, under the direction of John Crow, had not aggressively pushed up interest rates and opened up record high spreads between Canadian and U.S. short-term interest rates, Canada would not have escaped the spillover effects of the current U.S. recession.

Furthermore, even countries whose central banks have had a considerable degree of policy-making autonomy have found that the financial markets expect these banks to pursue a stable, low-inflation objective. When the financial markets firmly believe that a central bank is strongly committed to low inflation rates, these markets will be willing to overlook, for a short period of time, occasional departures from non-inflationary monetary policy. But countries that have not convinced the capital markets of their commitment to a strong, anti-inflation goal face higher real and nominal interest rates.[7] Political interference in the decision-making process for monetary policy has made it more difficult for a country to convince sceptical financial markets of the central bank's commitment to fight inflation.

A dual-currency, dual-central-bank, flexible-exchange-rate relationship between Québec and Canada could generate substantial economic costs that would be likely to far outweigh any possible benefits other than the symbolic one of independence. Separate currencies with no fixed parity between them would introduce an exchange-rate risk for transactions between the two countries. For example, a transaction that involved delivery of a good, service or financial asset today, but payment in Canadian dollars at a future date, would impose an exchange-rate risk on Québécois.[8] Forward exchange contracts could reduce short-term exchange risks, albeit at a cost. But they would prove to be inadequate for hedging longer-term trading relationships and contracts.

Québec and Canadian companies producing and/or selling in both countries would face a greater paper burden and larger transactions costs because of the need to deal in two currencies and one additional set of price quotations. In addition, the smaller the currency area, the less stable would be its exchange rate relative to other currencies in the presence of economic and financial disturbances. This greater instability and associated exchange-rate risk might add to the risk premium in the country's interest rates and so push up these rates. Moreover, the external value of the exchange rate might be more susceptible to speculative moves by financial and non-financial corporations or by individuals. This is so for two major reasons: first, the limited volume of trading and resulting limited degree of liquidity in the exchange market for a small country; second, the greater degree of market power possessed by the major, non-government participants in the foreign exchange markets.

The Single-Currency Option as the Only Other Choice

Carlos Costa, commenting on the drive to create a single European currency, has argued that this would produce at least the following three positive effects: lower transaction costs because of the reduced uncertainty about exchange-rate changes among the members of the EC; lower interest rates because of the elimination of the bid-ask spread in exchange rates; enhanced usefulness of money as a means for transmitting information across different national markets.[9]

The dual currency, fixed-exchange-rate options present their own problems. The European experience to date provides useful lessons about these options and many insights into their problems. In 1969, the six members of the European Economic Community, as it was then called, formed a quasi-fixed-exchange-rate system dubbed the "snake in the tunnel." This system allowed for a margin of fluctuation of 2.25 percent around currency parity levels among the members' currencies, which in turn would move in a U.S. dollar tunnel of 4.5 percent. With the floating of the U.S. dollar in July 1972, the tunnel was immediately dropped and the snake participants organized a joint float against the U.S. dollar.

The United Kingdom and Ireland quickly left the snake arrangement. France left as well, but after a somewhat longer stay. These countries were unwilling to co-ordinate their economic policies with those of the other members of the Community, in particular West Germany, whose currency was becoming the *de facto numéraire* in the system. As well, they were unwilling to bear the sole burden of the necessary adjustments that were placed on the countries experiencing a balance of payments deficit. The United Kingdom, for example, lost approximately 30 percent of its international reserves within a two-month period in 1972 as a result of the attempt by the Bank of England to maintain the value of the pound.

The European Monetary System (EMS) formally came into existence in March 1979 as a replacement for the snake. The EMS was seen as a catalyst for increased integration of the European economies and the creation of a single currency zone to rival the U.S. dollar and the yen in international capital markets. The EMS consisted of an exchange-rate pegging arrangement based on a parity grid which tied every currency to every other one in the system. Exchange rates were permitted to fluctuate within bands of 2.25 percent around their respective bases, with the pound and the Spanish peseta given 6 percent bands.

To avoid one of the major problems that led to the demise of the snake, the responsibility for exchange-rate intervention under the EMS was shared both by countries with balance of payments deficits and those with surpluses. The responsibility for day-to-day intervention rests with the central banks of the participating members; overall responsibility for the management of the EMS lies with the European Commission. Realignments among the exchange rates can take place only as a result of agreement among all member countries. This has resulted in policy conflicts among the member states which at times have threatened the survival of the EMS.

Some have attributed the success of the EMS to the leadership role assumed by the West German Bundesbank. M. van Meerhaeghe has noted: "Germany's grip on the EMS and its fairly independent monetary policy explain why the EMS works."[10] However, increasing trade interdependence and similar economic objectives have made the European governments more willing to accept an increasing degree of policy co-ordination and convergence of monetary policy, even along the lines pursued by Germany.

The EMS from its outset was seen as a stepping stone towards a single European currency area with a single European central bank having sole responsibility for the conduct of monetary policy for the entire Community. Indeed, the European Community is now committed to achieving this objective by the middle of this decade. Agreements are in place to ensure that the required institutional developments, as well as the convergence and co-ordination of national economic and monetary policies among the member states, will take place in three distinct stages during the next few years.

These plans do present problems. For example, if inappropriate internal exchange rates are selected and locked into by the adoption of a single currency, regional economic problems could be aggravated. As well, by imposing limits on the national budget deficits, the Community as a whole might have to guarantee the debts of each member country. Thus, the financially weaker states might affect the credit rating of and the real interest rates in the Community. But the costs associated with these problems may be less significant than the potential benefits a single currency area can produce for Europe. Moreover, only a single currency area can ensure that the commitment to fixed exchange rates will be credible to the financial markets.

The Choice for Québec and Canada

It appears that the only two reasonable options for Québec and Canada to consider are the extremes: a dual-currency, flexible-exchange-rate system or a single-currency regime. In light of the European experience, the other two options are not practical since they are unstable, leading eventually to the adoption of one of the two other models.

The choice for Québec and Canada boils down to their respective evaluations of the relative economic and political costs and benefits of the two systems. The preceding discussion and the developments in Europe argue against the dual-currency option. It seems to be the inferior one for both countries, for it does not appear to offer significant economic benefits. Regional development funds, increased factor mobility and co-ordination of economic policies are likely to be more effective and less costly for coping with regional disparities and asymmetrical regional adjustments to economic or financial disturbances than splitting up the present Canadian dollar currency area in two. In addition, the literature on and the experiences of small, open economies in a world of increasingly liberalized capital flows suggest that such countries would have little decision-making autonomy in the realm of monetary policy.

For the single-currency option to be acceptable to Québec, the central bank would have to be restructured and a supranational institution to co-ordinate economic policies would have to be developed. For the option to be acceptable to Canada, harmonization of the regulation of financial institutions would be needed.

We suggest that the key to a new structure for the central bank would be a twelve-member central bank open-market committee, modelled on the U.S. Federal Reserve System. The committee would consist of six members appointed by Québec and six appointed by Canada. The six Canadian appointees might be selected as follows: three by the central government, and one each by the three main regions — the West, Ontario, the Atlantic region. The committee would select its chair who would serve as the governor of the bank for a single term of three years.

All twelve members would vote on the policy initiatives of the bank; this would suffice to ensure that the governor of the bank could only attempt to influence the decisions of the committee as could any other member, but be unable to override any decision approved by the committee. This committee would be responsible for formulating monetary policy; developing positions on exchange rates, interest rates and other financial market conditions for Canada's participation in the G-7, and Canada's and Québec's participation in the IMF and other international forums; and proposing rules for the regulation and supervision of all financial institutions in Canada and Québec.

The Canadian and Québec appointees should be mandated to testify annually before the appropriate committee(s) of their respective parliaments. This requirement, together with a limitation on appointment terms (a maximum of two three-year appointments) and publication of the minutes of all the meetings of this committee, should contribute to enhancing the accountability of the central bank's key decision makers to their respective governments.

Furthermore, for economic efficiency, we recommend that Québec and Canada adopt rules comparable to those in the EC for the regulation and supervision of financial institutions. The rules would permit all financial institutions to establish branches and subsidiaries anywhere in Canada and Québec and supply financial services throughout the two countries. They would set minimum standards for capital adequacy, solvency ratios, insider conduct, information requirements and consumer protection. In addition, this would allow for home country control of financial institutions through authorization and supervision by the regulatory authorities of the country where a financial institution has its home base and by mutual recognition of each country's supervisory standards. Harmonization would be necessary to prevent a race of "competitive liberalization." This occurs when a country adopts lax standards in order to attract financial institutions and market activity. A joint Québec-Canada set of minimum standards is necessary to protect the basic requirements for the security and stability of the financial system. Otherwise, competitive liberalization might result if the country with the least restrictive rules dictates the standard for the other.

The supranational body should have an eight-member board consisting of the prime minister, finance minister, industry minister and a central bank committee member for both Québec and Canada, and a permanent secretariat. This body would be responsible for co-ordinating fiscal and other economic policies and establishing upper limits on the budget deficits of both countries. To ensure compliance, neither country should be allowed to have direct access to central bank credit in order to monetize part or all of its budgetary deficits.

But both countries should have limited recourse to external borrowing in foreign currencies.

Finally, Québec and Canada would share economic and monetary policy-making responsibility. As a result, Québec would gain some additional powers beyond those it has at present as a province within Canada. But Québec would not gain complete policy-making sovereignty in the economic arena. Indeed, as the junior partner (in terms of its size) in the currency and central bank arrangement, Québec might have to cede a larger share of the responsibility to Canada in order to reach an agreement along the lines we have described above. Ironically, economic re-association with the rest of Canada should constrain the sovereignty Québec is seeking by disassociating itself politically from Canada.

The Case for a Common Trade Strategy with a Sovereign Québec

Fred Lazar

At the end of 1990, Canada was a net debtor to the rest of the world to the tune of $252 billion — about $10,000 for every single Canadian. When Brian Mulroney first came to power, Canada's aggregate net international debt stood at $151 billion. So in the first six years of the Mulroney government, our net international debt increased by over $100 billion ($4,000 for every single Canadian).

Canadian industry needs to become more competitive to get us off the circular treadmill of large and growing current account deficits which result from and contribute to the explosive expansion of our net international debt. But the traditional policy levers (taxes, government spending, exchange rates and interest rates) have been badly managed. In 1984, the last time Canada recorded a current account surplus, we also had a record merchandise trade surplus of about $20 billion. By 1990, the merchandise trade surplus had fallen to about $11 billion. For Canada to have had an overall balance in the current account in 1990 would have required a tripling of that year's merchandise trade balance. In other words, our merchandise trade balance will have to range between $30 and $35 billion per year just to halt the rising flood of our net international indebtedness. If we were to eliminate our current account def-

I would like to thank the participants at the "Negotiating with a Sovereign Québec" conference, and in particular professors Mel Watkins, Daniel Drache and Roberto Perin for their valuable comments and suggestions for improving this paper.

TABLE 10.1
Canada's Merchandise Trade and Current Account
Balances, and Net International Debt Position,
Selected Years 1970–1990
($ Billions)

	Merchandise Trade Balance	Current Account Balance	Net International Debt Position
1970	3.0	1.0	30.0
1975	-0.3	-4.6	49.7
1980	8.8	-1.8	110.3
1984	19.8	1.7	151.1
1985	16.4	-3.1	173.6
1986	9.9	-11.4	191.4
1987	11.2	-11.6	204.7
1988	10.4	-13.9	213.0
1989	7.1	-20.7	231.9
1990	10.9	-22.0	252.2

Sources: Statistics Canada, *Canada's international invest-ment position, 1991* (Catalogue 67-202); Statistics Canada, *Canada's balance of international payments, First quarter 1991* (Catalogue 67-001).

---

icit, by producing and selling approximately $22 billion more of goods and services abroad, this would generate 395,000 new jobs and reduce the unemployment rate to about 7.3 percent.[1] It has not helped matters that the mix of federal government policies — high interest rates, a high value for the Canadian dollar relative to the U.S. dollar and large budget deficits — have harmed the competitiveness of Canadian industry.

In light of Bank of Canada Governor John Crow's fixation on inflation and Mulroney's fixation on the market, the traditional policies do not offer much scope for resolving our simmering international debt crisis. Worse yet, there does not appear to be any prospect for the necessary change in policy direction. The Mulroney government appears to be entirely incapable of recognizing its mistakes and changing its course of action on the economy.

Canada has been living off foreign savings for too long. Eventually these IOUs will have to be repaid; otherwise we may become the North American Argentina and Mulroney the Canadian Peron. Ottawa should be promoting policies to balance (at least) the current account. Ideally, we should be striving to achieve a long succession of current account surpluses so that we can begin to pay back some of our foreign debt. But this will necessitate a fundamental change in philosophy about the role of government and the direction of government policy.

Industrial Strategy

Professor Michael Porter, in his competitiveness study, emphasized Canada's poor productivity performance as a threat to our continued prosperity and pointed to high levels of unemployment and deteriorating trade balances outside of the resource sectors as symbols of our underlying structural problems.[2] Canada may have done well in the past, but Porter seems to warn that we may be on the slippery slope to second-class status.

The federal government has relied on the private sector to lead Canada out of the wilderness of her poor productivity performance, increasing trade deficits and international indebtedness. The Mulroney government's legacy has been one of reducing the role of government and expanding the scope for private-sector initiatives — for example, through free trade with the United States, deregulation, tax reform, privatization and the Bank of Canada's obsession with price stability. These policies do not yet show any signs of making Canada more competitive. The picture is no better in Québec. The current recession has exposed the structural weaknesses in the Québec economy, for Québec industry has performed as poorly as its counterparts in the rest of Canada.

But should we give the federal government's policies more time to be fully effective? Or should we contemplate the possibility that the private sector cannot do the job?

Indeed, even the federal government, the champion of free enterprise, has shown some concern about the ability of the private market to do the job. In the *Budget Papers* accompanying the February 1992 budget, the following comments appear to question whether Canada's private sector can be a first-rate competitor in the global marketplace:

> The government has provided strong support for investments in Canadian research and development ... [but] the record shows that, despite a very generous tax regime, Canadian businesses have failed to invest in research and development to the same extent as in our major trading partners....
>
> The government has increased its spending on training programs significantly during the past two years.... [Yet,] the record also shows that Canadian firms have not invested enough in their labour force. Only one-third of employers provide training for employees and the share of private training in GDP is a fraction of that in economies such as the U.S., Japan and Germany.[3]

Canada and Québec have no choice but to become more interventionist and develop the industrial strategies needed to rectify the long-term structural problems in their economies. The Mulroney government's policies will not succeed, and neither will the private sector, if left on their own.

Competitiveness and productivity growth are determined simultaneously by the relative success of domestic-based companies in creating and continually upgrading their competitive advantages. Competitive advantage results from continuous improvements in production techniques and the introduction of new product — in effect, from innovations. To enhance competitiveness and the subsequent rate of productivity growth, an industrial strategy must promote the development of indigenous research, design, development and manufacturing capabilities, as well as the creation and growth of technologically advanced Canadian firms.

Canadian companies will have to compete primarily on their creativity and innovativeness, and to a much lesser extent on costs. But the private sector in this country has not demonstrated the ability to compete on either basis. Porter has suggested that Canadian business leaders have become too complacent and inward-looking, unwilling to take risks and promote the development of domestic sources of supplies. Thus, a government-initiated industrial strategy is imperative to stem the flood of red ink on our current account and reduce our international debt, and to increase our lethargic productivity.

An industrial strategy will encompass an array of subsidies and so may be susceptible to countervail actions by our major trading partners (as sanctioned by the GATT) or unfair trade actions by the United States (not sanctioned by the GATT).[4] The Canada-U.S. Free Trade Agreement (FTA) was supposed to reduce the harassment potential of U.S. trade laws by making the trade rules more explicit and by creating a dispute-settlement mechanism. However, the ongoing softwood lumber dispute, and the equally acrimonious Honda case, where United States authorities unilaterally deemed Honda cars produced in Canada to be ineligible for duty-free entry under the FTA, show that the agreement has not created objective trade standards. In the Honda case, even if the trade panel finds in favour of Canada, the damage will have been done, for non–North American transnational corporations will be reluctant to invest in Canada in order to serve the North American market, preferring instead to locate production facilities in the United States.

Furthermore, the FTA does not cover the U.S. unfair trade practice law — section 301 of the 1974 Trade Act as amended most recently by the Omnibus Trade and Competitiveness Act of 1988. This trade law poses the greatest threat to Canada and Québec, for it extends the concept of extraterritoriality of U.S. legislation beyond U.S. corporations operating in Canada. It can be used to dictate the "industrial policies" Canada or Québec can introduce, and actions can be initiated against government measures that may be permissible within the GATT rules.

In addition, the FTA did not include a subsidies code. The negotiation of such a code was left to a later date. But this may never occur, since the current GATT and U.S.-Canada-Mexico (NAFTA) negotiations are tackling this subject. And according to unofficial reports, the United States has been adopting a hard-line position with respect to subsidies, even rejecting the latest proposal put forth by Arthur Dunkel, the director of the

GATT, to exempt from countervail actions only pre-commercialization research subsidies, a limited number of regional development subsidies and generally available subsidies.[5] Obviously, developments in this area are of utmost importance to Québec and Canada, including the subnational levels of government, since the new subsidies code will be binding on them as well. Any new code that is negotiated will sharply constrain the ability of Canada to introduce an industrial strategy and of Québec to continue and improve upon its "Québec Inc." strategy, an industrial strategy that co-ordinates the activities of business, labour and government.

The Need for a Common Trade Strategy: The Building Blocks

Canada and Québec have much to gain by formulating a common trade strategy and much to lose by not negotiating a trade agreement. Negotiating a new central banking arrangement, which will lead to a more efficacious monetary policy for the two countries, will not be sufficient to turn around the structural malaise in their economies. Industrial strategies are required and unless Canada and Québec can agree on a position to put forth jointly in multilateral trade negotiations, they will have rules imposed upon them that will seriously limit their discretion in developing these strategies.

In developing a common trade strategy and negotiating the rules to govern trade between them, Québec and Canada will be compelled to make trade-offs between the degree of trade liberalization and their respective policy-making autonomy. Economic interdependence and the need for rules to govern trade in goods and services, which are the hallmark of this interdependence, automatically impose limits on the economic sovereignty of nations. But their autonomy may be limited even more in the absence of a trade agreement.

Krommenacker has eloquently described the essence of the dilemma facing independent nations as they attempt to negotiate a set of trade rules:

> The central problem of interdependence is to keep international economic intercourse free of crippling restrictions while preserving a maximum degree of freedom for

each nation to pursue its legitimate economic objectives. Growing interdependence confronts countries with three broad choices: 1. to accept the integration and consequential loss of national freedom and to engage in the joint determination of economic policy objectives; 2. to accept the integration but to attempt to preserve as much national autonomy as possible; 3. to reject the integration.[6]

Québec and Canada should pursue the second of the three choices spelled out by Krommenacker.

In negotiating a trade agreement, they will have to address three major issues:

1. Should they adopt the fall-back option, namely, the existing GATT rules to govern trade between the two of them; or should they build upon existing arrangements and negotiate an agreement more appropriate to their relationship?
2. If they select the latter course of action, what rules should they adopt to regulate trade in goods and services between the two nations? It is important to note that a single set of rules will not be sufficient to deal with trade in both goods and services.
3. What rules should they incorporate into an agreement to govern trade between each country and the rest of the world?

Canada and Québec can do better than the fall-back option. They should negotiate a new trade agreement. There is much to build on — the GATT, the Canada-U.S. Free Trade Agreement, the present situation between Québec and Canada, and the EEC Treaty. Moreover, since every trade agreement produces both winners and losers in each country, Québécois and Canadian negotiators might be able to minimize the trade disruptions and subsequent restructurings by judiciously borrowing from existing agreements.

As well, Québec and Canada should focus on negotiating a common market rather than a free trade area or customs union.[7] That is, they should adopt a common trade strategy for dealing with the rest of the world, even though this would diminish, albeit marginally, each country's sovereignty. A common trade strategy would simplify the task of establishing rules governing trade between the two countries. And it might enable the two, acting together, to persuade one or more members of the Triad (Europe, Japan and the United States) to support this strategy in multilateral trade negotiations. Neither Canada nor Québec alone will be able to obtain what it wants in the GATT or the NAFTA.

Trade Rules for Goods

The existing trade relationship for goods between Québec and the rest of Canada is rather straightforward. There are no tariffs on trade in goods between Québec and the other provinces, and there is a common external tariff wall subject to the periodic reductions negotiated in the Canada-U.S. trade agreement and those that will be part of the Uruguay Round of the GATT. Quotas exist on interprovincial trade in some agricultural products. Interprovincial trade in goods is not subject to countervail or dumping rules. As a result there is no need, at present, for any form of dispute-settlement mechanism.

Thus, Québec and Canada have a good starting point for future negotiations. An agreement regulating trade in goods between the two countries should incorporate zero "internal" tariffs and common external tariffs as are now in effect, subject to negotiated reductions. This tariff structure would eliminate the need for complex rules of origin and reduce the need for border posts. Tariffs would be the easy part of an agreement.

In the absence of a single Québec-Canada competition policy to control business practices in both countries, a dumping code would be required to guard against the possibility of predatory dumping and attempted monopolization by a company in one country. A code would be necessary, even though the number of cases of predatory dumping might be limited, since the adoption of common external tariffs would preclude the injured country from resorting to the option of lowering its own external tariff in the affected industry in order to increase the degree of foreign competition. The GATT code as currently incorporated in Canadian legislation should be more than adequate since few, if any, cases might arise.

Subsidies and countervail might present a problem for negotiators. The two countries could view subsidies and other industrial-policy initiatives as their prerogative and hence agree to ignore each other's policies in these areas even if they distort trade patterns between the two. Examples of this could include preferential government procurement or export subsidies targeted towards domestic firms. In effect, Canada and Québec could forgo the need to incorporate a countervail code in the trade agreement and to draw up a list of subsidies which would be exempt from countervail actions. The two countries would be free to pursue whatever industrial policies they desired without concern for prompting a countervail action by the other country.

However, if Québec and Canada were to follow this course of action, they would still face another problem. Their sovereignty in formulating and implementing industrial policies would be constrained automatically by the existing international trade agreements or by unilateral actions by the United States.

By opting not to deal with the issues of subsidies and countervail in their bilateral trade agreement, they would lose the opportunity to formulate a common position for the current GATT and NAFTA negotiations of separate subsidies codes. Moreover, if Québec were to negotiate successfully a new trade agreement with the United States that included different arrangements for subsidies and countervail, this could create the potential for trade frictions between Québec and Canada. Different external trade rules might place one country's industries at a competitive disadvantage, especially if they were unable to benefit from certain types of industrial policies. This could result in lobbying efforts by companies in Canada, for example, to persuade the government to impose trade barriers on Québec companies in order to "level the playing field" or correct for "unfair trade."

Therefore, there are strong arguments for Québec and Canada to include a subsidies and countervail code in an agreement regulating bilateral trade in both goods and services. However, several problems might arise in negotiating this code. The Canadian and Québec governments might have different ideologies regarding the proper roles of government and the private market. But given the track record of the private sector in this country, these differences may have disappeared. On the other hand, would subnational levels of government in these two countries be subject to the code, and if so, how would their interests be represented in the negotiations?

These problems are not insurmountable. The preferred option is to include in the agreement a subsidies code that gives each country a considerable degree of latitude in implementing industrial policies. Indeed, the preamble to the code should emphasize that government intervention in the form of industrial policy does not constitute unfair trade and should set out the economic rationale for this type of intervention. A code along these lines then could be used to influence the GATT and NAFTA negotiations, assuming they have not been completed by that time. In addition, the Québec-Canada subsidies and countervail code should be binding on all subnational levels of government. This should not be controversial given the outlines of the code described above.

In negotiating the common rules governing trade relationships with foreign countries, Québec and Canada should review the two major flaws in the Canada-U.S. trade agreement. One of them, as already discussed, is the lack of a subsidies code. The other is the exclusion of section 301 of the 1974 U.S. Trade Act; that is, actions initiated against Canada under this unfair trade law cannot be challenged by Canada through any bilateral dispute-settlement procedure. Of course, the Canadian government could always directly petition the U.S. Trade Representative or the president to override successful actions against Canadian companies or governments.

As stated above, this U.S. trade law has the greatest potential for constraining the sovereignty of Québec and Canada. Section 301 directs the president to take appropriate actions to enforce the rights of the United States under any trade agreement or to respond to any act, policy or practice of a foreign country that is inconsistent with the provisions of the Act, or is unjustifiable, unreasonable or discriminatory and burdens or restricts U.S. commerce. It is important to keep in mind that this trade act has no basis in the GATT. Moreover, as a result of amendments included in the U.S. Trade and Tariff Act of 1984, section 301 covers trade in services and matters pertaining to investment, even though these are not as yet covered by any agreement under the GATT. Retaliation is permitted by this law against any "unfair trade" action (as defined within section 301), whether or not it is covered by a trade agreement or is consistent with the GATT or any other agreement. And section 301 increasingly has been used to initiate bilateral negotiations or GATT dispute-settlement procedures. In some cases when these have failed to resolve the trade disputes to the satisfaction of the United States, the dispute has been investigated further under section 301, and the U.S. Trade Representative has recommended some form of retaliation.

The revisions in the 1988 Omnibus Trade and Competitiveness Act strengthened the hand of the U.S. Trade Representative and increased the pressure on this official to take a more aggressive stance against unfair trade practices. New and broader definitions of unfair trade practices were included in the 1988 Act, as was a "super 301" which mandated the Trade Representative to identify practices and countries as targets for trade liberalization and to investigate them.

Thus, Québec and Canada must conclude a subsidies code with the United States, and negotiate an amendment directly to the FTA, or indirectly via the GATT or NAFTA, that would exempt domestic industries from section 301 actions. This proposed amendment might not be necessary if there were a subsidies code and all countries would be willing to abide by it.

If the United States were unwilling to do so, Québec and Canada could adopt comparable legislation to retaliate against the United States whenever the United States chose to use its trade law against Québec and/or Canadian industries or government policies. Such action would risk precipitating a trade-law war. But Québec and Canada could enlist the support of members of Congress supportive of more liberalized trade by demonstrating to them the absurdity of an escalating tit-for-tat trade-law war among the world's largest trading partners. Or the two nations could appeal to international public opinion by pointing out that if the United States is willing to bully small countries that are its staunchest allies, other nations should not trust any commitments made by the United States.

Trade Rules for Services

Turning our attention to trade in services, we find that at present there are no tariffs that impede this type of trade but, by and large, trade in services is affected by a number of federal and provincial regulations. For example, professional services are subject to provincial regulations that limit the extent of interprovincial trade; financial and transportation services are subject to both federal and provincial regulations that impose certain limitations on interprovincial trade in these types of services, although federally incorporated companies are able to provide services across the country. Furthermore, trade in services was dealt with, to some extent, in the FTA[8] and this issue has been an important part of the negotiations in the Uruguay Round of the GATT.

Negotiating a set of rules to regulate trade in services presents problems for countries concerned with their policy-making autonomy. Because of the importance and prevalence of direct government regulation of services, Québec and Canada will face a trade-off between liberalization and sovereignty. They will be compelled to decide how far each is willing to trade one off against the other.

Regulations are an expression of a country's policy objectives. There is general agreement that there are legitimate reasons for governments to intervene in the economy to regulate domestic economic activity even if this may interfere with cross-border trade.

Respect for the policy objectives of national laws and regulations applying to services was among the basic objectives originally set forth to govern the Uruguay Round negotiations on a framework of principles and rules for trade in services.

But what if it is not possible for countries, including subnational levels of government, to achieve their regulatory objectives effectively and efficiently in a manner which creates fewer distortions for international trade in services? Should certain blatantly protectionist regulations be tolerated and accepted in order to respect national sovereignty? Or should national sovereignty be constrained whenever it manifests itself in protectionist regulations?

Québec and Canada would again confront the issue of how much sovereignty is permissible and practical in an increasingly interdependent world. Two potentially conflicting principles of international law would come to the forefront in negotiating rules for trade in services: the sovereign right of a state to be free to engage in activities within its own territory and to regulate its own nationals; and the duty of a state to exercise its rights in a manner that does not harm the interests of other states unreasonably.

The presence of an increasing number of transnational service corporations and technological developments in communications and computers would complicate matters further for trade negotiators. Transnational corporations increasingly shop around for the most lax regulatory environment. As a result, increasing global integration and the continued growth of transnational service corporations will further erode national sovereignty and necessitate international co-operation and co-ordination in formulating regulations and minimum enforcement/ supervisory standards.

A further complication is that from a conceptual point of view, the liberalization of trade in services must also lead to greater trans-border mobility for the individual suppliers of the services. Article 3(c) of the Treaty of Rome stipulates that the free movement of persons (in addition to services and capital) should be guaranteed, and Articles 59 to 66 of the treaty deal specifically with persons who move from one member state to another to provide services.

To what extent would Canada and Québec grant mobility rights in order to liberalize trade in services?

Once more, the problem is not insurmountable if the two parties approach the negotiations realistically and in good faith. There is also much to build on. Chapters 14, 16 and 17 of the FTA provide a good starting point for the negotiations between Québec and Canada. National treatment stands out in this agreement as the key principle governing trade and investment in services. Article 1402, for example, sets out the obligation to extend the principle of national treatment to the providers of a list of commercial services.[9] Subnational levels of government are also covered by the national-treatment obligation.

But according to the introductory discussion in chapter 14 of the FTA, national treatment[10] does not require the two countries to harmonize their rules and regulations. Moreover, each government remains free to choose whether or not to regulate and how to regulate. Paragraph 3 of article 1402 allows for exceptions to national treatment. For example, either government may accord different treatment as long it is no greater than necessary for prudential, fiduciary, health and safety or consumer protection reasons and so long as it is equivalent in effect. The onus, however, is on the government proposing or according different treatment to establish that its ultimate purpose is not to restrict trade. As well, paragraph 5 in article 1402 makes it clear that no government is required to change any existing law or regulation in respect to the national treatment obligation.

Finally, article 1403 sets out the rules governing licensing and certification. The conditions for licensing and certification should relate principally to competence, and these conditions should not restrain access to such licensing or certification in a discriminatory way. Canada and the United States have also agreed to develop methods for the mutual recognition of licensing and certification requirements. The European Community solution to the problems created by different licensing and certification rules; namely, home-country regulation and supervision, mutual recognition and agreement on a minimal set of standards[11] — provides a sound basis for Québec-Canada negotiations. Different provincial rules governing the licensing of professions exist at present, and these different rules impede the mobility of many service providers across the country; even in the absence of Québec separation they should be the subject of interprovincial discussions on harmonization and mutual recognition.

Consequently, some degree of harmonization of regulations would be necessary both between Québec and Canada and between both countries and the rest of the world. It is important to note, however, that these regulations do not apply to services. Since regulations cannot be applied extraterritorially to providers of services, they have an incentive to search for and locate in the country with the most lax standards, and thus avoid more stringent and costly regulations. The resulting difficulties for a government in regulating certain service industries will be exacerbated over time by technological progress, which keeps shifting the boundary between traded and non-traded services. Innovations in telecommunications and computers are making it increasingly possible to deal with clients at a distance. Therefore, as more foreign providers are able to avoid local establishment and domestic regulation, more service providers may be in position to circumvent local regulations. Thus there exists the real possibility of a dramatic erosion of regulatory sovereignty.

In the absence of international, GATT-type rules and enforcement mechanisms to control competition in international markets, the ability of service providers to avoid regulations and the inability of governments to restrict the access of foreign providers of services to their markets could result in several service sectors becoming highly concentrated both nationally and internationally. It is conceivable that a small number of very large enterprises could end up in the position to set the terms for competing and the prices for and the quality of the services provided in the marketplace.

The trend towards larger and fewer international participants is apparent today in an increasing number of service sectors — for example, accounting, law, advertising, management consulting, financial services, transportation, real estate, employment agencies, travel agencies. The more binding the legal constraints on regulatory sovereignty, the more rapid and widespread will be the trend towards increased concentration and so the more binding will become the marketplace constraint on regulatory sovereignty.

This suggests that Québec and Canada should include in their trade agreement an establishment requirement for all providers of services in each country's market.[12] That is, establishment should become a precondition for providing services in the market. Furthermore, subject to the sole condition that the requirements not be blatantly protectionist, Québec and Canada should agree upon and incorporate in the agreement the requirements that foreign providers of services would have to satisfy in order to be permitted to become established in their markets. By requiring establishment as a precondition for providing services, foreign service providers would be unable to escape domestic regulations, and also would be subject to national competition laws.

Fair Trade between Québec and Canada

Both Québec and Canada will have to recognize and accept that economic interdependence necessitates some diminution of economic sovereignty. Furthermore, increasing global integration of markets and the further growth of transnational corporations in all sectors will further erode national sovereignty and necessitate international co-operation and co-ordination as a countervailing force. Nevertheless, a trade agreement should provide sufficient leeway for each country to develop and implement industrial strategies and pursue regulatory initiatives for prudential, fiduciary, health and safety, and cultural reasons.

The concept of fair trade does not require binding constraints on government intervention or extensive policy harmonization. Fair trade necessitates that all parties to a trade agreement accept that the rules do not give any party an advantage. That is, companies in a particular country are not able to gain a competitive advantage in international markets because of trade rules that enable these companies to benefit from a greater latitude for intervention by that country's government. All the parties to an agreement must believe that they are competing on a level playing field. Therefore, it will be important to specify clearly the actions all levels of government can take so as not to violate the fundamental objectives of the trade agreement. The key concepts, principles and rules must be defined precisely to avoid legal disputes arising from conflicting interpretations of ambiguous concepts.

The agreement should incorporate the principle of transparency.[13] Transparency will require that all regulations, policies and procedures that affect international trade and trade laws be published and be made readily available and reviewable by consultation and dispute-settlement mechanisms.

Finally, Québec and Canada should co-operate to create a coalition to limit the ability of the United States to act unilaterally to define fair trade and use section 301 to enforce its perception of fair trade and the benefits provided by international trade rules. This U.S. trade law currently lies outside the GATT and the FTA. Accordingly, it enables the United States to have a disproportionately large influence in trade negotiations. Unless section 301 is regulated or outlawed by multilateral trade agreements, no country will be free from U.S. pressures and harassment. No country will have assured access to the U.S. market or to markets in other countries where there will be direct competition with U.S. companies.

Dividing the Debt:
More than Bean Counting

Harold Chorney

A detailed examination of the issue of dividing up the debt between Canada and a sovereign Québec permits a number of useful insights into the thorny question of economic management, public accounting practices and debt mythology, as well as into the politics of separation.[1]

In order to establish some guidelines about how the debt might be divided, it is first essential to get a clear picture of the current situation at both the federal and provincial levels. Many studies have been undertaken. Tables 11.1, 11.2 and 11.3 show the amount of outstanding federal and provincial debt. Because there is considerable complexity here, and much confusion about these measures, I have chosen to use the data from the Bank of Canada's table of government of Canada direct and guaranteed securities and loans outstanding, and the distribution of these holdings from the Bank's February 1992 monthly review, to establish the amount of federal debt. This figure differs from the one in the government's annual budget because net financing requirements, which are reported by the Bank of Canada, subtract non-budgetary revenues and therefore always differ from budgetary debt. Using the Bank of Canada's data, it is possible to avoid double counting, net out government holding of debt and get a clear picture of the actual situation. This is necessary again because so much confusion and misleading information circulates among otherwise well-informed policy analysts on this issue. Contrary to the popular assumption, 79 percent of the federal debt is owed to domestic savers in Canada.

TABLE 11.1
Government of Canada Direct and Guaranteed Securities
Distribution by Type of Holder as of December 31, 1991
($ billions)

General Public

Provincial Government	20.3[1]
Municipal Government	1.6[1]
CSB	35.9
Non-residential	73.4[2]
Total	290.2[3]
Bank of Canada	22.4
Government of Canada	5.8
Chartered Banks	29.5

Note:
[1] Indicates Dec. 1990.
[2] Indicates 3rd quarter, 1991, the latest figures available.
[3] There are a number of other categories under the heading "general public" not included here.
Source: Table G5, *Bank of Canada Monthly Review*, February 1992.

As of December 1991, according to the Bank of Canada, there was a total of $347.9 billion in outstanding direct securities and loans. An additional $290.2 billion was owed to the general public, including $35.9 billion in Canada Savings Bonds. (The holdings under the category "General Public" include provincial and municipal governments.) A further $22.4 billion in marketable securities was owned by the Bank of Canada, in other words the government of Canada itself. Another $5.8 billion was held by the federal government directly. As of the end of 1990 — the latest date for which these figures are available — $20.3 billion was held by the provincial governments and $1.6 billion by municipal governments. In other words, a total of $50.3 billion of the total outstanding debt of the federal government was owed to the public sector itself (Table G5, *Bank of Canada Monthly Review*). An additional $29.5 billion was owed to the chartered banks. Of the total debt outstanding as of December 1991, $347.4 billion, an amount of $73.4 billion or 21.1 percent is owed to nonresidents.

As evidence of the discrepancy between the federal budget estimate of the debt and the Bank's figures on debt outstanding, the current budget lists the outstanding debt as some $420 billion, including projected financing requirements of $19.7 billion on a budget deficit of $31 billion. If we added $19.7 billion to the outstanding debt, according to the Bank's data the total would amount to almost $368 billion. The difference between this figure and the official government debt of some $420 billion is accounted for by non-budgetary transactions, including earnings on foreign exchange accounts and other specified-purpose accounts and loans which earn the government significant money each year.

In computing the actual debt to be divided, it is important to have a clear conception of just what this debt is. There is room for some methodological disagreement, but I would argue from a burden point of view that the correct figure is represented by the Bank of Canada's record of outstanding securities, less securities held by the public sector itself.

The Bélanger-Campeau Calculations

The Bélanger-Campeau commission on Québec's political and constitutional future used the government's budget debt and added to this amount pension obligations and the amount of debt that has been monetized. It then apportioned Québec's share of the total figure. For the amount of monetized debt they used total bank notes in circulation. For the purposes of dividing up debt this would seem reasonable, although for the purpose of assessing the burden of the debt it would not.

The process of establishing the total amount of debt is helpful because it shows to what extent the overall debt of the federal government is exaggerated in the budget and by media commentators, editorialists and politicians. In fact, if we were to net out debt owed to governments, the actual net debt owed

TABLE 11.2
Net Provincial Debt, March 1990
($billions)

Newfoundland	3.46
P.E.I.	.31
Nova Scotia	4.91
N.B.	3.13
Québec	46.57
Ontario	42.3[1]
Manitoba	5.3
Saskatchewan	7.5[1]
Alberta	-3.4
B.C.	4.1
Yukon/N.W.T.	-.3
Total all provinces	113.9

Source: provincial budgets 1991; Boothe and Harris 1991.
[1] indicates March 1991.

to non-governmental sources is just under $297 billion or some 43 percent of the GDP — a substantially smaller figure than the government's use of a gross-debt-to-GDP ratio of just over 60 percent. (For figures on provincial debt, see Table 11.2)

The Bélanger-Campeau report also makes a useful contribution to the debate by comparing the debt-to-GDP ratios of an independent Québec, the rest of Canada, and a number of other countries. When one introduces the unemployment and the inflation rate for these countries it becomes clear that there is no definite linkage between the relative size of the debt and the rate of unemployment or the rate of inflation. (See Table 11.3).

In two of the countries with the highest debt-to-GDP ratios, Japan and the Netherlands, the rate of unemployment is among the lowest. Inflation is also very low in Japan and moderately low in the Netherlands. Japan, which has a higher debt-to-GDP ratio than Canada's and the second highest ratio

TABLE 11.3

International Comparison of Gross Debt to GDP, Unemployment and Inflation

	Debt to GDP (1991)	Unemploy- ment rate (January 1992)	Inflation rate (January 1992)
Canada	61.5	10.6%[1]	1.6%
Canada without Québec	65.8	10.2	
Québec without Canada	65.7	11.9	
West Germany	44.6	6.3	4.0
Austria	55.6	10.3	1.3 [3]
Denmark	55.3	9.7[2]	3.2 [3]
United States	54.5	7.1	2.6
France	46.7	9.8	2.9
Japan	65.2	2.1	1.8
Netherlands	83.0	4.5	4.1
Sweden	43.5	4.1	5.3

The data for debt-to-GDP ratio are based on gross debt.
Sources: Calculations are based on the Bélanger-Campeau report, p. 489, and supplemented by information drawn from the *Budget Papers*, 1992; *The Economist* (March 1992); United Nations Monthly Economic Statistics, March 1992; OECD Economic Surveys, 1991, Netherlands.
[1] March 1992.
[2] July 1991.
[3] September 1991.

overall after the Netherlands, has the lowest discomfort index — the sum of the unemployment and inflation rates.

On the other hand, unemployment is very high in Canada, France, Austria and Denmark. And yet France has a low debt-to-GDP ratio.

Therefore, it would seem safe to say that there is no correlation between the debt-to-GDP ratio and the rate of unemployment. Similarly, there is no apparent correlation between low inflation and the debt ratio. Clearly, economic performance is conditional upon something other than the relative weight of debt in the economy. Lowering the ratio will not necessarily reduce the rate of unemployment or the rate of inflation. On the other hand, lowering the rate of unemployment ought to reduce the debt ratio, as a higher rate of utilization of potential output will result in greater tax revenues and lower expenditures on social welfare. But while the Swedish and German cases appear to confirm this, the Japanese and Dutch cases seem to show that a high debt ratio and low unemployment can go together. Another critical factor not covered in this table is the real rate of interest at which the outstanding debt is financed. The higher the rate, the more quickly debt grows and the more slowly the economy grows. Japan has had very low rates of real interest, despite a large debt-to-GDP ratio, while Canada has had very high real rates.

Given the overall debt figures, on what basis can the debt be divided in the case of Québec's separation? Bélanger-Campeau adopt the convention of calculating Québec's share of future revenues raised on the territory of Québec in keeping with their assumption of Ricardian equivalency: a deficit today is a tax tomorrow. (See Appendix.) Since this is difficult to forecast, they use past revenues as a guide, and after several adjustments (including making an allowance for tax abatement) arrive at the figure of 22.8 percent, which is considered Québec's share of the accumulated deficit. This amounts to $45.7 billion. To this figure is added debt corresponding to Québec's share of financial and non-financial assets — another $15 billion. Finally, an adjustment is made for Québec's obligations in terms of pensions to civil servants working for the federal government. This adds another $9.5 billion. The final total under Bélanger-Campeau is $70.3 billion.[2]

When added to Québec's current outstanding debt of about $52 billion, a sovereign Québec under the best of circumstances would have a debt of some $122 billion. This would amount to about 65.7 percent of its GDP, a substantial percentage but by no means a catastrophic one. On the other hand, the addition of some $70 billion of debt, other things being equal, would require a substantial increase in debt-servicing costs. Bélanger-Campeau estimate this to be on the order of $7 billion, which would increase debt-service costs as a percentage of GDP substantially, from 2.8 percent to 7.4 percent of the GDP.[3] The net effect of adding in debt-servicing costs would be to increase financing requirements by $6.5 billion. While this might entail an increase in taxes or a reduction in services if the government chose to reduce its deficit in this way, Bélanger-Campeau point out that the resulting ratio of debt-to-GDP of over 70 percent is still comparable to that of a number of other industrial countries. (See Table 11.3) The size of this deficit would undoubtedly worry the bond rating agencies and place the new Québec government under some pressure. Despite this pressure, the situation would be manageable, although difficult.

Incidentally, many of the voices who decry the size of the federal debt and deficit in Québec are quite comfortable with the prospect of a rise in Québec indebtedness after sovereignty, treating it correctly as a manageable burden. On the other hand, if Québec bowed to the wishes of its bond raters and attempted to reduce the debt through austerity policies, as opposed to economic growth, Mulroney-style deficit reduction would impose a considerable hardship on Québec taxpayers. It is here that the politics of dividing the debt is both fascinating and instructive.

Monetarists in Canada outside of Québec will attempt to exaggerate the burden. Monetarists on the Québec side who are federalists will also play it up. Monetarists who are sovereignists will play up the federal debt burden but downplay the debt burden of a sovereign Québec. Keynesians who are federalists will play up neither. Any division of Canada will be a very complex and painful process with a great deal of controversy. Nevertheless, while burdensome and sure to increase uncertainty among international investors who finance some of it, the division of the debt is not an insuperable problem. It is probable that initially some premium will be demanded by these investors to cover the uncertainty; but with proper central bank management to help establish the new market boundaries, the transition from a one- to a two-country market is a solvable problem.

The Historical-Benefits Approach

The key complication will revolve around the issue of whether Québec will have its own currency and its own central bank. If it chooses to do so, it will have some concerns about ensuring that the exchange rate is close to par with that of Canada in order to minimize the obligations it will assume on the debt market. It can avoid this problem by choosing to keep the Canadian dollar, but then it faces the problem of having independence without having any say over monetary policy. As well, keeping the Canadian dollar will require a degree of co-operation from the Canadian clearing system and the Bank of Canada. Ultimately, these issues will be more of a lasting complication and a potential problem than the division of the debt, provided that common criteria can be agreed upon.

The problem of agreeing upon common criteria becomes clear when we consider a historical-benefits approach to the division of debts and assets. Even if we simply compare historical benefits over the past thirty years, Québec's share of the debt grows considerably to over $110 billion. When we add in the pension adjustment, the share is almost $130 billion. This would represent a very large increase in the debt-to-GDP ratio, to over 90 percent of the GDP, which would be certain to increase greatly the pressure from the bond raters. For this reason, a historical-benefits approach will be fiercely resisted by a Québec in the process of becoming sovereign. On the other hand, compromises on these formulations can be used as bargaining leverage on other fronts — for example, in obtaining territorial concessions and minority-rights concessions. To strike such a bargain would have the virtue, from Québec's point of view, of reducing its share of the debt by as much as 15 percent. (See Table 11.4, option Per Capita*.)

Now, a major problem occurs in determining precisely which assets go to whom and what the value of these assets are. For example, because of the absurdly backward accounting procedures of the public accounts, non-financial assets are valued at one dollar. Bélanger-Campeau arrive at a figure of $72 billion for these same assets. They adopt the mean value of $50 billion in 1984 arrived at by the Neilsen task force on government programs, public administration and public real estate, and adjust it for inflation.[4] But they point out that this methodology is not comprehensive and does not include certain Crown corporations, Crown lands, national parks or resource rents. Clearly, if one did include these, the value would be considerably higher. The difference between Ottawa's accounting practice of evaluating these assets at one dollar and the figure of $72 billion is thus only a partial measure of the complete absurdity of current accounting practices in the public sector.

Since assets are the opposite side of the coin to debts, the value ascribed to them is important. For the smaller the evaluation of the assets received, the smaller will be the assessment of equitable liabilities. Therefore, the public accounts system of evaluating assets, which incidentally helps overstate the gravity of the current-deficit problem because it ignores the net worth of the public sector, will also have to be changed in order to come up with a fair method of dividing the debt.

Table 11.4, which is largely extracted from the studies done for the C. D. Howe Institute and the John Deutsch Centre,[5] includes the results of the Bélanger-Campeau report and certain modifications I am suggesting as part of either a territorial realignment or a major relocation of population. The table shows the wide range of values assigned to Québec's share of the debt depending upon the assumptions one adopts. I have not broken down the rest of Canada's proportion of the debt, although a number of the authors do so, in order to show how a given formula either worsens or improves a given region or province's liabilities in the case of further disintegration of the rest of Canada after the departure of Québec.

For example, under the historical-benefits regime which treats only equalization and transfer payments but ignores tariff barriers and regulation benefits, regions like the Atlantic provinces do much worse than even Québec in comparison with the per capita approach, or share-of-GDP approach.

Any attempt at a historical-benefits approach would allow a lot of scope for disagreement over the valuation of benefits, precisely how far back to go and what to include. Therefore, though it is interesting as an exercise it is unlikely to be more than a temporary bargaining chip. But, since Québec fares much worse under it, it might become a bargaining ploy in the rough and tumble of negotiations. As in all negotiations, the

TABLE 11.4
A Comparison of Debt Shares
Under Different Assumptions
($billions)

QUÉBEC	Debt	Pensions	Total %
B-C	60.8	9.5	13.3%P
			22.8%D
B-C*	67.9	12.3	20%D&P
GDP	76.3	16.4	23.2%
Per Capita	83.8	18.1	25.4%
Historical			
Benefits	110.3	18.1	33.0 %
Per			
Capita*	71.2	16.3	21.8 %
REST OF			
CANADA	Debt	Pensions	Total %
B-C	257.7	61.6	77.2%D
			86.7%P
B-C*	261.7	58.7	80%D&P
GDP	252.7	54.7	76.8%D&P
Per Capita	245.8	53.0	74.6%D&P
Historical			
Benefits	219.4	53.0	74.6%D&P
Per			
Capita*	258.4	54.8	78.2%D&P

Note: D stands for debt, P stands for pensions.
B-C — The Bélanger-Campeau Commission's estimate.
B-C* — modified Bélanger-Campeau estimate in Boothe, *et al.*, in which assets are divided in a slightly less favourable way for Québec.
GDP — A division based on share of the GDP in Boothe, *et al.*, and Boothe and Harris.
Per Capita — Debt is divided on a per capita basis, assuming current population.
Historical Benefits — Debt is divided according to a rather arbitrary assessment of who benefited from federalism over the past thirty years.
Per Capita* — A modification of the per capita formula in which a sovereign Québec's population is adjusted for the loss of a million people either through migration or the creation of a separate province federated to Canada in western Québec. The figure of a million is an arbitrary guess at the appropriate number.[6] It might turn out to be less, particularly if the loss in population results from migration alone as opposed to the creation of a new province of Western Québec. In the case of migration, Québec would be obligated to Canada for costs associated with relocation. If there were other boundary adjustments involving francophone additions to Québec from New Brunswick and Ontario, the two movements might cancel each other out and the resulting division of the debt would be closer to the straight per capita case.

degree of good-will and the desire for a settlement would determine the final outcome.

The Common-Currency, Common-Central-Bank Hypothesis

As Table 11.4 makes clear, there is a wide range of values for the Québec share of the debt, particularly if one includes the historical-benefits approach. If Québec seeks political sovereignty but continued economic association with a common currency and a common central bank, the division of debt poses several additional problems. Of course, the rest of Canada will probably not be in the mood to agree to this option, and in my opinion it is quite unlikely.

Nevertheless, for the purpose of the exercise let us consider it briefly. A common currency and a common central bank is no reason to continue with a commonly held debt, particularly if all other linkages except normal trade and commercial activity are broken. Québec would still have to assume its share of the federal debt and pay bondholders in Canadian dollars out of its tax revenues. It would be no different from the scenario of complete separation. The only difference would be that in the case of separation with separate central banks new debt issues would be handled by the government of Québec itself or the government of Canada. In the case of one common central bank, the bank would have to act on behalf of both governments in managing the debt. This would undoubtedly cause complications that might be difficult to resolve in negotiations. I have proposed elsewhere a model for ensuring Bank of Canada participation in the management of provincial debt.[7] The Bank would be governed by representatives from the Canada and Québec with voting power in proportion to each one's share of the total GDP of the two states. This model would permit monetization of a portion of the provincial debt in our present federation (that is, purchase of some of the debt by the central bank), which provinces cannot now do. It could easily be adapted to the problem of a common central bank for Québec and Canada. The bond-rating agencies would presumably treat Québec-issued debt, even if denominated in Canadian dollars, somewhat differently from Canada's, although the exact treatment would depend on whether the governments of Canada and Québec guaranteed the debt. This would seem very unlikely, although not impossible. Again, political considerations dictate against it.

Finally, there is the delicate issue of how to arrange the transfer of the agreed upon debt to the newly sovereign Québec. Here the term of the debt will complicate matters. Handing Québec only short-term debt will increase pressure on the Québec government to arrange for refunding of a significantly increased debt load in a short period of time. These kinds of problems are discussed by Boothe and Harris, who propose that Québec issue short-term bonds called Independence Bonds to cover the value of Québec's share of the federal debt.

These Independence Bonds would be held by the government of Canada and cashed upon maturity. This would give Québec a transition period in which to refund debt to cover this burden. The exact maturity mix of the bonds would be a matter of negotiation. Considerations such as inflation and default risk would also have to be taken into consideration. The risk of default could be minimized by Canada's purchasing a substantial share of Québec's new bonds and using them as leverage against default on the original debt owed to Canada. There are also complications surrounding the possibility that the creation of a large market for Québec bonds will diminish the market for Canadian bonds, but these complications are not insurmountable.

Many other issues remain. But in this short paper I have tried to report on the work to date, add several twists of my own and suggest a cautionary note. It seems far more rational to reach a compromise acceptable to both Québec and the rest of Canada on the present constitution than to plunge into what will surely be a major period of disruption and embattled negotiation. Unfortunately, reason rarely rules in politics. Perhaps this time it will be different.

Appendix: A Note on Debt Responsibility

The question has been asked whether or not a successor state is liable to any portion of the debts of the state from which it has separated. This question is particularly well developed in the work by Daniel Desjardins and Claude Gendron for the

C. D. Howe Institute, "Legal Issues Concerning the Division of Assets of Debt in State Succession: The Canada-Québec Debate."[8] Desjardins and Gendron rely upon the Vienna Convention on Succession of States in Respect of State Property, Archives and Debts to establish the case for Québec's obligation to assume an equitable proportion of the debt of Canada in the event of secession.

It should be noted that Canada is not a signatory to this convention, and opposed it when the United Nations conference adopted it in 1983. Nonetheless, because it is widely adhered to, it is likely that the court of international opinion, as well as international law, will resort to it for guidance in adjudicating any dispute between Canada and Québec in the case of separation. Furthermore, international custom and the Vienna Convention also dictate that, in the case of the separation of a state, the guiding principle governing the division of assets is that the successor state receive assets of the predecessor state in what is the territory of the successor state.

The division of liabilities is less clearly spelled out. But the authors review a number of different proposals. The Bélanger-Campeau report discusses the division of the debt in a comprehensive way in Chapter 9, "Analyse pro-forma des finances publiques dans l'hypothèse de la souveraineté du Québec." The analysis, although controversial, is rich in detail and offers a number of useful insights into public-sector accounting practices in Canada.

Bearing in mind that the Bélanger-Campeau commission acknowledged that Québec would assume what it called "its fair share" of the debt, it seems clear that a sovereign Québec would indeed accept some share of the federal debt, if for no other reason than to reassure the international financial community of its financial integrity.

On the other hand, it is also clear that Québec will not accept whatever share is apportioned to it by the rest of Canada and will, as in any negotiation, seek to minimize its liabilities and maximize its gains. Gendron and Desjardins, after reviewing various options, conclude that there is no legal imposition upon Québec to accept any portion of the Canadian debt that Canada could enforce, short of force majeure. But in practice, "a newly separated state could probably not expect to obtain any portion of the assets of the predecessor state without an equitable division of liabilities and a direct or indirect assumption of liabilities to third parties ... In short, political and economic realities would compel the successor state voluntarily to assume, either directly or indirectly, obligations towards the creditors of the national debt for its share of the debt as agreed by the predecessor state" (p. 10).

In other words, they will have to pay their fair share. Thus far, no responsible political figure in Québec has repudiated this position. But, in the heat of protracted negotiations and threat and counterthreat, repudiation is a possibility, particularly if the amounts demanded are regarded as unfair or unduly onerous.

In the context of this discussion, there are aspects of the methodology that bear careful scrutiny. For example, Bélanger-Campeau adopted the convention that Québec's share of the debt must be related to Québec's contribution to federal taxes raised in Québec (p. 425). This assumption is that debts represent the present value of future taxes. The assumption is the Ricardian notion of equivalence: a debt today is a tax tomorrow. This implies that debts do not create economic assets that enrich society, particularly in times of high unemployment. I would, of course, reject this logic. McCallum points out that the correct concept is the present value of the difference between future revenues and future outlays.[9]

This allows for the very real possibility that future revenues will be higher than otherwise would be the case in the absence of the investment in infrastructure associated with the debt and the higher growth rate that results.

V
Cross-Border Policies
and Issues

Protecting the Rights of Linguistic Minorities

Kenneth McRoberts

Over the years, one of the most frequently raised concerns about the accession of Québec to sovereignty is the consequence it would have for the linguistic minorities: the anglophones of Québec and the francophones in a reconfigured Canada.

Clearly, Québec sovereignty would have major consequences for the two minorities. Inevitably, it would be an issue in any negotiations between a sovereign (or about-to-be-sovereign) Québec and Canada.

There are, in fact, several different approaches that negotiators might adopt to deal with the minorities question. However, before assessing them, we first need to review the general state of the two minorities. We need to examine their demographic strength and geographical location, and to see what would be the impact of Québec sovereignty. And we need to survey the legal and political arrangements for the protection of minorities that are now in place in Canada and Québec — and to assess how they would be affected by sovereignty.

Anglophone Québec and Francophone Canada

Size
Discussion of the linguistic minorities is complicated by the fact that estimating their size is no straightforward matter:

I would like to thank Jean-Guy Bourgeois for his superb work as research assistant, and several colleagues for invaluable comments on a first draft: Yves Frenette, Simon Langlois, Patrick Monahan, Don Stevenson, François Vaillancourt and David Welch.

different indicators produce different results. Moreover, the biases of different indicators are not consistent. Substituting one measure for another will lead to smaller estimates for one minority yet larger estimates for the other.

Basically, two indicators are available in Canadian census data. The traditional measure is mother tongue. In the 1986 census, just as in previous censuses, this measure set Québec's anglophone minority as substantially smaller than Canada's francophone minority: 678,000 versus 945,860. The other measure, the language that is used primarily at home, was introduced in 1971. In the 1986 census this measure raised Québec's anglophone minority to 796,470, but reduced Canada's francophone minority to 672,470.[1] Thus, on this basis Canada's minority is smaller than Québec's.

The difference in results reflects the fact that, for one reason or another, people may in the course of their lifetimes supplant their mother tongue with another as their primary language. As we shall see, the Québec anglophone community has benefited from such transfers but Canada's francophones have lost ground through them.

Needless to say, selection of one indicator over another is not without political implications. The desire to emphasize or de-emphasize the significance of a minority might well influence this choice. Nonetheless, for most purposes the language used at home does seem to be the more meaningful indicator of a minority's actual strength. In the rest of the text, data will be based upon this indicator unless otherwise noted.

At the same time, it should be borne in mind that whatever measure is used, Québec's minority represents a substantially larger share of its total population, 10.4 percent or 12.3 percent, than does Canada's, 5 percent or 3.6 percent.[2]

Location

Beyond the relative size of the minorities, we need to examine their geographical distribution. Here both Québec's and Canada's minorities share the same trait: they are highly concentrated geographically. In Québec's case, 60 percent of its minority is concentrated in the Montréal area (l'Île de Montréal et Laval), even though that area contains only 24 percent of the province's total population.[3] By the same token, of Québec's seventy-six census divisions, only sixteen have anglophone populations of more than 10 percent.[4]

As for Canada outside of Québec, its minority is concentrated in two provinces: Ontario, which contains slightly over half (50.6 percent), and New Brunswick, which contains another third (32.65 percent). The next-largest minority, Manitoba's, represents only 4.4 percent of Canada's francophones.[5] For that matter, within the two provinces of Ontario and New Brunswick the francophone presence is highly concentrated. Of Ontario's forty-nine counties, only eight have francophone minorities of 10 percent or more, and of New Brunswick's sixteen counties, only eight are more than even 5 percent French speaking.[6]

Trends
Over recent decades, the two minorities have declined not only as proportions of the total populations, but in absolute numbers. Between 1971 and 1986, the francophone population of Canada outside of Québec fell from 675,920 (4.4 percent) to 672,470 (3.6 percent). Québec's anglophone population fell from 887,875 (14.7 percent) to 796,695 (12.3 percent).[7]

However, the two populations declined for different reasons. In Canada's case, the primary cause is assimilation. Thus, if the figure for home language is calculated as a percentage of the figure for mother tongue, the resulting "index of continuity" is 71 percent for 1986. In Québec's case, assimilation was not the problem. The anglophone community actually attracted people to it, primarily from the "allophone" (non-francophone/non-anglophone) population, producing an "index of continuity" of 117 percent in 1986.[8] However, the anglophone minority has been seriously affected by migration to other parts of Canada. Thus, over five-year periods between 1966 and 1986, net migration of anglophones between Québec and the rest of Canada was: 1966–71: 52,200; 1971–76: 52,200; 1976–81: 106,300; and 1981–86: 41,600.[9] Emigration from province to province has not been as significant a factor for Canada's francophones. Over the whole period 1966–86, Canada lost a net total of 48,500 francophones through migration between Canada and Québec.[10]

Demographic Strength after Québec's Accession to Sovereignty

There appear to be no scientific projections that specifically factor in the effects of Québec sovereignty. Existing projections seem to presume a continuation of the federal order. Even then, however, they presume that the minorities will continue their decline, once again for different reasons.

In the case of Canada outside of Québec, demographers expect that continued assimilation and inability to attract linguistic transfers should cause the francophone minority to decline to 3 percent of the total population by 2001.[11] As we shall see, there is every reason to presume that with Québec sovereignty the level of governmental support for Canada's francophones would decline, further strengthening assimilationist forces. Thus, for all intents and purposes it would be restricted to two provinces, Ontario and New Brunswick — and even there to areas which are adjacent to Québec.

As for Québec, its anglophone minority is expected to continue to decline through outmigration. Apparently, projections based on the 1986 census are not available. However, working from the 1981 census, two demographers, Termote and Gauvreau, have projected that anglophones will represent 11 percent of Québec's population in 2001 and 10 percent in 2021. This projection is based on the rates of births, linguistic transfers and net migration which marked the period 1976–81. Since outmigration was unusually high during that period (which happens to coincide with the first five years of the Lévesque government), they in fact raise their projection somewhat: 12 percent for 2021.[12]

However, in the context of Québec sovereignty, the 1976–81 level of outmigration may not be unrealistic. In fact, in an April 1991 survey of Québec anglophones (English as home language) only 35 percent stated that they would remain in Québec if it were to become independent (44 percent said they would not; 21 percent did not know or did not respond).[13] Moreover, linguistic transfers and especially gains through international migration might well decline radically. If the rates of net Québec-Canada migration and of births were to be the same as for 1976–81 and there were to be *no* linguistic

transfers or gains through international migration, then Termote and Gauvreau project that anglophones would represent
7.4 percent of the Québec population in 2001, and 4.9 percent
in 2021.[14] Thus, even under the worst scenario, a sovereign
Québec would still have a significant anglophone presence.
The 7.4 percent figure for 2001 would represent well over
500,000 people.[15]

Needs of Linguistic Minorities

Any assessment of schemes for the protection and support of
linguistic minorities hinges in part upon a reading of the broad
social and economic processes which determine a minority's
prospects. What are the crucial factors? How can legal protection and state intervention influence these factors to a group's
benefit?

The key determinant of a linguistic group's future strength
is whether its children will in fact start out their lives in that
language. That being accomplished, the issue becomes one of
whether they will continue to live their lives primarily in their
mother (or "parental") tongue. Many factors become important: the range and dynamism of educational facilities in the
language; the opportunities to use the language in work; the
language of culture and leisure; whether marriages take place
within the linguistic group; and so on. All of these factors seem
to be dependent upon two key conditions: a sufficiently large
population base and relative segregation from other languages.

Canada's Francophones
In most parts of Canada, with the exception of New Brunswick
(and, to a lesser extent, Ontario), the francophone minority has
neither asset. Historically, it has been able to maintain a certain
segregation from English-speaking populations in agricultural
settings, where work activities are focused on the family farm
and social activities may be restricted to the local community.
But segregation is much more difficult in urban settings. While
there may be a francophone presence in some small towns, in
most major urban settings it is exceedingly small — with the
exception of New Brunswick. Of the nineteen metropolitan

areas outside Québec and New Brunswick, there are only two where more than 3 percent of residents speak French at home — both in Ontario: Ottawa (15.4 percent) and Sudbury (22.7 percent).[16]

Accordingly, in urban Canada work opportunities may well involve a need to function in English. Media are predominantly in English, as well as many opportunities for social activity and leisure. Thus, the influence of English may well be overwhelming. In the case of Saskatchewan, the 1981 census found that the proportion of people of French origin still using French as their home language was 29 percent in farming areas and 26 percent in other rural areas, but only 12 percent in Saskatoon and 9 percent in Regina.[17]

In the case of Ontario, with its substantial number of francophones, state intervention has partially offset these anglicizing pressures through the creation of a "parallel" francophone public sector. In Ontario, the provincial government's expansion of French-language services has itself created important new opportunities to work in French in urban areas. Moreover, the French-language section of Ontario's public televison, *la Chaîne française*, has attracted a large following among urban, as well as rural, francophones. However, in the remaining provinces the francophone populations appear to be too small to support public-sector efforts of this scale.

Québec's Anglophones
The position of francophones in most parts of Canada is not at all parallelled by that of Québec's anglophones. In absolute numbers, Québec's anglophone minority is double the size of Ontario's francophone minority and three times the size of New Brunswick's. While concentrated primarily in the Montreal metropolitan area, it represents close to 25 percent of that area's population.[18] Even in present-day Québec it is able to have a substantial degree of segregation.

Moreover, Québec anglophones have a greater range of institutions available in their language than do the minorities of other provinces — including New Brunswick. While anglophone employment in the provincial public service is limited and private-sector employment often requires some knowledge of French, Québec anglophones still have far wider opportunities to work in their language than do Canada's francophone minorities. And they continue to own a substantial share of the province's private enterprises. Moreover, the external support available to Québec's anglophones — the English-language institutions of a whole continent — vastly exceeds the limited support which Québec's French-language institutions provide for the francophone minorities.

Thus, there is every reason to expect that even though many Québec anglophones now have acquired a second-language competence in French, they will retain English as their first language. Fears for the future of Québec's minority are based upon outmigration, not assimilation.

In sum, assuming that a minority has the demographic critical base necessary for survival, the essential question is whether it has control over a broad range of separate institutions: educational, social services, cultural and, ideally, economic. This would seem to be far more important than the formal status of its language within common public institutions, which is the essential thrust of official bilingualism.

Present Legal Position of Minorities

Two contrasting formulas characterize the legal position of linguistic minorities in present-day Canada.

Language Equality or Official Bilingualism
Within one formula the majority/minority distinction is ignored to the greatest extent possible. Under linguistic equality, or official bilingualism, French and English have precisely the same status. This is the basis for language rights within federal jurisdictions. Under the Official Languages Act, as first passed in 1969 and revised in 1988, and subsections of sections 16 through 20 of the Canadian Charter of Rights and Freedoms, English and French are declared to be the "official languages of Canada," both languages are to have equal status in federal institutions, and francophones and anglophones are entitled to a wide range of services in their language, where conditions warrant. Official bilingualism is also the basis of New Brunswick's language regime, as found both in the Official Languages Act of 1969 and subsections of sections 16 through

20 of the Charter. Services are to be provided throughout the province, without qualification.

Pre-eminence of One Language with Minority Services
Among all provinces other than New Brunswick, the language regime is one of pre-eminence for the majority language, whether on an official or a *de facto* basis, coupled with some measure of minority services.

The clearest instance is, of course, Québec where Bill 101 declares French to be "the official language of Québec," including governmental institutions, and seeks to establish French as the working language of the province. The law does allow children of Québec-educated anglophones to be educated in English; by virtue of section 23 of the Charter of Rights and Freedoms this right is extended to children of parents educated elsewhere in Canada. In 1983, the law was amended to allow for institutional bilingualism in schools, hospitals and social agencies serving the anglophone community. Moreover, Bill 142, passed in 1986, enshrined the right of anglophones to English-language health facilities and social services in areas with significant anglophone populations. (By and large the services were already available.)

None of the other provinces declares its majority language, English, to be the official language. But English is conventionally understood to have a superior status. One province, Ontario, does declare French to be an official language for certain purposes — "the French language is recognized as an official language in the courts and education" — and requires the promulgation of laws in both languages. None of the other provinces has committed itself to promulgate laws in both languages. (Manitoba found itself bound to do so by virtue by a 1979 Supreme Court interpretation of the Manitoba Act, 1870.)

All provinces, Québec included, are bound by section 23 to provide elementary and secondary education to minority-language populations where they are sufficiently large. Most provinces have modified their education statutes to reflect this.[19]Two provinces, Manitoba and Ontario, have laws specifying a larger range of French-language services. Ontario's Bill

8 stipulates that within twenty-two designated districts all provincial ministries must provide French-language services.

Protection of Minorities with Québec Sovereignty

Canada

In principle, the legal status of Canada's constitutionally entrenched language rights would be unaffected by Québec's departure. However, there would be strong political pressure to pare down or abolish the provisions.

Canada's francophone minority would have fallen from 25 percent of the total population to 3 percent. French could lose official status within federal institutions, although there might remain some disposition to provide services to francophone minorities.

For the same reason, as the French presence in Canada as a whole is radically reduced, English Canadians would be likely to feel less bound to support French-language rights at the provincial level. New Brunswick's official bilingualism might survive, given the size (31 percent) of its francophone minority — although the recent electoral success of the Confederation of Regions (COR) suggests that it would be under intense pressure. In the case of Ontario, with a francophone minority of about 4 percent, such provisions of Bill 8 as the promulgation of laws in both languages might be eliminated. There certainly would be strong political pressure in Ontario to dispense with public services in French, as there would in Manitoba. By the same token, in many parts of Canada there would be resistance to section 23's requirement of French-language education.

Québec

There are good reasons to believe that if the Parti Québécois were to form the government of a sovereign Québec, it would maintain some range of services for the English-speaking community. (To be sure, the commitment would be greater if, by some chance, the Liberal Party were to form the government — given the traditional presence of anglophones within the party.) The readiness of other states to recognize Québec's sovereignty might well be influenced by how the Québec government treats its anglophone minority. Not the least important of these states would be the United States. For this reason alone, a sovereign Québec could hardly run the risk of appearing to suppress English. Québec nationalists have already been alarmed over the influence that Mordecai Richler's pronouncements have secured in the United States.

For that matter, René Lévesque used to insist that if Québec were to become sovereign there would be no need for a Bill 101. During his tenure as leader, the Parti Québécois program explicitly guaranteed that the anglophone minority would have access to public education, at all levels, to the extent warranted by its proportion of Québec's population on the accession to sovereignty.[20]

By the same token, in his introduction to the 1991 edition of the party program, Jacques Parizeau declared:

Ce rêve collectif [of sovereignty] est intimement lié au respect profond toujours témoigné des droits, des institutions et de la langue de nos compatriotes anglophones.... Un Québec souverain, sûr de lui-meme comme de sa culture, pourra faire de la cohabitation de sa majorité francophone et de sa minorité anglophone une source d'enrichissement toujours plus prometteuse.[21]

Nonetheless, the 1991 version of the program itself contains no reference to the treatment of the anglophone population. However, at the conclusion of a colloquium, "La place de la communauté anglophone dans un Québec souverain," the party leadership established a study group to define the rights of Québec anglophones.[22]

Whatever may be the position which the Parti Québécois does finally adopt, the anglophone population of a newly sovereign Québec is bound to feel that its position is insecure. After all, party programs are never a guarantee of the policies a party will follow once it actually assumes power. Thus, it is bound to want firmer guarantees of its future. Moreover, at least some elements of public opinion in Canada, the United States and elsewhere will be concerned about its plight.

By the same token, we have already seen that if Québec should no longer be part of Canada, there are bound to be pressures to reduce French-language rights in Canada.

To the extent that Canadians become exercised over the possible treatment of their compatriots in Québec, and Québécois become similarly concerned about francophones in Canada, then relations between Québec and Canada could be seriously affected.

Accordingly, there are good reasons to explore approaches which might provide greater security for the two linguistic minorities.

International Law
International law would not be a clear source of support. In all likelihood, Québec would sign the several international agreements on human rights to which Canada is already a party. The most important of these is the International Treaty on Civil and Political Rights. However, according to legal scholar José Woerhling, even under this agreement Québec's obligation would be primarily not to interfere in the minorities' own efforts to maintain themselves. The treaty is not as firm in requiring states to support a minority actively.[23]

Adjusting Boundaries
An approach that has received a considerable degree of attention in recent months is to resolve the minorities problem by redrawing the Québec-Canada frontier so as to join minority populations with their compatriots.

Much of the discussion of the boundaries of a sovereign Québec has in fact been framed in terms not of the interests of minorities, but of the historical evolution of Québec's boundaries.[24]

However, a case for altering boundaries could also be based upon the principle that individuals should be able to decide whether in fact they will be incorporated within a new state. Former Saskatchewan premier Allan Blakeney has stated that

> subject to pressing geographic realities, we should do everything we can to ensure that all the people who want to be part of the new state be included, and all those who don't want to be excluded, leaving as few minority pockets as possible.[25]

In a recent study Ian Ross Robertson uses this principle to argue that "the future of southwestern Québec, including the western (English) part of Montréal, [should] be decided by a free vote."[26]

Nonetheless, there are major difficulties with this approach. First, it is bound to be extremely contentious. For many people, territory has very high symbolic significance. Certainly, the principle would be rejected by a great many Québécois. For that matter, it is not at all clear that English Canadians who countenance such an accommodation of Québec's anglophones would support a loss of territory to Québec so as to accommodate the francophones of Ontario and New Brunswick — if they should so choose.

By the same token, the introduction of territory as a negotiating issue would greatly heighten the sense of "winners" and "losers." Since any exchange of territory is unlikely to be fully equivalent, it would create feelings of injustice that will bode ill for the future of the Québec-Canada relationship.

Finally, there is the very real possibility that the two sides will be unable to agree on any redrawing of the boundary. Any "free votes" by citizens presume prior agreements that may be unattainable. Are these votes to take place in all localities that are contiguous to boundaries, or just those where the minority is of a sufficient size? If the latter, what is the criterion for size and what is the criterion for "minority" — mother tongue, home language? At the same time, how far can boundaries be accommodated so as to incorporate minority populations? Most proposals for redrawing boundaries restrict the adjustments to "contiguous" populations. But what is "contiguous"?

Clearly, there is enormous potential for deadlock in any negotiations over boundaries. And with deadlock there would arise the possibility of civil strife as frustrated minority populations decide to take matters into their own hands. Certainly, the violence that has surrounded recent border disputes in such settings as Yugoslavia and the former Soviet Union is not encouraging.

Robertson counters that Québec sovereignty with the present boundaries would itself be very destabilizing and "probably cause more human suffering and dislocation of population than partition." (The exact nature of this "human suffering" is not specified.)

Yet he proposes a scheme for partition in which "part of the border would run through Montréal."[27] It is difficult to imagine an arrangement more economically destabilizing and likely to induce hardship and strife than to divide Montréal, Québec's essential metropolis, between two countries. How could it possibly be in the interest of anglophone residents of Montréal to have the city from which they gain their livelihood fatally undermined in this fashion?

The second difficulty with seeking to resolve the issue of linguistic minorities by altering boundaries so as to incorporate contiguous populations is that in fact it cannot fully address the matter — at least not within the conventional sense of "contiguous."

Most of Québec's anglophone population is concentrated in the Metropolitan Montréal area. The western edge of this region is over fifty kilometres from the Québec border. The two intervening counties of Soulanges and Vaudreuil have English-speaking minorities that constitute respectively 5 percent and 24 percent of their populations.[28] Clearly, the normal sense of "contiguous" could not accommodate such a situation.

Thus, the question arises as to whether there are more practical ways through which the rights of linguistic minorities might be secured.

Constitutional Entrenchment
One possibility would be for a sovereign Québec to entrench minority language rights within its constitution. However, as Judge Jules Deschênes testified to a committee of the National Assembly charged with examining Québec sovereignty, the very notion of privileging one minority over others in a constitution is problematic in principle. While this state of affairs exists within the Canadian constitution, there might not be support for reproducing it within a sovereign Québec's constitution.[29]

In any event, even with entrenchment, Québec's anglophones might still be fearful that at some point their rights could be eliminated through constitutional amendment or could be eroded through unsympathetic jurisprudence in Québec's courts.

Agreements or Treaties Regarding Linguistic Minorities
A stronger basis for security would be for both Québec and Canada to sign a protocol or treaty through which they would be committed to recognize the rights of their respective minorities.

This notion has already been discussed within the context of Canadian federalism. In 1977 the Parti Québécois government of René Lévesque invited the other provinces to join with it in signing reciprocal interprovincial accords, but the provinces declined to do so. Not only were the provincial premiers under intense pressure from the federal government to avoid agreements with the "separatist" Québec government, but they apparently were troubled by the unevenness in rights which would emerge if some governments were to enter the accords and others were not. Nonetheless, the PQ government's Bill 101 contains an unused provision for reciprocal accords.[30]And, apparently, a few years ago the governments of Ontario, New Brunswick and Québec explored the possibility of a reciprocal accord on language rights among the three of them.

By the same token, there already have been proposals for a treaty on language rights between a sovereign Québec and Canada. In his testimony to the Bélanger-Campeau commission, Université de Montréal constitutional lawyer José Woerhling raised the possibility of

> accords de réciprocité dans lesquels le Québec, d'une part, l'État central et les autres provinces, d'autre part, s'engageraient à reconnaître des droits et privilèges comparables aux minorités respectivement placées sous leur juridiction.[31]

This same notion is invoked in a document prepared by the committee of the National Assembly established to examine Québec's accession to sovereignty.[32] And Judge Deschênes favoured such a scheme in his testimony to the committee of the National Assembly.[33]

The fullest elaboration of the concept, in fact, appeared back in 1979 in *L'option*, a volume written by two PQ backbenchers, Jean-Pierre Charbonneau and Gilbert Paquette. The first detailed outline of sovereignty-association, the study proposed that Canada and Québec commit themselves to a "Charte des droits":

> Cette Charte devra assurer aux deux minorités le droit à des services d'information, d'enseignement, de justice et de la santé dans leur langue, de même que celui d'utiliser leur langue dans les communications avec les services de l'administration publique des deux États et de [the Québec-Canada Association] et celui de promouvoir leur développement social, économique et culturel, par les moyens jugés par eux appropriés.[34]

In addition, the two states would create minority councils which would be the *"instruments politiques et financiers"* through which these rights would be applied. Finally, they proposed arrangements to ensure minority-language radio and television in each state.[35]

Assuming that these are to be the broad parameters of a Québec-Canada treaty or protocol on linguistic minorities, the question remains as to how it would be administered within Canada, which would remain a federal state. To a very great extent these matters involve provincial jurisdictions. Thus, as is indicated in Woerhling's formulation, the provincial governments would have to be parties to the agreement.

What would be the effectiveness of such an accord in meeting the concerns of the linguistic minorities? Beyond any principled commitment to generosity towards minorities, majority-language public opinion would be motivated by awareness that the fate of their compatriots in the other state is now very much dependent upon their treatment of their own minority. This equation has been implicit in much of the development of language rights within Canada over the last thirty years — now it would be made explicit. However, just as with the rights entrenched in the Charter of Rights and Freedoms, the terms of this agreement could be enforced by a tribunal.

It could even be argued that relative to what now exists by way of protection of language rights such an agreement would be an improvement. After all, the constitutional obligations on the provincial governments to provide French-language services are now limited to education alone, with the exception of New Brunswick. If properly supported, the minority councils might well provide the control over distinct institutions that we have seen is crucial to a group's survival.

However, it must be recognized that the process of Québec's accession to sovereignty could itself weaken the position of Québec's anglophone minority, by triggering a massive out-migration. A joint Québec-Canada charter of minority language rights might help to ease these fears, but it could not eliminate them.

Nonetheless, if the decision has been made that Québec is to be sovereign, then both Québec and Canada would have a clear interest in negotiating an accord to protect minority language rights. To be sure, there is no certainty that public opinion in either country would support such a measure. Canadians might decide that with the departure of Québec they should be freed of any need to support the French language. And Québécois might feel that a continued public status for English would detract from their hard-won achievement of sovereignty. Yet, without reciprocal accords on linguistic minorities or an equivalent measure, Québec's accession to sovereignty is bound to be even more conflictual than it would be otherwise. This would be a cost for both parties.

Our Common Future: Avoiding the "Tragedy of the Commons"[1]

Barbara Rutherford

It is clear that we have been living in an age of rampant individualism that arose historically from circumstances of abnormal abundance. It seems predictable, therefore, that on our way toward the steady state we shall move from individualism toward communalism. The self-interest that individualistic political, economic, and social philosophies have justified as being in the overall best interests of the community, as long as the "growth" frontier provided a safe outlet for competitive striving, will begin to seem more reprehensible and illegitimate as scarcity grows; the traditional primacy of the community over the individual that has characterized virtually every other period of history will be restored.

—William Ophuls[2]

Our geographical bonds with Québec will not change as a result of Québec's sovereignty. We must therefore seize the opportunity to consider how best to protect our children and the environmental heritage that is our common future. This paper will discuss what form of intergovernmental or supranational integration and co-operation will foster the right balance of good-neighbourliness and sovereignty in respect of environmental protection and resource conservation.

The Environment Transcends Political Borders

Canada is comprised of "bioregions" or "ecozones."[3] Ontario, Québec and Manitoba share a common environment which includes the Hudson Plains, the Boreal Shield and a mixed

wood plains bioregion. Within these bioregions, the citizens of
Ontario and Québec share the same environmental concerns
and the acts of one province affect the other's environment.[4]
We all share the obligation to protect and preserve the environment. While these environmental considerations should be
at the centre of our constitutional concerns, they are not.[5]

The Hudson Bay/James Bay bioregion is a case in point. Its
size in comparison to the rest of Canada and the global importance of its ecosystem in relation to the rest of the world
make it environmentally significant. Its watershed stretches
west to the British Columbia border, north to Melville Peninsula, and south into North Dakota and Minnesota and covers
well over a third of Canada. The rivers flowing into this bioregion discharge more than twice the amount of water than
either the Mackenzie or St. Lawrence rivers.[6] This fact of nature makes the ecological integrity of the bioregion highly
significant. The bioregion also plays a pivotal role in the economic independence and prosperity of the affected provinces.

The rich diversity of ecosystems and of the mammals, migratory birds and fish in this area is astounding. It is home to
approximately sixty species of fish, ringed seals, polar bears
and the endangered beluga and bowhead whales. The coasts
are a major migratory pathway and breeding ground for many
species of geese and ducks. These species are at risk from the
presence of toxic metals and chemicals, such as mercury and
organochlorine compounds, and their future is bleak:

> Hydro developments that change the timing and rate of
> flow of water may cause changes in … the habitats of
> marine mammals, fish, and migratory birds … and anad-
> romous fish [fish that go upriver to spawn] popula-
> tions…. Further large-scale developments are likely to
> compound these stresses when combined with continued
> loadings of long-range transported toxic contaminants
> and probable regional climatic changes or shifts in sea-
> level caused by global increases in air temperature.[7]

Québec's plans to develop James Bay are only part of the story.
The present and future hydro-electric capacity of Ontario and
Manitoba place further stress on these shared fragile ecosys-
tems.

Culturally, this bioregion is extremely significant, having been occupied by aboriginal peoples for thousands of years; they include the Cree and Inuit whose livelihood depends on hunting and fishing. These unique people and their cultures are also at risk of further contamination and, eventually, annihilation. The five-thousand-year history of the Cree, for example, shows the profound respect they and their ancestors have for this land "based on both an ethic of sharing and the deep spiritual significance of hunting."[8]

For all of these reasons, action to safeguard the environment must be at the top of any political, constitutional or legal agenda. Currently, the federal government is reluctant to exercise its environmental jurisdiction, even in issues with clear interprovincial and international dimensions, for fear of treading on provincial autonomy. Indeed, both levels of government engage in jurisdictional buck-passing to avoid having to make tough decisions with respect to the protection of the environment. In some sense then, provinces operate almost as sovereign states within Canada. Consequently, in this bioregion we are witnessing a clear case of the "tragedy of the commons" as Manitoba, Ontario and Québec compete to exploit the natural environment of Hudson Bay/James Bay and externalize the environmental costs, while ignoring the cumulative impact of their joint actions. If the secession of Québec removes the minimal need for co-operation, this trend will undoubtedly accelerate.

Perhaps the most insidious aspect of this question is that provincial Crown corporations, including Hydro-Québec and Ontario Hydro, operate independently with no real accountability to their shareholders, the taxpayers. This underscores the fundamental contradiction in the role of the state: it is the protector, but also owner and manager of the environment and natural resources. Governments are in a blatant conflict-of-interest situation when having to regulate environmental protection and resource conservation. Thus it is imperative to find new ways to regulate the state and make it accountable for its actions.

These Crown corporations also retain a monopoly on their environmental assessment data. This frustrates the fundamental right to information and ensures that their scientific findings are not subject to rigorous peer review. We simply do not know what the likely effects of any of their proposed development schemes are. We can, however, list the sensitive environmental issues.

The boreal forest region (coniferous and broad-leaf forest) is the single most important one in the country. It forms a continuous belt from Newfoundland and the Labrador coast westward to the Rocky Mountains and north-westward to the Yukon and Alberta. The main environmental issues in the boreal shield concern the safeguarding of the long-term sustainability of forests and ensuring that mining operations are non-polluting. Sustainable forestry practices entail protecting biodiversity, permitting only selective logging, and eliminating reliance on chemical pesticides and herbicides. The environmental impacts of mining are the waste products, including acidified and radioactive mine wastes, sulphur dioxide (acid rain), and land use issues, such as the desecration of wilderness areas and the violation of aboriginal rights.[9]

Within the mixed-wood plain (the southern parts of Québec and Ontario), the main concerns are polluted drinking water, urban congestion, air pollution, and loss of wildlife habitat and farmland. The problems here require an integrated approach and involve ecologically sustainable community planning, preserving and enhancing wildlife habitats, reducing carbon dioxide and other global warming gases, eliminating chemical pesticide and herbicide use, and protecting and remediating groundwater polluted by hazardous chemicals and leaking underground storage tanks.

Beyond these general concerns, specific water and land pollution issues are of joint interest to Ontario and Québec. First, there is the undeniable and persistent contamination of the Great Lakes and the St. Lawrence River, and marine pollution in the Gulf of St. Lawrence.[10] That pollution does not respect any political boundaries is indisputable. The Great Lakes drain into the St. Lawrence River, which in turn flows into the Gulf of St. Lawrence. Canada may remediate Lake Ontario only to find the Gulf of St. Lawrence polluted because of Québec's lack of care. Similarly, Québec may attempt to clean up the St. Lawrence only to find that Canada is still polluting Lake Ontario.

An issue of major concern for all sovereign nations, local government and individual citizens is the transboundary movement and storage of hazardous waste. There may be an economic incentive in driving growth partly through the waste trade. Already, Ontario exports hazardous waste to Québec, as does the United States.[11]

These local environmental concerns all have global dimensions, formally recognized by the report issued by the World Commission on Environment and Development. Desertification, acid rain, global warming, ozone depletion, loss of biodiversity, deforestation, and toxic contamination of our air, water and land are life threatening. These crises are interlocking, and concerted action is required. Yet traditional international legal principles of state sovereignty militate against the proper co-management of, and respect for, our global commons and shared ecosystems. "The Earth is one but the world is not."[12]

Global Citizenship: A Challenge for Québec and Canada

Canada enjoys a good reputation as a global citizen. As citizens, all of us are both the trustees and beneficiaries of a large proportion of the world's fresh water and natural resources, including 10 percent of the world's forests and approximately 25 percent of the world's wetlands. All are integral parts of the world's life-support system. Furthermore, as an industrialized nation, Canada is responsible for a disproportionate part of our earth's environmental degradation. We must be conscious of this debt. If we do nothing, the likelihood of worsening environmental degradation is real.

There will be significant pressure on both Ontario and Québec to stabilize their present trade relationship and find other markets for secure economic development. This means more resource exploitation (probably resulting in further deforestation, more nuclear and hydro-electric power projects in Ontario, as well as hydro-electric power projects in Québec), more industry (including transportation and storage of hazardous waste) with the consequent environmental degradation. Furthermore, some have suggested that present lax environmental standards in resource industries are a significant cause of Canadian uncompetitiveness.[13] As we know from the present economic climate, the cost of environmental remediation can be seen as too much to bear. The debate becomes polarized; jobs are pitted against the environment.

Within our own regions, as in all the world, environmental degradation falls disproportionately upon the lower income segments of our population, further increasing the gap between rich and poor.[14] If this trend is to be reversed, we must all assume the responsibility for ensuring that Québec's independence results in proactive environmental protection and not a "race to the bottom." Thus, we have a duty as trustees to negotiate the sovereignty of Québec in an environmentally responsible manner. This must be done with foresight and understanding of the links between environment, economy and trade.

If Québec becomes an independent state, the first question will be whether it is bound by Canada's obligations under international environmental treaties. Canada is a party to many such conventions: the London Dumping Convention, the Geneva Convention on Transboundary Air Pollution, the Montréal Protocol on Substances that Deplete the Ozone Layer, and the Basel Convention on Transboundary Movements of Hazardous Waste.[15] Although there is some debate about Québec's options in international law, the official position of the Québec government is that it would consider itself bound by these international obligations.[16]

But the deficiencies of these United Nations efforts to achieve effective global environmental protection are well documented.[17] After all, the right to a healthy environment has received international recognition, in theory, since 1972.[18] The main problem with exercising and protecting this right is that sovereign nations can choose not to co-operate (and often do). Even if such co-operation is forthcoming, the enforcement and dispute-resolution mechanisms are ineffective and inadequate. The United Nations Conference on Environment and Development (UNCED) in Brazil has shown that despite the seriousness of environmental degradation, concrete action remains elusive and is actively thwarted by some nations.

The fact that international environmental law operates reactively, like the law of torts, is a further problem. The injured party is forced to trade rights against the remedy of damages after the fact, as compensation. This is not only directly contrary to the prevention principle — recognized as essential for adequate environmental protection — it clearly does not work. Environmental degradation so often results in pervasive, irreversible and cumulative damage (over generations) to life on earth. Therefore, prevention is the *only* regulatory option.

> A preventive, or regulatory, regime of this character requires a more sophisticated approach to enforcement and compliance than one based primarily on the award of damages of the third party adjudication of claims to resources. It necessitates an appreciation that environmental problems may require a community response, and that a perspective which accords rights only to "injured states" will be inadequate for the purpose of protecting common interests, common property or the interests of future generations, peoples or non-human species.[19]

The bilateral model of the Canada-U.S. 1909 Boundary Waters Treaty[20] offers important lessons. This treaty created the International Joint Commission (IJC) to manage transboundary water resources for the United States and Canada. This body has met with some success in effecting a decrease of nutrient concentrations in the Great Lakes. However, there has been an increase in contamination from heavy metals, such as arsenic and cadmium.[21]

> Fish with tumours and diseases caused by toxins in water, birds with crossed bills and other deformities caused by eating contaminated fish and reproductive failures in mammals feeding on the top predators of the aquatic food web all suggest that human health may be in jeopardy.[22]

Although it is said that the IJC is highly respected by the United States and Canada, its recommendations on pollution matters are not binding. In fact, the IJC can only address a pollution problem when it is submitted by both parties.[23]

A multilateral model of co-operation worthy of study is the European Community (EC). Since the ratification of the Single European Act in 1987, the protection of the environment has become one of the EC's six most important obligations.[24] The environmental amendments to the Treaty of Rome have fundamentally altered the purpose of the EC, guiding it slowly away from a purely economic union. Contained in this Environmental Charter are the fundamental principles of preventive action: rectifying environmental damage at source, recognizing the "polluter pays" principle, and requiring the integration of environmental protection as a component of the EC's other policies.

Effective environmental protection requires that the real costs of production include externalities — that is, the cost of preventing the pollution of the air, water and land, and their species. The "polluter pays" principle guarantees that goods are properly priced to reflect the true cost of preserving the integrity of the environment. Consumer demand will then adjust accordingly. Similarly, pollution prevention at source ensures that polluters and the communities they affect cannot pass on their environmental costs to other regions: out of sight, out of mind. This in turn will foster proactive environmental protection to prevent degradation as the effects of pollution will mostly remain localized. Finally, the integration of environmental and economic planning requires that the environmental impact of all government policy, law and action be assessed prior to implementation. This guards against the conflicts present in any government among, for example, tax policy, regional development, resource conservation and environmental protection.

The provisions of the EC Environmental Charter are designed to set minimum standards, allowing states to introduce more stringent protective measures.[25] The results of the 1991 Community negotiations in Maastricht, Holland, promise to produce more stringent environmental protection. They propose to give greater priority in the Community to matters of environmental concern.

The EC has developed policy, law and a supranational political structure that enables better environmental decision making than exists within the United Nations. The Community issues legally binding directives to its members for the purpose of environmental protection. Its standards exert a strong upward pressure on the harmonization of environmental laws in member states that do not have a strong environmental tradition, such as Spain, Italy and the United Kingdom. The EC is a model of co-operation and struggle in ecosystem management and preservation.[26]

As part of its environmental evolution, the EC has also recently created the European Environment Agency, a semiautonomous institution at the Community level responsible for environmental policy. The EC has also recently issued a directive on freedom of access to information on the environment, another fundamental cornerstone of adequate environmental protection.

Although the European Parliament is elected, most binding decisions on environmental protection and resource conservation are taken behind closed doors by non-elected officials of the Council of Ministers and the European Commission. This model of supranational environmental decision making, called "executive federalism," has the obvious drawback of denying the right of meaningful public participation, which is essential to ensure environmental justice. However, the EC institutions and law-making power are an improvement upon their United Nations counterparts, because they require the surrender of a fair degree of sovereignty. This pooling of sovereignty for a common end is the reasonable course of action for all independent nations.

> Unless all can be persuaded or forced to lay down their arms simultaneously, nothing can prevent the war of all against all. The crucial problem in the state of nature is thus to make it safe for men to be reasonable, rather than merely "rational," so that they can share peacefully what the environment has to offer.[27]

Trade and the Threat to the Environment

One element that cannot be ignored in the whole question of conservation is the globalization of trade. The goal of eradicating barriers to trade through the General Agreement on Tariffs and Trade (GATT), the Canada-U.S. Free Trade Agreement (FTA), and the impending North American Free Trade Agreement (NAFTA)[28] has meant that progressive environmental protection measures are under attack by those pursuing the myth of perfect competition. This harmonization downwards of environmental standards is seen clearly in our experience with the FTA. Under this agreement, both Canada and the United States have challenged each other's environmental regulations as "unfair trade practices."

The first trade dispute to be adjudicated under the FTA involved a challenge by the United States to regulations under Canada's Fisheries Act established to promote conservation of herring and salmon stocks in Canada's Pacific Coast waters. This conservation program required that all fish caught commercially in Canadian waters be landed in Canada for biological sampling to deter false reporting and for in-season management. After fulfilling this requirement, American fisherman were free to export their catches to the United States.

In the first decision to be released under the FTA, the Canadian regulations were deemed to be "incompatible with the requirements of Article 407 of the FTA." In deciding the case, the FTA dispute panel concluded that a conservation measure having a trade-restricting effect could be sustained only if it could be said to be "primarily aimed at conservation." Considering the Fisheries Act regulation, the panel stated: "An important reason for the specific rule requiring all salmon and herring to be landed in Canada was to make exports more amenable to data collection and this, in fact, is its principal effect." Notwithstanding this finding, however, the panel went on to hold that the country seeking to justify a conservation program that might have trade restricting effects also had to show that such a program "was established for conservation reasons alone and that no other means were available to accomplish those objectives."[29] It is hard to conceive of a regulatory regime that would pass this onerous test — which probably violates the internationally recognized "precautionary principle." This principle mandates that regulators not wait for conclusive scientific proof before acting to further resource conservation goals and to combat environmental harm.

In another revealing case, the U.S. Environmental Protection Agency (EPA) announced in July 1989 that it was introducing regulations to phase out the production, import and use of asbestos over seven years. The ban represented the culmination of more than ten years of struggle involving several congressional investigations, 45,000 pages of analyses, comments and testimony, and thousands of lives. William Reilly, the U.S. EPA administrator, estimated that the ban on this cancer-causing material could save 1,900 lives by the turn of the century. No sooner was the program announced than it was denounced as being insincere and politically motivated. The government of Québec, a province with a substantial interest in asbestos mining, intervened. Assisting the interests of the Québec asbestos mining industry, the government of Canada joined in a legal challenge to the U.S. EPA initiative. In its brief to the U.S. Court of Appeals for the Fifth Circuit, Canada argued that U.S. asbestos regulations under the Toxic Substances Control Act violate U.S. obligations under GATT and FTA. It further argued:

> Moreover under Article 603 of the Canada-U.S. FTA the parties may not adopt standards-related measures that create unnecessary obstacles to trade. Unnecessary obstacles are deemed not to be created if the measures achieve "a legitimate domestic objective". While the protection of human life or health is a legitimate domestic objective, *Canada submits that to the extent that the EPA rule bans the importation of products that do not cause unreasonable risks to life or health, the rule is not necessary to achieve a legitimate domestic objective, and therefore runs counter to U.S. FTA commitments.*[30] [emphasis added]

Not long afterwards, the U.S. Court of Appeal struck down this asbestos ban. The Court ruled that more evidence is needed to support the ban.[31]

In a similar vein, the U.S. non-ferrous metals industry has used a provision of the U.S. legislation implementing the FTA to challenge Canadian pollution-control programs which include loans and investment credits. The Non-Ferrous Metals Producers Committee has assailed as unfair trade practices a variety of federal and provincial programs intended to reduce emissions from, and improve workplace safety in, several Canadian lead, zinc and copper smelters. The U.S. Trade Representative determined that there is "a reasonable likelihood" that this complaint is well founded and investigated these Canadian pollution control programs.[32]

The chilling effect of these rulings and political actions cannot be underestimated. Governments are keenly aware of the potential implications of new regulatory initiatives and have a strong inclination to accommodate corporate interests before the point of confrontation is reached. This phenomenon of "regulatory agency capture" becomes more pronounced in times of recession, when governments must be extra-sensitive to any threat of job loss and industry relocation.[33] Accordingly, proactive measures must be implemented to ensure intergovernmental co-ordination for the pursuit of environmental protection and resource conservation objectives.

This analysis shows that free trade creates legal rights that act as incentives to undermine the goals and principles of effective environmental protection. Accordingly, if a free trade area is negotiated by Canada and a sovereign Québec, there must be a full debate as to how to exempt environmental regulation from challenge as a non-tariff barrier to trade. This is extremely important, as Québec may become a party to the FTA or its successor NAFTA, and will be likely to sign the GATT. These exemptions must be based on internationally accepted environmental-protection and resource-conservation principles.

Any economic negotiations of a free trade area must deal with the eventuality of the "race to the bottom," specifically by excluding environmental protection measures and by mandating that the GATT and FTA law governing what is permissible environmental protection regulation will not be applicable. This requires foresight and the political will to reflect in trade policy the fundamental reality that the world's economy and the earth's ecology are inextricably linked.

Trade agreements must incorporate environmentally sustainable development as a fundamental goal and explicitly recognize the legitimacy of environmental protection measures taken by nations. In addition, several other measures must be taken to protect environmental regulation from free trade, including:

• an environmental assessment of the trade deal in question;

- the inclusion of environmental protection and resource conservation measures in trade agreements;
- the enhancement of environmental standards and effective enforcement mechanisms; and
- meaningful public participation.[34]

Canada and Québec: Intergovernmental Co-ordination

To ensure successful negotiation of the appropriate amount of intergovernmental environmental protection between Canada and a sovereign Québec, there must first be an environmental audit of each government's responsibilities and undertakings. Québec and Canada have many institutional and financial incentives to negotiate and co-ordinate effective environmental protection for their common resources.

At present, there is a great deal of co-ordination and cost-sharing of environmental and resource-conservation policies between the federal and Québec governments. Reviewing the activities of the federal Ministry of the Environment alone is instructive. There are at least five federal-provincial agreements in operation specifically with Québec involving the administration of Environment Canada. This excludes Environment Canada's general projects and their administration for all provinces, as well as other environmental and resource-conservation initiatives administered by other federal departments, such as Fisheries and Oceans, and Forestry. Québec also derives economic and environmental benefits from the federal government's Pesticide Directorate and the Canadian Dairy Commission. Some of these programs will have to be maintained jointly.[35]

Significant among these joint federal-provincial programs are the Canada-Québec agreements respecting the cleanup of the St. Lawrence river and technological assistance to the Québec wastewater treatment program. These alone commit the federal government to spending at least $118.5 million over the next five years.[36]

Indeed, the multitude of federal, provincial and municipal government departments that exercise jurisdiction over resource-conservation and environmental matters is staggering. Federally, there are at least the following departments and other governmental bodies with environmental responsibilities: Agriculture, the Atomic Energy Commission, the Canadian Dairy Commission, Energy, Mines and Resources, Fisheries and Oceans, Forestry, and Health. Their provincial counterparts in Ontario are the following: Agriculture and Food, Energy, Environment, Health, Housing, Industry, Trade and Technology, Labour, Municipal Affairs, Natural Resources, Northern Development and Mines, and Tourism and Recreation. In addition, municipal governments have responsibility for sewage and water treatment, sewers, park maintenance, housing developments, and so on. Clearly, the essential ingredient for success in this war against ourselves is effective co-ordination and policy regulation, combined with the political will to make the tough decisions and stick by them.

Given our present reality, what would be the appropriate model for ensuring effective environmental protection and resource management between Canada and Québec? Undoubtedly, we would be wise to negotiate the following as a minimum:

- an Environmental Charter to articulate shared fundamental environmental principles;
- a supranational environmental agency for information gathering, monitoring and law making;
- dispute-resolution mechanisms for conciliation, arbitration, or judicial settlement;[37] and
- ensuring the "greening" of any trade agreements, as discussed above.

A proposal for an Environmental Charter embodying the necessary general environmental principles, rights and responsibilities has been drafted by the World Commission on Environment and Development. It encompasses the fundamental environmental principles:

- freedom of information
- mandatory reporting
- the fundamental human right to a healthy environment
- intergenerational equity (environmental equity for successive generations)
- conservation and sustainable use of natural resources

- environmental standards and monitoring
- adoption of the precautionary principle
- prior environmental assessments
- prevention and abatement of transboundary environmental harm
- prior consultation
- procedure for emergency situations
- aboriginal peoples' involvement
- adoption of the "polluter pays" principle

We would be wise to share some sovereignty in the furtherance of concerted action on remedying and preventing environmental degradation.[38] The proposed environmental agency and any decision-making bodies must allow effective public participation and must especially give effective voice to aboriginal communities, whether they reside within Canada or Québec. These suggestions are equally applicable in regulating the environment in present-day Canada.

Thus, our fragile environment must be factored in among the costs of the breakup of Canada. Even if we only consider the environmental costs of the period of transition, they will be high. However, if sovereignty must be negotiated with Québec, we then must seize the opportunity to plan for an integrated intergovernmental approach to environmental protection and resource conservation. Without such proactive measures, we will doom ourselves to failure in the greatest task the human race has ever faced, saving the planet.

Defence North of the 49th Parallel: What Happens to the Military?

Douglas Bland

In some respects the strategic questions of war and peace are easy for Canada and Québec to settle, if only because of both states' relative powerlessness on the world stage. But it is important to understand that defence relationships have many facets besides those relating to the "high politics" of strategy. The independence of Québec would require that officials negotiate the division of the defence infrastructure and the lives and welfare of soldiers and civilian employees. This would include not only the distribution of assets, which are enormous, but also such personal items as pensions and benefits for members of the Canadian Forces.

What are Canada's and Québec's defence problems today and into the foreseeable future? Despite the radically transformed global security environment, Canada's defence problem continues to reflect its basic geopolitical position on the continent. The country's isolation from the rest of the world, its closeness to the United States, and its great size make it virtually unassailable. Such permanent factors are largely unresponsive to defence planning. Canada can therefore live in relative safety without expending many resources on its national defence.

Strategic Imperatives and Choices for Canada

In practice, these factors have given Canada two strategic imperatives and a number of strategic choices. We are compelled by the dictates of national sovereignty to defend Canada against direct aggression and to maintain law and order within the country.

First, under the National Defence Act, the federal government is obliged to provide "aid of the civil power" to the provinces.[1] The complete disbandment of the Canadian Forces could not, therefore, take place without the agreement of the provinces. National defence arguments aside, it is difficult to believe that the provinces would freely surrender this federal resource or the regional economic advantages that flow to them from defence expenditures. The compelling nature of these highly political considerations means that the question is not whether or not Canada needs an armed force, but rather what capabilities such a force will have in the future.

Second, we are required to reassure the United States that it will not be subject to attack from Canadian territory. If Canada failed to undertake this second task, the Americans would do it themselves, with or without our knowledge or permission. Thus, the tasks are complementary. By guarding Canada, Canadians defend themselves against American help.

As well, Canada has a number of other defence options. Since 1949, it has used its defence resources to support and maintain an international order favourable to its values and beliefs. This has been done in co-operation with like-minded nations in alliances and in the United Nations. All of these commitments are now open to reconsideration.

If the decision is to concentrate on home defence, the resources required will consist of quite limited naval and air units. If, on the other hand, the option is to maintain some capability to act outside North America and participate in alliances or under United Nations auspices, Canada will have to increase its commitment to defence spending correspondingly.

Québec's Defence Capacity

For Québec the considerations will be similar, but with some interesting differences. Québec will need armed forces to survey its territory and to maintain law and order. It will also have to assure the United States that Québec can protect America from attacks launched from or through its spaces. Although Québec's usable sea areas and coastlines are relatively small (mainly because they are ice-bound most of the year), it still has important economic and social responsibilities in these waters.

Québec will appear to most of the world as a relatively prosperous and enlightened country with obvious international responsibilities. Certainly Québec would wish to appear to the members of the United Nations as an independent and active member of the assembly. It would, therefore, find it hard to resist the call to provide foreign aid and assistance to peacekeeping missions. If it were to ignore these international collective security duties, Québec would be labelled a free rider, especially when compared with Canada, which plays a leading role in the United Nations. Québec, therefore, will need to establish its own armed force. The question, as with Canada, is not of need, but of capabilities.

For most people, even very experienced ones, the expression "military capabilities" means hardware. But if they understood warfare's dual character, its environmental and natural elements, they would see that establishing a military capability requires more than merely buying tools.

There are numerous ways to structure and arm military forces. Given the situation and the defence problem outlined above, both states will probably decide to establish a force with land, air, and sea capabilities, the Canadian forces being somewhat larger than those of Québec. The air and naval forces would be equipped to conduct surveillance and limited intervention operations in and around Canada and Québec. The land force would be organized and armed as a force of last resort to maintain civil order and to be dispatched on small-scale expeditionary missions in support of the UN or an allied force. In any case, the actual force structure and types of equipment would be determined, much as in the past, not by the so-called strategic assessment, but by such pedestrian considerations as regional-industrial policies, special pledging and patronage. In both states the military forces will be professional ones, much as the Canadian Forces are today.

Neighbouring states can live with undefended borders and feel no threat at all. Witness the Canada–United States relationship. The early period of Québec independence is the most dangerous time for establishing relations between new neighbouring states. During this time the absence of norms or mutual lack of faith may turn seemingly inconsequential incidents into full-blown violence. It would seem prudent, therefore, for Canada and Québec to begin immediately to build mechanisms and institutions allowing them to develop a defence regime and to respond early to international frictions. The shape of such institutions is often determined by their agendas. It might therefore be useful to survey these areas in an effort to ensure that the appropriate mechanisms are in place.

An Agenda for Co-operation

There will certainly be two phases in defence negotiations between Canada and Québec. The first will be concerned with establishing a negotiating position, and the second with developing and utilizing the defence regime. Obviously, the two phases will overlap, but the second will evolve into a continuous process.

During the first phase, negotiators will face several sensitive topics. Borders will have to be clarified and agreed on. One can anticipate prolonged discussions over territorial claims in Labrador and on the east coast, in the north, especially where borders intersect with the unsettled claims of native peoples, and at sea, particularly in the resource-rich waters of the Gulf of St. Lawrence. Besides identifying the borders, negotiators will also have to agree concurrently on such technical issues as where border crossings will be placed, how borders will be patrolled, and how cross-border violators will be handled.

A related negotiation will be required after the border areas are settled to seek agreement on Canadian rights of passage through Québec's territory. Some international agreements already exist for these purposes and could be used with little modification. However, the Canadian defence negotiators will be interested in gaining agreement that armed Canadian ships and aircraft will be allowed unhindered passage east and west. Negotiators might agree on certain corridors and warning times for such movements. But, as Canada knows from its relationship with the United States, this can be a continuously contentious issue. Peacetime arrangements are not difficult to manage. However, Canada would also seek unhindered passage in times of tension or war because Canadians would not accept the notion that the country might be placed in danger by a neutral, indecisive Québec. From Québec's point of view some of these demands will be difficult to accommodate because they appear to infringe on its sovereign rights.

Canada and Québec might wish to conclude an agreement to manage their respective military forces. This would detail the capabilities, size and location of each force, with the aim of providing assurances to each side. Such an agreement might also include provisions for inspections and warnings of exercises and force deployments.

Clearly, the most difficult first-phase negotiation will concern the division of the spoils. When the Canadian Forces are split, who will get what parts of the infrastructure, equipment, and personnel? In crude figures, about 20 percent of Canada's approximately $12 billion annual defence expenditure is spent in Québec. This $2.4 billion sum includes infrastructure maintenance, defence contracting, and personnel salaries, both military and civilian. It is to be expected that Canada would remove all transportable equipment, including vehicles, ships, aircraft and machinery. The inventory of immovable infrastructure, including major bases at Bagotville, Valcartier, and Montréal, would have to change hands under some type of arrangement or payment.[3]

Approximately 11,000 military personnel are now stationed in Québec. All have sworn obligations to Canada, are subject to the National Defence Act, and would have to be given some type of release from their obligations if they were to select to remain in Québec. In the Canadian Forces, numbering 87,000 men and women, approximately 24 percent is "francophone," and most of these people also declare Québec as their normal place of residency. It should be anticipated that a large proportion, say 90 percent, will decide to return to Québec rather than renounce Québec citizenship to remain in the Canadian Forces. Canada, if it wished, could easily recruit replacements, but it is not clear that Québec is prepared to finance an annual expenditure of approximately $650,000 (assuming Canadian Forces rates of pay) for all this personnel.

Civilian employees of the Department of National Defence, like other federal employees, could expect to be retired on the day of Québec's independence. While some cross-border working could be expected, there would be no pay for defence workers in Québec. This work-force is approximately 7,000 personnel with an annual aggregate salary of $250,000.

Canada would also repatriate most of its Québec-based defence industries. Even where it would be logical and cost-effective to leave contracts in Québec, one must anticipate, at least over the short run, a loud demand from Canadians that no federal funds be spent in Québec. Their politicians would surely respond to such pressures. If Québec and Canada did not enter into some kind of defence-sharing agreement, this would have a devastating effect on Québec's aircraft, shipbuilding and telecommunications industries.

Negotiations over the spoils will be difficult and emotional. It seems clear that, despite the possibility of mutual advantages through defence co-operation, the Canadian people will want the economic benefits of defence spending removed from Québec and transferred to some region in Canada as rapidly as possible. People will be hurt and families will be split by the decisions that will be forced on them. Members of the Canadian Forces, all of whom have served Canada loyally and well, will be forced to choose between Canada and Québec in a way that is without equal for any other group in Canadian society. One can only hope that those who go and those who stay will be treated fairly and with compassion by the citizens they serve and have served in both countries.

The United States will have to join some stage of the negotiations. American officers and officials, while not particularly concerned about the state of the Canadian federation, will be concerned about the state of defence plans and preparations in the region. They will attempt to determine whether or not they will have to plan to supplement Canadian and Québécois defence efforts with their own. It is likely that they would wish to join any discussion that touched on extant "CANUS" undertakings, such as the NORAD agreement. They would be particularly interested in Québec's plans and capability to replace Canadian assets covering Québec's air space. These discussions might begin at a bi-lateral level, but they would be likely to evolve into tri-lateral meetings, probably at the Americans' insistence.

Discussion of defence matters between liberal democratic states usually takes place within a framework initiated and controlled by elected political figures. These leaders provide the guidance and authority for the technical deliberations of officials. Defence negotiations between Québec and Canada probably will be preceded by a meeting of heads of state that presumably will become periodic and routine. Occasionally, one would expect the president of the United States to join such meetings.

Assuming that Québec organized its forces under a unified system of command, their chief of defence staff would represent the military authority for their country's armed forces and would provide the final military advice to the government.

Because chiefs of defence staffs are responsible for the day-to-day operations and co-ordination of national defence efforts, they provide the centre of opinion and knowledge about the capabilities and military interests of their nation. The technical arrangements for any defence regime negotiated by Canada and Québec must begin with meetings of the chiefs of staff of the two countries. These officers will direct the efforts of their staffs and ratify the recommendations of negotiators before they are passed to governments for approval. As with the meetings of heads of state, it is anticipated that periodic meetings of chiefs of staff would become routine.

The NATO model for military co-operation is sound and well accepted by most senior officers of the alliance.[4] It may well serve as an example for Canada and Québec. It would be especially helpful if a NATO-style permanent military committee could be established to manage the day-to-day military affairs of the two countries. The advantage of the NATO command system is that it allows for the formation of *ad hoc* "working groups" to address any problem without the need to convene senior officials or politicians before a staff consensus has been achieved. American officers from the joint chiefs of staff might be persuaded to take part in such meetings. But the United States has always been very reluctant to share with foreigners their exclusive right to manage and plan their continental defence schemes. Too close an association with a CAN-Q defence arrangement would surely raise questions in the U.S. Congress.

Since August 17, 1940, Canada and the United States have managed their defence arrangements, at least formally, through the Permanent Joint Board on Defence (PJBD).[5] This political-military committee meets periodically to discuss and to advise governments on defence arrangements. Most serious work is done elsewhere. But the PJBD and its subordinate Military Coordination Committee do provide a mechanism to incorporate Québec into North American defence planning without upsetting long-standing CANUS arrangements. None of these institutions or arrangements would interfere with the right of either Canada or Québec to make other bilateral arrangements with the United States.

This framework of periodic meetings of heads of state and chiefs of staff, and the permanent assembly of a small group of officials and officers, would facilitate the second continuous period of negotiation. Its main aim would be to head off conflict caused by misunderstanding and ignorance. Its success, however, would be entirely dependent on the successful conclusion of the main elements of a separation agreement.

Challenges and Prospects

It may appear to some that this paper is too pessimistic in tone and outlook. Some would argue that reasonable people can surely make relatively simple, workable arrangements to address what appears to be a simple defence problem. Furthermore, the advantages of co-operation between the two forces and with the American forces seem so obvious that disagreements are apt to be minor and unimportant.

Certainly, the NATO experience is instructive. There is much to be gained from the integration of command and training organizations. Indeed, Canada and Québec may some day be able to integrate their armed forces in a manner that will benefit both and profit their people. The fact remains, however, that if reasonableness and efficiency had been the commanding concepts in relations between these two states, they would have remained united and these defence negotiations would not be required at all. It is wishful thinking in its most dangerous manifestation to believe that people who cannot act reasonably in a rich and fruitful union will suddenly begin to act with reason once they are separated. If this sense of foreboding seems misplaced, ask an Irishman or a Yugoslav to recount the bloody histories of his country.

In summary, military forces will be created by both states, and their size will be determined by internal political and budgetary factors. The conditions that have made Canada a fireproof house extend as well to Québec, except where internal frictions and spontaneous combustion might ignite fires to damage, if not consume, both houses. We must build, through negotiations and institutions, a regime that will provide for the expectation of the peaceful resolution of the causes of conflict. We must anticipate a difficult transition and then a gradual resumption of stable relationships. The instrument to achieve this goal, in the military sphere, is a heads-of-state committee supported by a chiefs-of-defence committee, a permanent international staff, and a lot of good will.

VI
Reconstructing English Canada

Sovereignty and the New Constitutionalism

Michael Mandel

This paper explores the idea of "sovereignty," not only in the relations between Canada and Québec, but in the modern state in general. Since the idea of sovereignty, both in the national and international context, is increasingly anachronistic, I want to examine some of the mechanisms that have made it so. Specifically, I want to look at the constitutionalism of charters of rights (including "social" charters). It is my thesis that this kind of constitutionalism has aided, and indeed been the form of, a rapidly diminishing sovereignty both in Québec and in the rest of Canada — though especially in Québec. Since the debate about Québec has taken the form of a debate about constitutional arrangements, it seems like a good time to try to understand the relationship between constitutionalism and sovereignty.

It is not my purpose to belittle anyone's aspirations to sovereignty, independence or autonomy. Such aspirations are as natural and legitimate as they are difficult to realize. Nor do I want to add to the chorus of discouragement that English Canadians are singing to Québécois as they discuss their future. My own view is that we should butt out of what is an essentially internal debate.

This paper has benefited so much from discussions and collaborations with my colleague Harry Glasbeek that I can no longer tell where his thoughts leave off and mine begin.

Sovereignty and Constitutionalism

Until the twentieth century, sovereignty was, both theoretically and practically, an attribute of property. The feudal lord's authority and the bourgeois's right to be represented in Parliament both rested upon the ownership of property. This all changed between the end of the last century and the end of the Second World War, at least in the developed world, when the state became the property of everyone, not only legally but practically, and when it started to regulate the economy under pressure from the newly enfranchised working class. As the suffrage spread, the meaning of sovereignty started to change. Parliamentary sovereignty came to be discredited in theory and negated in law at the very moment parliaments started to represent people and not just property. The main mechanism was constitutional law: formal limits on legislative sovereignty — unthinkable in the prior period — administered by the legal profession. After the Second World War, this mechanism spread rapidly throughout the capitalist world from its origins in the United States, though it only triumphed in Canada with the Charter of Rights and Freedoms in 1982.

The Canadian Charter of Rights and Freedoms

The dominant intellectual and political view of this development was that it was a straightforward advancement for human rights, because "entrenching" them in a constitution would make it more difficult, if not impossible, for them to be violated. In my view, the development could not be regarded as the advance it was supposed to be.[1] I have called it the "legalization of politics," to emphasize the ascendancy it meant for the legal profession and the legal technique. Though the legal technique is celebrated for its inevitability and impartiality, it is well known to insiders as a veneer for a politics no more immune from the influence of power than ordinary political reasoning. That is because law is not a "thing," objectively standing out there and judging us, but a *form of argument*, a form of political argument. I like to think of law the way Clausewitz thought of war, as "politics by other means." But, as with war, the form politics takes is never irrelevant; it reflects and determines the substance.

What is the substance of legal politics? In my view, it is a *conservative* politics, ideologically and practically, by which I mean one that tends to preserve and even to increase inequality of social power. Legal politics is the antithesis of democratic politics in its tendency to preserve and even to increase the sway of unequal market power (one dollar, one vote) at the expense of democratic power (one person, one vote). I am using *democracy* here not merely in its majoritarian sense, but in its more fundamental class sense, its original Greek sense, of rule by the many *without property*. The fundamental problem of charters of rights is not that the unelected, undemocratic courts are exalted over the elected, democratic legislatures. In the first place, it is clear that the popular appeal of charters of rights derives from the deserved disrepute of legislatures as democratic representatives. We do not feel represented by our legislatures, so we leap at charters on the mistaken assumption that they give us more control over government. In the second place, governments and courts often work in tandem to get around people, by letting the courts deal with questions that the politicians believe to be too hot to handle. Legal politics is really a way of *avoiding* more democracy by serving up a fake substitute.

Origins are crucial to an understanding of the conservative nature of charters of rights and their role in limiting "sovereignty." In Canada, there are two important connections: the Québec connection and the American connection. It is obvious from many clues that the political objective of the main sponsors of the Charter, from the late 1960s through to entrenchment in 1982, was to use it to defeat the popular and class-based Québec independence movement. The Charter was intended, under the guise of the protection of human rights, to reduce the constitutional jurisdiction of the province of Québec when the election of a popular nationalist government threatened the interests of the socially powerful English minority and through them their allies in English Canada. Of course, Charter politics were not *invented* for Québec, just applied to it. Judicial review has older roots. As mentioned earlier, it appears in history with the spread of the suffrage and the threat this poses to private power. That is why it appeared first in the United States in the 1780s and that is why it spread throughout the capitalist world after the Second World War, usually via the vehicle of American economic, military and cultural hegemony.[2]

The general tendency of the Charter is to remove state discrimination and to equalize people before the law, but at the same time to leave the inequality of private power unscathed, in fact enhanced. It is basically a form of privatization, of the sort that characterized the conventional wisdom and practice of business economics in the 1980s. Legally speaking, the Charter only applies to the state, and its tendency is therefore to remove it from the scene, leaving not "freedom" but the free — that is, unrestrained — exercise of market power. Some of the best examples in the first decade of the Charter come from Québec itself, where the relatively powerful — in economic terms — English minority was given a measure of protection by the Charter against the relatively weak French majority: English was well entrenched in the marketplace, so "freedom," in Charter terms, meant no interference with English economic power (one dollar, one vote). The French had to work through the public sphere of one person, one vote. The Charter, in striking down interferences with "freedom of choice" in education and the language of business signs, handed victory to those with market power. In the end, it seems that what really defeated the English was the rise of French market power, against which charters of rights are helpless. On the other hand, the Charter probably had something to do with the noticeable reduction in what was once the strong and clear class character of the Québec nationalist/independentist movement.[3]

Of course, any realistic assessment of the role of legal politics in the reproduction of social power must confront the potential counter-examples, the most important of which are in the realms of criminal procedure and women's rights. It is my thesis, however, that these are not counter-examples at all, but rather subtle *examples* of the conservative nature of the Charter. In criminal procedure, we find that the fair-trial provisions actually go hand in hand with and legitimate a repression rate that is, in the era of the Charter, vastly greater than at any period in Canada's history.[4] As for women, not only has the effect of the Charter been classically double-edged, striking down both the anti-women abortion law and the pro-women "rape-shield" law,[5] but it has also exhibited its general deregulatory character, removing the often oppressive presence of the state only to leave the always oppressive presence of market power. The pure judicial decriminalization of abortion has meant only its privatization with access heavily dependent on social class; only the election of pro-choice governments has made any real difference in democratic access.

The New Constitutional Politics

The term *legalization of politics* emphasizes the role of the legal profession in the operationalization of the empty phrases in the constitution. Others use the term *judicialization of politics* to emphasize the centrality of courts and judges. But neither formulation adequately captures the full range of constitutional politics, especially the current phase of symbolic constitutionalism almost completely detached from litigation.

This aspect of constitutionalism played a rather subordinate role in the events of 1982. Most of the Charter of Rights was intended to be litigated — especially those parts having to do with Québec — but there were also added some deliberately unenforceable provisions, including those which "committed" the federal and provincial governments to "promoting equal opportunities for the well-being of Canadians; furthering economic development to reduce disparities in opportunities; and providing essential public services of reasonable quality to all Canadians" (Part III, section 36).

The symbolic side of things was slightly more important in the Meech Lake Accord, where the star attraction, the "distinct society" clause, had little to do with litigation and more with legitimating a set of fairly run-of-the-mill political motivations: the desire of the federal Tories to establish their federal political hegemony in Québec; the desire of the Québec Liberals to put an end to the pressure from the PQ by putting a Québec government's signature on the constitution; the desire of business in general to ensure that pro-business and pro–free trade governments (in Ottawa and Québec) remained in power and overcame the current obstacles to political and economic stability. These mundane objectives were dressed up in constitutional clothes, mainly to cover the sores opened by the constitutional power play of 1982, but also partly to depoliticize and dignify them. In this case, once again, the constitutional device seems to have had little to do with litigation. Despite all of the fury, the "distinct society" clause was so ambiguously worded that it did not change any of the powers of any level of government.

There has been much romanticism about Meech Lake's substantive and procedural constitutional defects. If it failed in part because of these defects, it also failed, in my view, because of real political opposition to the Tory agenda. Apart from pure party loyalty, there was opposition on the right from the anti-bilingualists in English Canada as well as those favouring the regionalization of political power through such devices as Senate reform. There was opposition on the left from the anti–free trade coalition of labour and women's groups and from the native peoples. All of these groups saw the Meech Lake Accord as an expression of a concrete agenda opposed to their own, and they used the constitutional venue to express their opposition. In other words, they hoisted the Tories by their own constitutional petard. As Foucault says, "power is exercised rather than possessed,"[6] by which I take him to mean that power has its structural limits. In other words, a constitutional strategy has constitutional drawbacks.

But it is also true that the form of opposition fetters its content. The opposition to the real political-economic program of Meech Lake had to be submerged in abstract constitutional objections. These were easy enough for the Tories to remedy and they did so handsomely in their 1991 constitutional package of proposals, while not abandoning for a minute the concrete business agenda underlying the constitutional program.[7]

The 1991 federal proposals would deliver the one-two punch of modern business: the decentralization of political power and the depoliticization of the economy. Decentralizing proposals include transfers of constitutional jurisdiction from the federal to provincial level in a vast range of areas. Then there is the commitment to making the Senate more powerful and to making it more representative of the regions than of the Canadian population as a whole. Fragmenting the public power increases the ability of private power to dictate its terms of investment. Devolving powers to the provinces reduces the public power to the strength of its weakest link. To the proposals which indirectly increase the power of business are added others which do the same thing more directly. One is the proposal for strengthening the Canadian economic union by entrenching the European Community's "four freedoms": "persons, goods, services and capital may move freely without barriers or restrictions based on provincial or territorial boundaries." This proposal directly threatens not only local industries with provincial monopolies but also those dependent on government supply. It indirectly threatens all provincial social programs in the same way the free trade and EC agreements do, by the potential that they will be held by the courts to be barriers to trade, and by the potential for "social dumping" — that is, lowering social standards in order to compete in a global economy. By allowing business to range freely across borders, measures like these immeasurably increase the concentration and centralization of capital, all in the face of a weakening public power.[8]

This is clearly a much more ambitious package than Meech. Its business agenda is not just in the background, but right up front and constitutionalized. Many of the same groups that helped to sink Meech are lining up against these proposals. But what really distinguishes this initiative is the constitutional packaging, which is clearly designed to undercut the kind of constitutional opposition that was so decisive with Meech.

The new package effectively responds to the major official, constitutional sin of Meech: that it was *exclusive*, both procedurally and substantively, a *fait accompli* with no real participation below the élite level and with an end product that recognized only the two major linguistic groups in the constitution and left everybody else out. The new package is desperately consultative and desperately inclusive. We are drowning in consultation: committees, televised conferences, workbooks, questionnaires, and so on. As for representation and inclusion in the constitution, besides some essentially unenforceable promises for native peoples,[9] this mainly takes the form of a proposal for a statement in the constitution recognizing the importance, distinctiveness and contributions of various groups, and certain aspirations, characteristics and values which Canadians are supposed to hold in common. The following are only a few of the characteristics and values to be entrenched in the "Canada clause":

- a federation whose identity encompasses the characteristics of each province, territory and community;
- the equality of women and men;
- a commitment to fairness, openness and full participation in Canada's citizenship by all people without regard to race, colour, creed, physical or mental disability, or cultural background;
- a commitment to the well-being of all Canadians.

The clause can afford to be so generous because it is not intended to be enforceable like the other constitutional proposals, but merely "symbolic." This is the new species of constitutional politics that cannot really be termed "legal." Of course, we have no lack of such statements in our poetry, our bibles, our novels, our histories, our philosophies and our polemics, so what is the point of an "official" statement of who we are and what we want?

In trying to answer this, it is important not to neglect the precise context: the statement is situated in a very concrete constitution, with new constitutional proposals, designed to limit public power in favour of private power. We must ask the point of a statement *in this context*. Then there is the content: Does the statement really "reflect" us? On the contrary, it lies in virtually every paragraph. Women and men are only equal before the law; in social power, in property, in job status, in victimization through inter-sex violence, we are anything but equal. There is no commitment to full participation in social life, at least on the part of those responsible for this document; there is a commitment to "business confidence" and a consequent tolerance of high levels of unemployment and social inequality according to the very features denied by the paragraph: race, colour, creed, physical and mental disability, and cultural background. There is no commitment to the well-being of all Canadians. Under the philosophy and practice of the sponsors of this document we have seen the most violent, repressive and probably the most unequal era since Confederation.[10] And so on down the line. This constitutional statement is a kind of "official story" which attempts to deny the concrete reality of the deterioration of social life in Canada.

Of course, these ideals and commitments burn in the hearts of many Canadians, but not the ones responsible for this document, who, in the program they advance in the rest of the document and in their everyday policies, are doing everything to *defeat* these ideals. And, furthermore, though the word "entrenched" makes it seem as if these ideals and aspirations will be really protected, it is actually their antitheses in the rest of the document that get concrete protection. Now, what other role could noble and egalitarian symbols play when combined with an ignoble and inegalitarian concrete reality, but the *legitimation* of that reality?

Enter the Social Charter

Up to this point we are on very familiar constitutional territory. Whether you call it the "legalization of politics" or not, we still have an attempted legitimation both of the retreat of the public sector in favour of private power and of the decline in social conditions that inevitably accompanies such a retreat.

However, there is yet a new element in the constitutional equation: the "social charter," introduced into the constitutional debate by the NDP government of Ontario in September of 1991. The idea is to have constitutional guarantees for the very public-sector social welfare programs that are threatened by the competitive pressures of continentalization and globalization of the economy. The social charter is in fact the direct opposite of the old-style deregulatory charters of rights and the business agenda of the federal constitutional proposals. It is offered as the antidote to the current trend towards domination of social life by the market, as "a strategy for ensuring that growing interprovincial and international economic competitive pressures do not become an excuse for weakening or abandoning our social contract."[11]

The proposal for a social charter has proved extremely popular among left-wing theorists and activists. Not long after the release of the Ontario proposal, constitutional entrenchment was being advocated by anti-poverty groups as a serious strategy for combating the alarming rates of child poverty in Canada.[12] Not much later, economist James Laxer was chastising the Canadian left for simply opposing global and North American trade liberalization. According to Laxer, we could turn the free trade agreement to our advantage by ensuring that it contained a social charter: "for once, let's stop being on the defensive and challenge [the Americans] to add a social contract to our economic union."[13]

There are, in fact, many precedents for a social charter. The one with the most direct relevance, indeed the one explicitly invoked by Ontario advocates Bob Rae and James Laxer, is the European social charter, which European trade unions tried to tack onto the 1992 program to end all internal barriers to trade in the European Economic Community.

The European experience is very instructive, not for its success but for its abject failure. The main sponsors of the European Social Charter were the unions from the better-off countries who sought to protect themselves from the social dumping that free trade with less-developed countries would entail. A draft was adopted by the European Trade Union Confederation in 1988 which included the rights to organize, to bargain collectively (with an emphasis on the legal right to Europe-wide bargaining) and to strike, to healthy and safe working conditions, and to vocational and continuing education, among others. The key demand was that these rights be legally enforceable, just like those of business. But European business would only support the Charter on the condition that it would not be legally binding and would do no more than state aspirations. The plan that ultimately received the endorsement of the European Commission followed the recommendation of business, not that of labour, and proposed only a "solemn declaration" and an "action program," not enforceable rights. Even this was not acceptable to some of the European governments, and the content was further weakened to gain more acceptance. In the end Britain still refused to sign, leaving a weak, quasi-official *and* unenforceable instrument. The result was branded by the unions as "not worth the paper on which it was printed."[14]

Originally, the Ontario proposals for a social charter included the option of court enforceability, but this was downplayed as somehow inconsistent with positive social rights, as opposed to the negative deregulatory rights against the government which are typical of court-enforced charters.[15] It is worth noting that there is no technical reason why positive social rights in a constitution cannot be judicially enforceable. An example is section 23 of the 1982 Charter, which in great detail imposes obligations on governments to provide minority-language education facilities at public expense — enforceable and enforced against the Québec government's Bill 101. Backing by powerful interests can work wonders for constitutional law; in other words, the only real obstacles to enforceable positive constitutional rights are political and not technical.

But the Ontario proposal preferred to avoid enforceability for the purely symbolic function that the federal government proposals assigned to the "Canada clause." As the Ontario government now sees it, the social charter would consist of the following additional paragraphs to the current unenforceable "commitments" in section 36 of the Charter of 1982:

(d) Providing throughout Canada a health care program that is comprehensive, universal, portable, publicly administered and accessible.

(e) Providing social services and welfare based on need, so as to insure that all Canadians have access to a minimum level of housing, food and other basic necessities.

(f) Providing high quality public primary and secondary education to all persons resident in Canada.

(g) Protecting, preserving and improving the quality of the environment within a sustainable economy.

(h) Generally promoting the quality and standard of life of Canadians.

The proposal of the federal NDP is somewhat stronger in content and would include, for example, a commitment to "full employment and fair working conditions."[16] In the Ontario plan these commitments are to be monitored by an independent body, either from a reformed Senate or, as preferred by Ontario, by an independent commission appointed jointly by Canada and the provinces, which would conduct hearings, do research and report annually on governments' progress in meeting social charter commitments, but which would have no powers of enforcement.[17]

Some advocates of a social charter are still arguing for judicial enforceability, but it seems that the main sponsors have decided to skip this stage altogether. The conventional objection is that an enforceable social charter would involve the courts too deeply in social policy-making questions.[18]

In fact, the judges are already up to their elbows in social-policy making with the negative rights of the Charter of Rights and Freedoms of 1982 — and I repeat that there are no technical and only political obstacles to making positive rights just as enforceable as the negative ones. A better reason for not bothering about enforceability is that, given their record with the 1982 Charter, the courts cannot be expected to give progressive spins to any of the principles that have any chance of making it into the constitution.

This is legalized politics all over again, and judges and lawyers cannot seriously be expected to challenge the status quo of social power. They will interpret any document according to the dominant wisdom of the day. The provision for "fair working conditions" in the federal NDP proposal may sound radical to some ears, and without too much ingenuity it could be given a radical interpretation. But, like the famous "fair distribution of the proceeds of labour" in Marx's *Critique of the Gotha Programme*, it can always be read to mean the going rate, however meagre that is in a declining economy. This is exactly the way section 36 of the Italian Constitution (*retribuzione proporzionata*) has been interpreted by a constitutional court that has always had Communists represented on it. The same would hold for any commitment to "full employment." Doubtless, labour and the political left would argue that this requires a robust and active public sector, but, equally doubtless, business and the political right would answer that the road to prosperity, decent living standards and the highest possible level of employment is through a "lean and mean" and "competitive" economy, with the tiniest possible public sector. And whom would the courts agree with? If experience with the 1982 Charter is any indication, the courts would either go along with business or say that it is not their place to second-guess government economic strategy.[19] In addition, if the European case is any indication, it would be no easy trick getting business to accept even the slight risk posed to profit making by an enforceable social charter: in other words, a long, hard fight for something of virtually no value.

On the other hand, it does not take much reflection to see that purely symbolic principles are worth even less (if that is possible) than the enforceable kind. If "a fair day's wage" and a commitment to "full employment" mean opposite things to people with opposite political points of view, the point of view that ultimately gets put into practice will depend on political power, not clever argumentation about whose interpretation of the principle is more faithful. And if the social charter is monitored by "independent overseers?" It all depends on who appoints these overseers, the same way the Charter of Rights depends on the judges. If labour thinks it is going to appoint them, business has other ideas. In other words, the addition of monitors and overseers merely takes us back into the realm of legal politics: endless, inconclusive arguments about the meaning of meaningless phrases, by political partisans who try (unconvincingly) to hide the partisan nature of their arguments, before supposedly impartial decision makers who are biased in favour of the status quo but do their best to hide that, too.

The appeal of charters, whether social or anti-social, is their promise to transcend politics, to go beyond politics with all its mess about power. Call something a fundamental value and you seem to have removed it from the political battleground to the temple. Charters respond to our dream of justice unsullied by power. Social charters seduce us with the promise of freedom from all those immensely powerful forces that seem bent on destroying the standards of living we have fought so hard to achieve or at least hope one day to achieve. That is why charters are so often invoked by groups without political power, as a defence against power.

In fact, the most depressing thing about the call for a social charter in the Ontario case is that it comes *not* from an opposition party trying to substitute principle for lack of political clout, but from a majority government with the full legal power to intervene in the marketplace in defence of our so-called commitments to social justice. As the Ontario social charter document admits: "Jurisdiction over most of Canada's social policy domains is in provincial hands."[20] What does this mean? It means nothing less than that everything the Rae government calls for in the social charter is something that it has the full constitutional right not only to "guarantee" but to actually *deliver* to the people of Ontario *right now*. Name the goal and, as far as the constitution is concerned, Bob Rae's government has the right to achieve it. Ontario can raise the minimum wage, open closing plants, restore jobs and provide a decent standard of living to the record numbers on Ontario's welfare rolls. Of course, the government would have to get very tough with big business to make it all possible, using to the fullest the provincial constitutional powers of regulation, taxation and, indeed, *expropriation*. But constitutional and legal powers do not necessarily entail the political will to use them. This tiny minority that is big business has all the power necessary to punish governments who dare to stand up to them, or who in a any way threaten the scope of their activities or their ability to make profit. That is what globalization of the economy is *for*.

Not that you cannot stand up to business; but it takes a lot of preparation and just plain nerve. As the Rae government amply demonstrated when it backed down on its campaign promise to nationalize automobile insurance, it has none of the necessary qualities for the job. After the insurance fiasco, it has behaved like any other provincial government in a recession, making every possible concession to business power to keep the economy afloat.

So it seems that the social charter not only legitimates business power, by combining unenforceable constitutional commitments to social programs with enforceable constitutional and non-constitutional rules enhancing business power. Perhaps more importantly, it legitimates the failure of social-democratic governments to do anything but surrender to that power, the squandering of their real legal authority actually to do something to put the ideals of their supporters into practice. The social charter allows the government to pretend it is doing something to protect public-sector programs and the standard of living when in fact it is merely presiding over their destruction. It is no surprise that the unenforceable social charter has been received warmly by business.[21]

The new constitutionalism is not much different from the old. It has gone hand in hand with, defined and legitimized the destruction of sovereignty, by limiting its reach, even as the state becomes the property of the whole people. The new-old states emerging from the former Soviet power bloc and the regions straining for more autonomy within or without their current national confines can only ever be "independent" or "sovereign" in a very restricted sense, so long as the enormous agglomeration of private power in the global economy remains unchallenged. This applies to Québec as much as to Canada:

"Québec, as a sovereign nation, would choose the Canadian dollar. That is absolutely certain," Mr. Parizeau told a group of institutional investors from across Canada. "Yes, a lot of people argue we wouldn't have any control over the monetary policy of the currency we employ. And that's perfectly correct. But, as far as I'm concerned, Québec doesn't have any control over the policies of the Bank of Canada now. So what have we got to lose?"[22]

As the state is reshaped to accommodate global business power, all that seems to be left for sovereignty is the brandishing of constitutional symbols that do not reflect but completely falsify the realities of modern political power.

A Constitution for English Canada

Barbara Cameron

One of the remarkable outcomes of the current round of constitutional "renewal" in Canada is the emergence of distinctly English-Canadian views of constitutional arrangements. Two main, and competing, views have appeared. On one side, there is the conception promoted by business associations, their academic supporters and politicians with a vested interest in the existing federal arrangements. On the other, there is the conception supported by popular organizations, including the Action Canada Network, the National Action Committee on the Status of Women, the Council of Canadians, a number of unions and other organizations.[1]

The élite conception calls for a decentralized federalism with respect to social programs and a more centralized federalism when it comes to economic powers. The Meech Lake Accord presented a blueprint for a decentralized federalism with a restricted role for the central Canadian state in funding social programs. The Conservative government's September 1991 constitutional proposals offered a full statement of the élite position with its unexpected emphasis on greater centralization of economic powers.

The conception being advanced by a number of influential popular organizations departs from the existing federal constitutional framework and calls for the acknowledgement of the existence in Canada of three national communities: aboriginal peoples, Québec and Canadians outside of Québec. It advocates recognition of the inherent right to self-government of aboriginal peoples, different powers for the Québec government than for other provincial governments and a continuing strong role for the central Canadian state with respect to social programs for the rest of Canada.

In the current round of constitutional debates, proponents of the élite and popular conceptions are vying for support from the public in English Canada and for allies in Québec. The popular conception has the advantage of responding to a deeply rooted identification of Canadians outside of Québec with the Canadian state as their national government. The élite conception, for its part, appeals to an equally deep-seated English-Canadian resistance to anything that looks like special privileges for Québec.

National Communities versus the Federal Structure

The emergence of perspectives on the constitution that are identifiably English Canadian happened more or less by default. During the post-Meech round of constitutional discussions, English Canadians found themselves speaking mainly to each other as a result of two boycotts of the federal government's constitutional process, one by Québec and the other by aboriginal peoples. The Spicer commission acknowledged that it took a sounding primarily of English-Canadian opinion.[2] The constitutional conferences running from late January 1991 through February 1992 were essentially dialogues among English Canadians.

With both Québec and aboriginal peoples acting like nations, English Canadians were forced to act like a national community, too. However, this is not the whole story. The constitutional conferences were themselves the result of a third boycott, this one by English Canadians who stayed away in droves from hearings sponsored by the Beaudoin-Dobbie Special Joint Committee on the Renewal of Canada. In a desperate but nonetheless successful bid to salvage the credibility of the constitutional consultation process, the federal Conservatives bowed to pressure from the New Democratic Party and instituted constitutional conferences.

The constitutional conferences provided the occasion for the "three national communities" conception, advocated by the popular organizations, to meet up with the common sense of the average English Canadian. Constrained by the themes chosen for the conferences, this perspective appeared at the conferences as an argument in favour of different powers for Québec and a continuing strong role for the federal government with respect to social programs. At all four constitutional conferences, the popular organizations' perspective regarding different powers for Québec won out over the élite proposal to decentralize control over social and cultural programs to all provinces.

The current round of constitutional "renewal" has seen the emergence of three processes for amending the constitution, in addition to the official formulas enshrined in the 1982 Constitution Act. There is the Québec process, which calls for a referendum either on proposals from the rest of Canada or on sovereignty by October 26, 1992. There is the aboriginal process, which involves separate aboriginal conferences and seats alongside the provinces at the constitutional table. And there is the English-Canadian process, which began as the hearings and conferences that members of the other national communities mostly chose not to attend.

The significant feature of the three parallel constitutional processes which have emerged outside the formal framework anticipated in the Constitution Act, 1982 is that they correspond to national communities. For Québec and for aboriginal peoples, the creation of separate and autonomous processes was a positive assertion of their national identity. For the rest of Canada, the existence of forums that were essentially English Canadian was, as pointed out above, more by default than by design.

These three processes have no formal, legally recognized place within the Canadian constitution. What they do have is political legitimacy. This is in sharp contrast to the amending formulas enshrined for the first time in the Constitution Act of 1982. These formulas are based on the notion that the significant units for ascertaining consent are the provincial legislatures and the federal parliament. Meech Lake was the first time out for this approach and it proved unworkable.

The difficulty the federal Conservatives are having in finding a legitimate process to amend the constitution is not based on the "surliness" of the electorate, as David Peterson suggested before his stunning defeat in the 1990 Ontario election. Nor is it based on a cynicism about politicians and politics because of corruption. The problem is much more fundamental.

It is based on the deep contradiction between the fundamental sociological reality of Canada and the existing federal structure. The sociological reality is the existence in Canada of major national communities.[3] This reality is not recognized in the existing federal structure and the amending formulas that accompany it. Indeed, the existing structure of Canadian federalism is based on the denial of national communities.

The emergence of extra-constitutional processes for expressing the national aspirations of the major national communities in Canada provides the best hope for finding some resolution to the never-ending crisis of Canadian Confederation. The problem is that these processes have no legal standing and are only dimly recognized in the media's coverage of what is taking place. At the end of the constitutional conferences, which were successful from the point of view of many in English Canada, the ball was tossed back into the court of the already discredited Special Joint Committee on a Renewed Canada and from there to the first ministers.

The Report of the Special Joint Committee

The report of the Special Joint Committee on a Renewed Canada[4] demonstrates just how huge the gap is between the sociological reality of Canada and the perspectives of politicians trapped within the existing federal structures. The committee had to write a report that in some way could be seen as reflecting the vision of Canada that emerged in all the constitutional conferences. At the same time, it had to come up with proposals that would be acceptable to the provincial premiers who were soon to become the major players in the constitutional game. The committee handled this dilemma by conceding a large amount of ground on rhetoric and very little on the actual substance of the fall 1991 federal government proposals.

The battle of rhetoric was quite clearly won by the popular sector. The Beaudoin-Dobbie report abandons the neo-conservative language of the September 1991 Conservative government proposals and embraces the left-liberal rhetoric which still has a strong resonance among English Canadians. The vocabulary of competitiveness has been subordinated to the rhetoric of "inclusion" and "vision," which are identified as the two greatest challenges facing Canadians. The Tory-dominated committee went so far as to endorse a Social Covenant which would jointly commit the federal, provincial and territorial governments to a universal health care system, adequate social services and benefits, the integrity of the environment and even the rights of workers to organize and bargain collectively. The companion clause on the Economic Union endorses the goal of full employment.

At the substance level, however, the victories were few. The most significant one is the proposal to recognize the inherent right of aboriginal peoples to self-government. Women succeeded in shifting the discourse on the Senate to include representation of under-represented groups as well as of provinces. Another victory of sorts is that the worst elements of the fall 1991 Conservative proposals have been dropped, including the notion of a Council of the Federation to allow the provinces to oversee the use of the federal spending power.

The right-wing agenda has been trimmed a bit but the essential elements are still in place. The Social Covenant and Economic Union, which is proposed as an amendment to section 36 of the Constitution Act, 1982, has no teeth whatsoever.[5] In contrast, a somewhat improved but still dangerous amendment to section 121 of the Constitution Act, 1867, remains.[6] Corporations will be given the right to challenge legislation in court which interferes with the free movement of goods, services, capital and persons (especially corporate persons). Laws enacted to protect the environment or promote sexual, racial or other equality will not be exempt from this.

On the fundamental issue of the division of powers, which is at the centre of constitutional debate in Canada, the voices of popular-sector organizations and many "average" English Canadians were completely ignored. The decentralization of powers remains in the proposals, although in a more devious form than in either the fall 1991 proposals or in the Meech Lake Accord. Instead of clearly identifying which powers will be devolved, Beaudoin-Dobbie recommends measures which would permit a dramatic transformation of the division of powers without the inconvenience of having recourse to the apparently unworkable constitutional amending formulas. This would be done through the intergovernmental delegation of powers and the conclusion of bilateral agreements between the federal and provincial governments.[7] As in Meech Lake, provinces would be able to opt out of new federal cost-shared programs with compensation.[8]

Reaction against the Beaudoin-Dobbie proposals was swift in Québec, where the virtually unanimous opinion is that they do not constitute the basis for an acceptable federal offer. Québec politicians are not prepared to have the power of the Québec government dependent on agreements which require federal government approval. The response from aboriginal people was also quick, and very interesting. While welcoming the proposed recognition of the inherent right of self-government, aboriginal leaders raised questions about the implications for aboriginal land claims and self-government of giving a privileged constitutional status to bilateral federal-provincial agreements.[9] Aboriginal issues must be addressed before a new division of powers between the federal and provincial governments is introduced.

Canadians outside of Québec reacted more slowly to the Beaudoin-Dobbie report. This has more to do with the lack of institutions to articulate a distinctly English-Canadian perspective than the merits of the proposals. All three political parties endorsed the proposals. The provincial premiers either took a wait-and-see attitude or engaged in parochial posturing, as was the case with Don Getty in Alberta.[10] Popular-sector organizations such as the Action Canada Network and the National Action Committee on the Status of Women opposed the proposals but had trouble getting their perspective across, with media attention back on the more familiar focus of federal-provincial manoeuvring.[11]

The federal and provincial governments are unlikely to come up with a proposal that satisfies Québec public opinion. Any statement on the division of powers explicit enough to gain support in Québec will alert Canadians in the rest of Canada to a decentralization of powers which they do not support. An increase in provincial powers is in any case opposed by aboriginal peoples, unless there are agreements reached about their own outstanding issues. Even among English-Canadian premiers there is little agreement on issues. In the face of the challenge from the Reform Party, the Alberta premier cannot agree to a formula for provincial representation in the Senate acceptable to either Ontario or Québec.[12]

By law, Québec is committed to a referendum vote on its constitutional future. In the absence of a genuine consensus, federal politicians are likely to launch a scare campaign about the dire economic consequences for Québec and the rest of Canada of Québec independence. Appeals will be made to anti-Québec and anti-French sentiment in English Canada against the separatists in Québec. As the French-speaking population of Québec thus becomes identified as the enemy, the stage will be set for a coercive response to a Québec vote in favour of sovereignty, perhaps using the cover of protecting aboriginal rights.

A Constitution for English Canada

It is becoming increasingly clear that there is no resolution to the constitutional crisis acceptable to democratically minded Canadians within the framework of existing federalism. Escape from the current constitutional impasse must start from a recognition that Canada is fundamentally composed of the distinct national communities of aboriginal peoples, Québec and English Canadians. Aboriginal peoples and Québécois already define constitutional problems in terms of national rights. The lack of a strong sense of national identity on the part of English Canadians is the biggest obstacle to the adoption of a constitutional framework based on national, as opposed to provincial, equality.

One of the reasons English Canadians have such difficulty coming to an awareness of ourselves as a national community is the absence of common political institutions. Almost all the institutions that English Canadians think of as national are in fact either binational or multinational. This is true of the Canadian state as well as of Canada-wide popular organizations, such as the Canadian Labour Congress and the National Action Committee on the Status of Women. The constitutional conferences, inadequate though they were, showed the value in English Canadians talking to each other about their shared vision of the country.

Further progress on the development of an English-Canadian perspective on the constitution requires forums created specifically for that purpose. Popular organizations have advanced the demand for a constituent assembly for English Canada. This might take the form of a series of regional assemblies leading up to one nation-wide assembly for English Canada.

There is a danger, however, that such assemblies will not get beyond the generalities with which the discussion began. To move forward to a clear articulation of an English-Canadian perspective, a way is needed to focus debate on the central choices facing Canada outside of Québec. One way to achieve this is to present representative assemblies of English Canadians with the task of designing a constitution for English Canada.

The resistance to doing this will come from those people who identify a constitution with an independent state. They will see this as an acceptance of the inevitability of Québec's independence. But a constitution does not necessarily *imply* a separate state. After all, the Canadian constitution recognizes the existence of provincial constitutions. A constitution for English Canada does, however, make the assumption that English Canadians need common national political institutions.

In arriving at a constitution for themselves, English Canadians would have to address and resolve some fundamental political questions. The following discussion suggests some ways that recurring issues in constitutional debates in Canada outside of Québec might be addressed more creatively in the context of developing a constitution for English Canada.

Protection of Individual and Collective Rights
As long as constitutional debates in English Canada are defined by what is necessary to keep Québec in Confederation, little progress can be made on strengthening the protections in the Charter of Rights and Freedoms or on the inclusion of a social charter with teeth. The reason for this is that the Charter imposes federally enshrined limits on the activity of the Québec legislature, and a social charter, if it were effective, would be the imposition from outside of positive obligations on the Québec government. The issue is not the merits of these charters but the source of the limitation or obligation. Many in

Québec look to a Québec Charter of Human Rights and Freedoms to protect their rights.

Yet many equality-seeking groups in Canada outside of Québec wish to see the Charter of Rights and Freedoms strengthened. Some women's organizations would like to see changes to section 28 of the Charter.[13] Groups representing people with disabilities have advanced changes to section 15.[14] As part of a social charter proposal, anti-poverty organizations have argued that the Charter of Rights and Freedoms should be interpreted in a manner consistent with "the fundamental value of alleviating and eliminating social and economic disadvantage."[15] Within the framework of a constitution that does not treat Québec and English Canada as separate national communities, these proposals are not seriously entertained.

One of the least helpful dynamics in constitutional discussions today is the competition of rights set up between ethnic and racial minorities and Québec. There is a strong feeling among such minorities that they are excluded from a constitutional debate that seems fixated on the English-French relationship. A debate over a constitution for English Canada could significantly alter the terms of their participation. They could fight for a definition of the culture of English Canada as multi-ethnic and multi-racial, rather than as "English."

Within a framework that does not acknowledge national communities, the French and the English populations of Canada simply become ethnic groups. Yet they enjoy a privileged position within Canada by virtue of their early date of arrival here. A hierarchy of rights is established whereby other ethnic communities are cast as second class, as Johnny-come-latelies. Within a framework that recognizes the existence of distinct nations within Canada, the culture of either nation can be seen as an evolving product of the cultures of the various waves of immigration. The predominant languages of Québec and English Canada are French and English respectively, but the cultures of each are multicultural and multiracial.

A very different "Canada clause" would result from this perspective than the one proposed by the Beaudoin-Dobbie committee. That proposal talks about the French and British settlers "who to this country brought their own unique languages and cultures but together forged political institutions that strengthened our union and enabled Québec to flourish as a distinct society within Canada." It then refers to "the peoples from myriad other nations, scattered the world over, who came to *our* shores and helped *us* greatly to fulfil the promise of this fair land."[16] The "us and them" language would disappear within a framework that accepts the existence within Canada of major national communities and defines the culture of each of these communities as pluralistic.

Within such a framework that recognizes the existence of distinct nations, there would be room for the minority proposal of the NDP members of the Beaudoin-Dobbie committee, which calls for an amendment to section 27 of the Charter of Rights and Freedoms to say that the Charter "shall be interpreted in a manner consistent with the preservation and enhancement of the multicultural heritage of Canadians and the preservation and promotion of racial and ethnic equality."[17] In the context of the current constitution, which does not recognize Québec as a nation, such a proposal might appear to place diverse ethnic groups in a competition for rights with the French-speaking population of Québec. Within the framework of a constitution for English Canada — and a separate constitution for Québec — such an amendment would be an acknowledgement of the equal status of all ethnic groups within the nations of English Canada and of Québec.

The Division of Powers
Both Keith Spicer's Citizens' Forum on Canada's Future and the 1992 Constitutional Conferences were told by Canadians outside of Québec that they do not want to see a weakening of the federal government. As the Spicer report noted, "the desire of the majority of participants outside of Québec is for a strong central government which will act with resolution to remedy the country's economic ills, help to unify its citizens, and reduce the level of division and discord among groups or regions."[18] The option of different powers for Québec has been embraced largely as a way to protect the role of the central government with respect to the rest of the country. English Canadians need to debate further what powers they wish the different levels of government to have. If it were an option, would the majority of Canadians outside of Québec like to see

a strengthening of the role of the federal government, for example by assigning to it a constitutional responsibility to spend in the area of social programs?

One of the problems about restricting the debate to the current federal framework is that English Canadians are forced into a defensive mode in order to prevent the dismantling of many federal programs. In a similar way, the neo-conservative attack on social services and benefits has forced many reformers to defend existing programs even when they are inadequate. But in reality, most popular organizations have raised strong criticisms about the undemocratic delivery of many public services. It is clear that English Canadians do not support the wholesale devolution of powers demanded by Québec. It is not so clear that some democratic decentralization of powers would not improve the quality and accessibility of services.

The current set of financial arrangements around social programs, for example, is extremely complicated. Most Canadians have little notion of what the federal spending power is all about or what is involved in shared-cost programs. In order to lobby for quality, accessible child care services, advocates have to become instant experts on very complex fiscal arrangements. For the majority of Québécois, greater collective control means greater provincial government powers. For Canadians outside of Québec, greater collective control could mean not only placing a positive constitutional obligation on the federal government to spend in areas of social services and to establish basic national standards, but providing explicitly for the provincial or municipal design and delivery of services in ways that involve local communities.

A debate among English Canadians about the responsibilities they would like to see assigned to their municipal, provincial and federal governments might well result in creative proposals to democratize political institutions. For example, constitutional recognition could be given to municipal governments and a secure financial base provided for their activity independent of the provincial governments. Consideration of such issues gets lost in a climate where English Canadians feel compelled to defend the integrity of what they see as their national state. A dialogue among English Canadians about a constitution for English Canada would be a way to have a creative debate.

Political Representation

As long as discussion about reform of the Senate was confined to the political élites, the basis of representation in the Senate was assumed to be territory. The West's proposal of a triple-E Senate seemed to be the only item on the agenda. However, once popular organizations became involved in the debate, attention was focused on the need for representation of women, people with disabilities, and racial and other minorities. Instead of seeing the Senate as a house of the provinces, the traditionally excluded groups began to raise the possibility of a second chamber as a House of Equality.

One of the few supportable recommendations of the Beaudoin-Dobbie report was that the Senate be elected by means of proportional representation.[19] But if the Senate is elected by this means, why not the House of Commons as well? And if the House of Commons is chosen by a more democratic electoral system, is a Senate necessary at all? If the question becomes defined as fairer representation for all excluded groups, then the ground of the debate shifts dramatically.

As a consequence of suffering under the neo-conservative agenda of the Mulroney government since 1984, many Canadians are angry about the unrepresentative nature of Canadian political institutions and the unresponsiveness of parties and legislative bodies to popular sentiment. A debate on a constitution for English Canada could channel this anger into a constructive discussion about how to democratize political institutions. With the issue of democracy at the centre of the debate, the focus could be on which political arrangements would most faithfully translate popular aspirations into public policy and how best to give voice to those who are currently under-represented, whether these are poor regions or women and minorities. Within the current federal framework, the problem of representation is posed as a trade-off in which the Québec political élites will be granted greater power only if the élites of other provinces also receive stronger recognition.

The development of a constitution for English Canada that reflects new institutional arrangements and new protections for individual and collective rights could only result from a democratic political process involving Canadians in forums for exploring and debating alternative proposals. A series of regional constituent assemblies culminating in an English-Canada-wide constituent assembly would provide such forums. Within such constituent assemblies and in the surrounding public debate, a variety of competing interests would come forward with their pet proposals. In many cases, the interests of competing groups could be reconciled; in other cases, choices would need to be made about what kind of country Canadians wish to build for the future. The choices arrived at would be the result of struggle for support among the representatives of competing social interests. In arenas free from élite pressure to accept the changes that are being marketed as the only way to keep Québec in Confederation, democratic voices will be heard more easily than in the current consociational arrangements.

An example of this is the environment. In the élite arena of the Beaudoin-Dobbie Select Committee on the Renewal of the Constitution, the demand for environmentally sustainable development was translated into a proposed commitment of governments to "preserving the integrity of the environment in an economically sustainable manner."[20] In a democratic debate where the demands of environmentalists confronted directly the demands of the corporations for freedom from regulation, the commitment to the environment could not be so easily fudged and the choice between competing interests would be clearer.

If a clearly worded Québec referendum resulted in a unilateral declaration of independence, the proposal for a constitution for English Canada would take on a practical urgency. It would provide a positive focus for the fears of English Canadians that the complete dissolution of Canada is inevitable. Designing a constitution would be an exercise in self-determination for Canada outside of Québec. It would provide English Canadians with a basis to negotiate a new relationship with Québec as well as with aboriginal peoples.

Even if the verdict of a Québec referendum is less clear, the project of designing a constitution for English Canada is a valid one. Should the existing federal framework in Canada survive yet another challenge, it will continue to be an obstacle to democratic advance in Canada. It is in the interests of English Canadians, as well as of Québécois and aboriginal peoples, to develop new political institutions which allow us greater collective control over our economic and social life. Beginning now to debate a constitution for English Canada will allow us to define what those institutions should be.

Notes

Chapter 1

1. There is a voluminous literature on Canada's constitutional crisis. For a sampling of different perspectives, see Kent Weaver *et al., The Collapse of Canada?* (Washington: The Brookings Institute, 1992); Duncan Cameron and Miriam Smith, eds., *Constitutional Politics* (Toronto: Lorimer, 1992); Ronald L. Watts and Douglas M. Brown, eds., *Options for a New Canada* (Toronto: University of Toronto Press, 1991).
2. For a contemporary analysis of the effects of globalization on Canada, see D. Drache and M. Gertler, eds., *The New Era of Global Competition: State Policy and Market Policy* (Montréal: McGill–Queen's University Press, 1991).
3. See the recent Toronto-based manifesto written collectively by Christina McCall, *et al.*, "Three Nations," *Canadian Forum* (March 1992): 4–6.
4. For a lucid analysis of the forces that have rekindled Québec nationalism, see Alain-G. Gagnon and Daniel Latouche, *Allaire, Bélanger, Campeau et les autres* (Montréal: Québec/Amérique, 1991).
5. J. R. Mallory, "The Five Faces of Federalism," in P. A. Crépeau and C. B. Macpherson, eds., *The Future of Canadian Federalism* (Toronto: University of Toronto Press, 1965) p. 11.
6. See K. McRoberts, *Québec: Social Change and Political Crisis*, 3rd ed. (Toronto: McClelland and Stewart, 1988).
7. These issues are analysed in detail by the Economic Council of Canada's special study of the constitutional crisis. See *A Joint Venture: The Economics of Constitutional Options* (Ottawa: 1991).
8. Edouard Cloutier, Jean H. Guay, and Daniel Latouche, *Le Virage: L'évolution de l'opinion publique au Québec depuis 1960* (Montréal: Québec/Amérique, 1992).
9. For an extremely powerful analysis of the division of powers question, see François Vaillancourt, *The Division of Powers in Canada: Theory, Evidence and Proposals for Quebec* (Kingston: John Deutsch Institute for the Study of Economic Policy, Queen's University, 1991), Vol. 1, p. 260.
10. This section draws its inspiration from Vaillancourt's article.
11. *The Toronto Star*, April 19, 1992.
12. Informetrica, Update on the Constitutional Debate, Special Supplement No. 1 (Ottawa: January 1992).
13. *Ibid.*, p. 270.

14. For a detailed analysis of the limitations in any further division and redivision of powers, see Andrée Lajoie, "Contribution aux travaux de la Commission sur l'avenir politique et constitutionnel du Québec" (Montréal, January 15, 1991);"Le Canada anglais et la crise constitutionelle," ACFAS (Sherbrooke, May 22, 1991); "Does Canada Have A Future? A View From Québec" (Niagara-on-the-Lake: April 1991).

15. For a sampling of the vast literature, see the studies and memoranda published by the Commission d'étude des questions afférentes à l'accession du Québec à la souveraineté established by the National Assembly, first session, Thirty-Fourth Legislature, associated with Bill 150: "An Act respecting the process for determining the political and constitutional future of Québec," (Québec: Official Publisher, 1991).

16. The association aspect is the most important question, even more critical than the intricate legal aspects of sovereignty, the favourite terrain of constitutional lawyers. Aboriginal rights is an important exception. See Turpel's and MacNeil's contributions to this volume. The recognition of aboriginal entitlement in the fullest sense of the term raises such large ethical, constitutional and political questions that no Québec government or federal authority can afford to ignore to them.

17. The Business Council on National Issues has taken a leading role in making the constitutional crisis part of its neo-conservative agenda. See *Canada and the 21st Century: Towards a More Effective Federalism and a Stronger Economy* (Ottawa: 1991). The C. D. Howe Institute is another think-tank with a clear political agenda. See its most sophisticated analyst and thinker, Thomas J. Courchene, *In Praise of Renewed Federalism* (Toronto: C. D. Howe Institute, 1991). For a detailed critique of this perspective see also M. Smith's article in this volume.

18. A private communciation from Daniel Latouche.

19. The phrase is that of Douglas G. Lenihan, who also used it as the title of his article on institutional reform in Canada. See *Network Analyses* no. 3 (January 1992).

20. U.S. trade laws give the United States enormous power to punish its competitors, including Canada. This is why the United States has no hesistation to enter into free trade agreements, knowing full well that its countervail powers are not affected by these international agreements. A reconfigured federal government would try to pattern itself on the U.S. model because, as the larger trading partner, it has the clear advantage over Québec.

21. See the Economic Council of Canada 1991 study, *A Joint Venture.*

22. Bill 150 defines the access of Québec to full sovereignty as including "a position of exclusive jurisdiction, through its democratic institutions, to make laws and levy taxes in its territory and to act on the international scene for the making of agreements and treaties of any kind with other independent States and participating in various international organizations, and to make recommendations to the National Assembly in that regard." Chapter 11, para. 3.
23. Donald G. Lenihan, "Squaring Politics and Principles," p. 15.
24. Informetrica, Update.
25. The phrase "the politics of spite" is borrowed from Keith Banting, who used it recently in his contribution to *The Collapse of Canada?*
26. The numbers are taken from a June 4 1992 column by Lysiane Gagnon in *The Globe and Mail*.
27. The contrast with federal practice in Ontario is marked. There, the top ten suppliers to the federal government account for less than 24 percent of all federal procurement contracts. The list is far more diverse, including such giants as Esso Petroleum, IBM Canada, GM, Spar Aerospace, Petro Canada and UTDC as well as the Corps of Commissionaires. There is no clear political, industrial or strategic development bias in awarding contracts working to Ontario's benefit.
28. Economic Council of Canada, *A Joint Venture*.
29. In terms of trade with the rest of Canada, Québec and Ontario export a little more than 9 percent of their total manufacturing shipments to other provinces. What is alarming is that there has been a sharp drop in the flow of east-west trade. Canada's markets are being increasingly supplied by American — and in the case of British Columbia, Japanese — goods.
30. See Drache and Gertler, *The New Era of Global Competition*.
31. *Le Devoir*, February 8, 1992, p. A-5.
32. The various options are realistically examined by Informetrica's study, *Financial Sector: Deposit-Taking Institutions*, Economics of Confederation, Study no. 6, October 1991, pp. 13–14.

Chapter 2
1. It might be useful to recall that the term *Québec question* was used by sociologist Marcel Rioux as the title of a book, *La question du Québec*, published by Seghers in 1969.
2. *Quebec Mercury*, April 3, 1809; cited by D. C. Creighton, *The Empire of the St. Lawrence* (Toronto: Macmillan, 1956), p. 160.
3. Cited in Ramsay Cook, *Canada and the French Canadian Question* (Toronto: Macmillan, 1966), p. 175.

4. This point is most persuasively argued in Ralph Heintzman, "The Spirit of Confederation: Professor Creighton, Biculturalism and the Use of History," *Canadian Historical Review* 52, no. 3 (September 1975): 245–275. Before Heintzman, though, Maurice Careless argued in favour of a more accommodating, more tolerant George Brown. See his *Brown of the Globe*, 2 vols. (Toronto: 1959 and 1963).

5. Mason Wade, *Les Canadiens français de 1760 à nos jours*, 2 vols. (Ottawa: Cercle du Livre de France, 1966), vol. 1, p. 456.

6. *Ibid.*, p. 523.

7. *La Minerve*, July 1, 1867; quoted in Alastair Sweeny, *George-Étienne Cartier*. (Toronto: McClelland and Stewart, 1976), p. 167.

8. Michel Brunet, "Trois dominantes de la pensée canadienne-française: l'agriculturalisme, l'anti-étatisme et le messianisme" in *La présence anglaise et les Canadiens* (Montréal: Beauchemin, 1958). An abridged English version appeared in Dale Miquelon, ed., *Society and Conquest: The Debate on the Bourgeoisie and Social Change in French Canada, 1700–1850* (Toronto: Copp-Clark, 1977).

9. The focus throughout this essay is on process, rather than on intentions or motivations. Historial process is independent of will or intention, be it individual or collective. At the same time, however, individuals are free to behave as they wish in its regard. The Church as an institution may have had different intentions or acted out of entirely different motives regarding French Canada. This does not diminish the objective historical role it played in protecting French-Canadian culture. By the same token, individuals within the institution may have been opposed to French-Canadian nationalism or to the Church's involvement in *la survivance*. These issues, while certainly valid and worthy of study, are not within the ambit of this paper. It must be stressed, however, that French Canada was not a nationalist monolith, nor were French Canadians obliged to behave in a certain way by the historical process. The two phenomena are quite distinct.

10. Michiel Horn, *The League for Social Reconstruction: Intellectual Origins of the Democratic Left in Canada, 1930–1942* (Toronto: University of Toronto Press, 1980), p. 112.

11. Gregory Baum, *Catholics and Canadian Socialism: Political Thought in the Thirties and Forties* (Toronto: Lorimer, 1980), Chapter 6.

12. Jack Granatstein and Paul Stevens, eds., *Forum: Canadian Life and Letters, 1920-70* (Toronto: University of Toronto Press, 1972). See especially articles by Eugene Forsey, J. Addison Reid, J. E. Keith. The only exception to this view is stated by Frank Scott, who

attempts to put events in Québec in the broader Canadian context.

13. Marlene Shore, *The Science of Social Redemption: McGill, the Chicago School, and the Origins of Social Science in Canada* (Toronto: University of Toronto Press, 1987). Shore points out that Stuart Jamieson and William Roy had a different theoretical framework for analysing Québec society. See also Everett Hughes, *French Canada in Transition* (Chicago: University of Chicago Press, 1965), and Horace Miner, *St. Denis: A French Canadian Parish* (Chicago: University of Chicago Press, 1966).

14. Baum, *Catholics and Canadian Socialism*, pp. 185–8.

15. The abridged version is published as Donald Smiley, ed., *The Rowell-Sirois Report: Book I* (Toronto: McClelland and Stewart, 1964).

16. See Jacques Cousineau, *L'Église d'ici et le social 1940–1960* (Montréal: Bellarmin, 1982), pp. 19–24, 143–53.

17. Taschereau brought in legislation that provided state funding for Church-run social service and educational insitutions in 1921. Minimalist laws on labour, education and social security were brought in by his administration and that of Duplessis. The Godbout government (1939–44) took the biggest step in meeting the requirements of the new order by nationalizing the largest hydro company in Québec and introducing a new labour code. See Bernard Vigod, *Québec Before Duplessis. The Political Career of Louis-Alexandre Taschereau* (Montréal and Kingston: McGill–Queens University Press, 1986).

18. Daniel Latouche, "La vraie nature de ... la révolution tranquille," *Revue canadienne de science politique* 7, no. 3 (September 1974): 525–36.

19. An abridged edition appeared as David Kwavnick, ed., *The Tremblay Report* (Toronto: McClelland and Stewart, 1973).

20. Denis Monière, *André Laurendeau et le destin d'un peuple* (Montréal: 1983).

Chapter 3

1. See the works on constitutionalism by Arendt Lijphant, Kenneth McRae, S. J. R. Noel, and Robert Presthus.

2. *Maclean's*, January 7, 1991, p. 33.

3. Reporting on an Environics poll conducted in March 1992, Susan Delacourt pointed out that 56 percent of Canadians said "they have had enough consultation on the Constitution"; but the poll showed that "62 percent said they still hope to get involved in a national referendum." *The Globe and Mail*, April 4, 1992, p. A6.

4. This definition was developed by a cross-disciplinary inter-university research group that met over the course of two years in 1988–89 to discuss international negotiation. See Janice Stein, *International Journal*, 1989.
5. Quotations are from Québec National Assembly, first session, Thirty-Fourth Legislature, Bill 150: "An Act respecting the process for determining the political and constitutional future of Québec" (Québec: Official Publisher, 1991).
6. *The Toronto Star*, March 20, 1992.
7. David V. J. Bell, *The Roots of Disunity* (Toronto: Oxford University Press, 1992), Chapter 4.
8. Joe Clark, quoted in *The Globe and Mail*: "PM, Ministers differ on unity proposal," September 12, 1991, p. A8.
9. Jean Chrétien, *The Toronto Star*, September 25, 1991, p. A1.
10. *Maclean's*, January 7, 1991, p. 34.
11. See *inter alia* Barbara Gray, "Negotiations: Arenas for Reconstructing Meaning," *Centre for Research in Conflict and Negotiation Working Paper* (The Pennsylvania State University, 1988).
12. Cf. Pierre Fournier's book, *A Meech Lake Post Mortem*. For a critique of the response of the Québec media to the Beaudoin-Dobbie report see Laurier LaPierre, "Meet the Notables, Who Dictate What Quebeckers Think," *The Globe and Mail*, March 21, 1992, pp. D1, D5.
13. It is this metaphor, combined with another that we will discuss shortly, that Resnick invokes in his discussion of sovereignty-association. He asks rhetorically if "an English Canada [will be] well disposed to reaching economic agreements with a Québec that has just removed itself from the Canada body politic? A Québec eager to forge associations with a truculent English Canada? Marital separations leave deep wounds. Why would the breakup of a country leave less?" (pp. 58–59).
14. Any effort to calculate the economic costs and benefits of the breakup of Canada is complicated because it is impossible to predict the amount of what one study calls "acrimony." Some observers warn of the potential for violence and the probability of extreme bitterness. Others, like Jacques Parizeau, insist that both sides would want to avoid this painful outcome, and therefore separation will be peaceful and calm. John McCallum and Chris Green base their economic calculations "on the assumption of a nonacrimonious breakup," but they point out that bitter conflict could easily occur if the legitimacy of the process is questioned, or over the substantive issues of territory, debt and currency. See *Parting As Friends:*

The Economic Consequences for Quebec (Toronto: C. D. Howe Institute, 1991), p. 8.

15. "No more, roll the dice: Mulroney tries soft-sell," *The Toronto Star*, September 24, 1991, p. A1.
16. See George Lakoff, *Metaphors We Live By.*
17. *The Globe and Mail*, March 13, 1992, p. A12.

Chapter 4

1. Ronald L. Watts, "Canada's Constitutional Options: An Outline," in Ronald L. Watts and Douglas M. Brown, eds., *Options for a New Canada* (Toronto: University of Toronto Press, 1991), pp. 15–30; Pierre Thibault, "Expert advice to the Bélanger-Campeau Commission," *The Network* (February/March 1991).
2. Secrétariat de la Commission sur l'avenir politique et constitutionnel du Québec, "L'accès du Québec aux marchés extérieurs et à l'espace économique canadien," in Commission sur l'avenir politique et constitutionnel du Québec, *Éléments d'analyse économique pertinents à la révision du statut politique et constitutionnel du Québec*, Document de travail, numéro 1, pp. 19–54; Bernard Fortin, "Les options monétaires d'un Québec souverain," in *Éléments d'analyse économique*, pp. 283–301; Jacques Parizeau, *Ottawa Citizen*, May 28, 1991.
3. Ivan Bernier, "Le maintien de l'accès aux marchés extérieurs: Certaines questions juridiques soulevées dans l'hypothèse de la souveraineté du Québec," in *Éléments d'analyse économique*, pp. 1–17.
4. Daniel Soberman, "European Integration: Are There Lessons for Canada?" in Watts and Brown, *Options*, pp. 191–205, especially p. 201.
5. Patrick Grady, *The Economic Consequences of Quebec Sovereignty* (Vancouver: Fraser Institute, 1991); David E. W. Laidler and William B. P. Robson, *Two Nations, One Money?: Canada's Monetary System Following a Quebec Secession* (Toronto: C. D. Howe Institute, 1991).
6. M. Luc Bergeron, "L'intégration européenne," in Commission sur l'avenir politique et constitutionnel du Québec, *Éléments d'analyse institutionnelle, juridique et démolinguistique pertinents à la révision du statut politique et constitutionnel du Québec*, Document de travail, numéro 2, 1991, pp. 111–238. See especially pp. 184–188.
7. Most other Québec commentary on this issue follows the same lines. Québec Liberal Party, Constitutional Committee, *A Quebec Free to Choose* (Québec, January 28, 1991), p. 53. Bourassa remarks on a new political superstructure, *The Globe and Mail*, February

1, 1991, p. A1. Remarks on the EC by the Parti Québécois brief to the Bélanger-Campeau commission in Alain-G. Gagnon and Daniel Latouche, *Allaire, Bélanger, Campeau et les autres: Les Québécois s'interrogent sur leur avenir* (Montréal: Éditions Québec/Amérique, 1991), pp. 151 –157, especially p. 157. See also the final report of the Bélanger-Campeau commission, Québec, Commission on the Political and Constitutional Future of Quebec, *Report* (Québec, March 27, 1991), pp. 10–11.

8. The classic statement remains Gouvernement du Québec, *La nouvelle entente Québec-Canada: Proposition du gouvernement du Québec pour une entente d'égal à égal: la souveraineté-association* (Québec: Éditeur officiel, 1979).

9. Soberman, "European Integration"; Peter M. Leslie, *The European Community: A Political Model for Canada?* (Ottawa: Supply and Services, 1991); Thomas J. Courchene, *In Praise of Renewed Federalism* (Toronto: C. D. Howe Institute, 1991); G. Bruce Doern, *Europe Uniting: The EC Model and Canada's Constitutional Debate* (Toronto: C. D. Howe Institute, 1991).

10. Doern, *Europe Uniting*, p. 30.

11. Ronald L. Watts, "The Federative Superstructure," in Watts and Brown, *Options*, p. 312.

12. On some of these other issues, see Gordon Ritchie, *et al.*, *Broken Links: Trade Relations after a Quebec Secession* (Toronto: C. D. Howe Institute, 1991); Secrétariat de la Commisson sur l'avenir politique et constitutionnel du Québec, "Analyse des activités fiscales et budgétaires du gouvernement fédéral," in *Éléments d'analyse économique*, pp. 303–52; Ministère des Finances du Québec, "La présence du gouvernement fédéral au Québec," in *Éléments d'analyse économique*, pp. 353–91; M. José Woehrling, "Les aspects juridiques de la redéfinition du statut politique et constitutionnel du Québec," in *Éléments d'analyse institutionnelle*, pp. 1–110.

13. Peter M. Leslie, "Options for the Future of Canada: The Good, the Bad, and the Fantastic," in Watts and Brown, *Options*, pp. 123–40.

14. Jane Jenson and Miriam Smith, "L'union économique, une menace commune au Québec et au Canada," *Le Devoir*, October 31, 1991; Jane Jenson, "Beyond Brokerage Politics: Towards the Democracy Round," in Duncan Cameron and Miriam Smith, eds., *Constitutional Politics* (Toronto: Lorimer, 1992); David Schneidermann, "The Market and the Constitution," in Cameron and Smith, *Constitutional Politics*; Doern, *Europe Uniting*, pp. 31–33.

15. Canada, *Canadian Federalism and Economic Union: Partnership for Prosperity* (Ottawa: Supply and Services, 1991); Canada, *Shaping Canada's Future Together: Proposals* (Ottawa: Supply and Services, 1991).

16. Business Council on National Issues, *Canada and the 21st Century: Towards a More Effective Federalism and a Stronger Economy* (Ottawa: April 26, 1991), p. 8.

17. Business Council on National Issues, *Canada's Constitutional Future: A Response by the Business Council on National Issues to the Government of Canada Proposals "Shaping Canada's Future Together,"* January 1992, p. 16.

18. *Ibid.*, p. 19.

19. *Ibid.*, p. 21.

20. *Ibid.*, p. 25–26.

21. For example, Thomas J. Courchene and John N. McDougall, "The Context for Future Constitutional Options," in Watts and Brown, *Options*, pp. 33–51.

22. *A Quebec Free to Choose*, p. 61.

23. Mémoire présenté par la Fédération des travailleurs et travailleuses du Québec (FTQ) à la Commission sur l'avenir politique et constitutionnel du Québec, novembre 1990, pp. 11–13; Mémoire de la Confédération des syndicats nationaux (CSN) soumis à la Commission sur l'avenir politique et constitutionnel du Québec, novembre 1990, *Un Choix clair pour la CSN: L'indépendance du Québec*, pp. 31–41.

24. CSN, *Un choix clair*, p. 15.

25. Mémoire de la division du Québec de L'Association des manufacturiers canadiens à la Commission sur l'avenir politique et constitutionnel du Québec, pp. 33–46.

26. National Assembly, first session, Thirty-Fourth Legislature, *Journal de débats* (in translation), Commission on the Political and Constitutional Future of Québec, November 7, 1990, no. 2, p. 52.

27. *Ibid.*, pp. 53–54.

28. National Assembly, first session, Thirty-Fourth Legislature, *Journal de débats* (in translation), Commission on the Political and Constitutional Future of Québec, November 15, 1990, no. 6, pp. 335–37.

29. Mémoire du Mouvement des caisses Desjardins présenté à la Commission sur l'avenir politique et constitutionnel du Québec, novembre 1990.

30. Gilles Breton and Jane Jenson, "La nouvelle dualité canadienne," in Louis Balthazar, Guy Laforest and Vincent Lemieux, *Le Québec et la restructuration du Canada, 1980–1992: Enjeux et perspectives* (Québec: Septentrion, 1991), pp. 75–92.

Chapter 5

1. With Québec's departure, the franchise on the name "Canada" remains with Ottawa, the provinces outside Québec and the territories. The term "English Canada" refers to that part of the present federation excluding Québec. In this context, "English" Canada simply means the predominance of the English language, and has no ethnic or cultural implications. Such barbarous formulations as ROC ("the Rest of Canada") or COQ ("Canada Outside Québec")which define the rest of us outside Québec as a negativity or a residual category are rejected here.
2. There is another aspect to the national unity/cultural disintegration argument that is worth considering. The argument that English Canada has nothing distinctive without Québec is a curious one for both English Canada and Québec. To the former it implies that they are nothing more than a kind of vampire hanging on the neck of Québec. To Québécois, it is a good argument for sovereignty: who wants to be married to a vampire?
3. Abraham Rotstein, "Is there an English Canadian nationalism?" *Journal of Canadian Studies* 13, no. 2 (Summer 1978): 109–18.
4. David Bercuson and Barry Cooper, *Deconfederation: Canada Without Quebec* (Toronto: Key Porter, 1991).

Chapter 6

1. A quick perusal of Alain-G. Gagnon and Daniel Latouche, eds., *Allaire, Bélanger, Campeau et les autres* (Montréal: Éditions Québec/Amérique, 1991) would confirm this.
2. Examples of this sort of thinking are reflected in the pieces by Reg Whitaker, Bryan Schwartz and Richard Gwyn in Jack Granatstein and Kenneth McNaught, eds., *English Canada Speaks Out* (Toronto: Doubleday, 1991).
3. For a proposal along these lines, see Gordon Laxer, "Why not give Quebec what it wants?" *The Globe and Mail*, January 23, 1992, p. A17.
4. For details of a confederal-type argument, see my *Toward a Canada-Quebec Union* (Montréal: McGill–Queen's University Press, 1991), especially Chapter 10.

Chapter 7

1. H. Brody, *Maps and Dreams* (Vancouver: Douglas and McIntyre, 1988), p. xiii.
2. Government of Québec, *Quebec-Canada: A New Deal* (Éditeur Officiel, 1979), p. 89. This is the official Parti Québécois publication circulated prior to the referendum on sovereignty-association in 1980.

3. Although my preferred expression is *First Nations,* I use the phrase *aboriginal peoples* throughout this paper because I want it to be clear that I am referring to both the First Nations (sometimes called "Indians") and Inuit. In the province of Québec there are First Nations and Inuit people, each with distinctive perspectives, status and rights.

4. Here I am particularly mindful of the comments of the members of the Committee on the Accession of Québec to Full Sovereignty, established pursuant to Bill 150 (An Act Respecting the Process for Determining the Political and Constitutional Future of Québec). It has been before this committee that the sovereignist position has become most clearly articulated in the past months, in terms of the comments of members of the committee, background studies and the submissions of witnesses.

5. Now section 91(24) of the Constitution Act, 1867.

6. Of course, law and politics are hardly distinct. Legal arguments are interconnected with politics at every level in this context. I have deliberately made this essay less technical and "legal" than it could have been. Some of the detail of the legal argument, at least on the issue of territory, can be found in Kent McNeil, "Aboriginal Nations and Québec's Boundaries: Canada Couldn't Give What It Didn't Have," in this volume. For a detailed and superb legal analysis of aboriginal peoples' concerns *vis-à-vis* full sovereignty for Québec, see Grand Council of the Crees of Québec, *Status and Rights of the James Bay Crees in the Context of Quebec's Secession from Canada,* Submission to the United Nations Commission on Human Rights, 48th Session, February 21, 1992.

7. This is a land claim agreement or modern treaty entered into in 1975 by Cree, Inuit, and the federal and provincial governments.

8. As Zebeedee Nungak, spokesperson for the Inuit Tapirisat of Canada and the Inuit in northern Québec, rather graphically illustrated at the federally sponsored constitutional constituency assembly, "Identity, Values and Rights," he identifies as an Inuk first, a Canadian second, and a Québécois third. (February 7, 1992, Royal York Hotel, Toronto.) I say "graphically" because he held up a map of Québec which divided the province into the north and south, arguing that (to paraphrase) "the distinct society of the south cannot override the distinct society of the north."

9. The National Chief of the Assembly of First Nations, Ovide Mercredi, appeared on February 11, 1992. A copy of his text is on file with the author.

10. From the translation, reprinted in *The Globe and Mail,* February 18, 1992, p. 19.

11. The sovereignists often refer to a March 20, 1985, National Assembly resolution as a starting point for engaging with aboriginal peoples on issues relating to full sovereignty. However, it is important to note that this resolution was unilaterally imposed on the First Nations in Québec. The aboriginal leadership in the province wrote a letter to Premier Lévesque on June 25, 1985, reminding the premier of the First Nations' objections to the tabling of the resolution and the unilateral way in which the government behaved. This letter expressed concern about the substance of the resolution. As a unilaterally imposed document, it is not a basis for a relationship which respects self-determination for aboriginal peoples.

    The Crees suggest, in their brief to the United Nations, that "it is unacceptable for the National Assembly or government of Quebec to unilaterally impose policies on First Nations. The contents of an acceptable Resolution were in the process of being negotiated. Also, a prior commitment had been expressly made by the Premier of Quebec that he would not table any resolution on this matter in the National Assembly without aboriginal consent." Submission of the Grand Council of the Crees of Québec, p. 166.

12. The secessionist position has been articulated in detail by Professor J. Brossard in his text, *L'accession à la souveraineté et le cas du Québec* (Montréal: Les Presses de l'Université de Montréal, 1977). This text has been referred to by the Committee on the Accession of Québec to Sovereignty as an accurate statement of the rights of French Canadians to self-determination.

13. Brossard acknowledges that the basis of the claim to accession is the rights of French Canadians to self-determination. He goes further to suggest that in theory it is only the French-Canadian nation that could participate in the decision on full sovereignty, thus excluding the anglophones. *L'accession à la souveraineté*, pp. 183–85. He admits that politically such an alternative is impracticable.

14. This is quoted in the Submission of the Grand Council of the Crees of Québec to the United Nations Commission on Human Rights.

15. He appeared before the Committee on Accession on October 9, 1991.

16. See, for example, I. Brownlie, *Principles of International Law*, 4th ed. (Oxford: Clarendon Press, 1989), p. 135, who suggests that "the principle [of *uti possidetis*] is by no means mandatory and the states concerned are free to adopt other principles as the basis of settlement."

17. *Frontier Dispute (Burkina Faso/Mali)*, 80 I.L.R. 440 at 554 (separate opinion of Judge Luchaire).
18. Quoted in H. Thurston, "Power in a Land of Remembrance," *Audubon* 52 (Nov.-Dec. 1991): 58–9.
19. As the National Chief of the Assembly of First Nations stated in his presentation to the Committee on Accession, "The Quebec government's proposed principle concerning the territorial integrity of Quebec is an affront to First Nations. It is obvious that territorial integrity serves to consolidate your legal position to the extreme prejudice of the First Nations."

Chapter 8
1. See Henriette Immarigeon, "Les frontières du Québec," in Jacques Brossard *et al.*, *Le territoire québécois* (Montréal: Les Presses de l'Université de Montréal, 1970), 3–47, at 12–17; Luce Patenaude, "L'extension territoriale du Code civil actuel dans le Québec,"in Brossard *et al.*, 49–103, at 63–71; Jacques Brossard, *L'accession à la souveraineté et le cas du Québec* (Montréal: Les Presses de l'Université de Montréal, 1976), pp. 490–4.
2. S.C. 1898 (61 Vict.), c.3; S.Q. 1898 (61 Vict.), c.6.
3. *The Quebec Boundaries Extension Act*, 1912, S.C. 1912 (2 Geo. V), c.45; *An Act Respecting the Extension of Quebec by the Annexation of Ungava*, S.Q. 1912 (2 Geo. V), c.7. Note that the eastern boundary of this additional territory was defined by these Acts as the boundary of the territory over which Newfoundland had lawful jurisdiction, i.e., Labrador. The location of that eastern boundary was determined by the Privy Council in *Re Labrador Boundary* [1927] 2 D.L.R. 401. The historical changes to and disputes over that boundary will not be discussed in this article. On these matters, see Henri Dorion, *La frontière Québec-Terreneuve* (Québec: Les Presses de l'Université Laval, 1963); Henri Dorion *et al.*, *Rapport de la Commission d'étude sur l'integrité du territoire du Québec: 3. La frontière du Labrador* (Québec: 1971); Henri Brun, *Le territoire du Québec* (Québec: Les Presses de l'Université Laval, 1974), pp. 97–146; Norman L. Nicholson, *The Boundaries of the Canadian Confederation* (Toronto: Macmillan of Canada, 1979), pp. 78–82.
4. 34 & 35 Vict., c.28 (U.K.). See collection of documents relating to the 1898 boundary in Canada, *Sessional Papers*, 1911, vol. XLV, no. 65. Note that this provision was changed by the *Constitution Act, 1982*, Schedule B to the *Canada Act 1982*, c.11 (U.K.), s.42(1)(e), which provides that the "extension of existing provinces into the territories" requires a constitutional amendment in accordance with the amending formula in s.38(1).

5. This issue is examined here from the perspective of Canadian law. For discussion of relevant international law, see Grand Council of the Crees of Québec, *Status and Rights of the James Bay Crees in the Context of Quebec's Secession from Canada*, Submission to the United Nations Commission on Human Rights, 48th Session, February 21, 1992.

6. See generally Patrick Macklem, "First Nations Self-Government and the Borders of the Canadian Legal Imagination" (1991) 36 *McGill L.J.* 382–456; Michael Asch and Patrick Macklem, "Aboriginal Rights and Canadian Sovereignty: An Essay on *R. v. Sparrow*" (1991) 29 *Alta. L. Rev.* 498–517; Brian Slattery, "Aboriginal Sovereignty and Imperial Claims" (1991) 29 *Osgoode Hall L.J.* 681–703.

7. See *Delgamuukw v. The Queen* (1991) 79 D.L.R. (4th) 185, esp. 282–85.

8. See Mei Lin Ng, "Sovereignty and the Rupert's Land Charter," unpublished research paper, 1991.

9. On French claims, see Brian Slattery, "French Claims in North America 1500–59," *Canadian Historial Review* 59 (1978): 139–69; W. J. Eccles, "Sovereignty-Association, 1500–1783," *Canadian Historical Review* 65 (1984): 475–510; Cornelius J. Jaenen, "French Sovereignty and Native Nationhood during the French Régime," in J. R. Miller, ed., *Sweet Promises: A Reader on Indian-White Relations in Canada* (Toronto: University of Toronto Press, 1991), pp. 19–42.

10. The charter is reproduced in E. E. Rich, ed., *Minutes of the Hudson's Bay Company, 1671–1674* (Toronto: The Champlain Society, 1942), pp. 131–48. The grant contained certain exceptions which are not relevant to the present discussion.

11. See Kent McNeil, *Native Rights and the Boundaries of Rupert's Land and the North-Western Territory* (Saskatoon: University of Saskatchewan Native Law Centre, 1982), pp. 13–19.

12. *Ibid.*, pp. 17, 45–47. See also Nicholson, *Boundaries of the Canadian Confederation*, pp. 104–6.

13. *House of Commons Debates*, 1911–12, Vol. IV, 6159–75. See also Executive Council of Quebec, Committee Report, "Respecting the Settlement of the Northern and the North-Easterly Boundary of the Province of Quebec," 21 Nov. 1894, in Canada, *Sessional Papers*, 1911, Vol. XLV, No. 65, pp. 2–3. Compare A. M. Burgess, Deputy Minister of the Interior, to T. Mayne Daly, Minister of the Interior, Canada, 29 Jan. 1896: *ibid.*, pp. 4–5.

14. For further discussion, see Dorion *et al.*, *Rapport de la Commission d'étude* Vol. 1, pp. 102–8; Nicholson, *Boundaries of the Canadian Confederation*, pp. 104–7.

15. Otherwise, it would have to be argued that the 1898 Acts in fact *reduced* the size of the province, which would have been totally unacceptable to Québec, and to my knowledge has never been contended. Instead, Québec's principal argument in favour of the 1912 extension was geographic: see Patenaude, "L'extension territoriale du code civil," pp. 70–71.
16. See generally Brun, *Le territoire du Québec* pp. 9–31; Nicholson, *Boundaries of the Canadian Confederation*, pp. 16–30, 100–4.
17. See R. Cole Harris, ed., *Historical Atlas of Canada* Vol. 1 (Toronto: University of Toronto Press, 1987), Plate 36.
18. R.S.C. 1985, App. II, No. 1.
19. 14 Geo. III, c.83 (U.K.), preamble.
20. Authority to alter the external boundaries of British colonies by order in council or letters patent was conferred on the Imperial Crown by the *Colonial Boundaries Act, 1895*, 58 & 59 Vict., c.34 (U.K.). In the case of "self-governing colonies," including Canada (see Schedule to the Act), this could be done only with the consent of the colony concerned. Since the Imperial Parliament provided this mechanism for altering colonial boundaries, colonial legislatures could not accomplish the task on their own. But quite apart from this Act, extending external boundaries would involve foreign affairs, which self-governing British colonies did not control prior to the end of World War I and the Imperial Conferences of 1923 and 1926: see Arthur Berriedale Keith, *The Constitutional Law of the British Dominions* (London: Macmillan, 1933), pp. 7–13, 45–57, 67–78; Robert B. Stewart, *Treaty Relations of the British Commonwealth of Nations* (New York: Macmillan, 1939), esp. pp. 133–35, 159–78, 367–68; Maurice Ollivier, ed., *The Colonial and Imperial Conferences from 1887 to 1937* (Ottawa: Queen's Printer, 1954), Vol. 3, esp. pp. 150–57. For that reason, the British Government treated Queensland's purported annexation of part of New Guinea in 1883 as "null in point of law": Prime Minister Gladstone to the House of Commons, *Hansard's Parliamentary Debates*, 3rd series, 1883, Vol. 281, p. 55. See discussion in Donald Craigie Gordon, *The Australian Frontier in New Guinea 1870–1885* (New York: AMS Press, 1968), pp. 151–73. This is consistent with the general rule that sovereignty cannot be thrust upon the Crown without its consent: see authorities in Kent McNeil, *Common Law Aboriginal Title* (Oxford: Clarendon Press, 1989), p. 116 n. 34.
21. Rupert's Land and North-Western Territory Order, 23 June 1870, in R.S.C. 1985, App.II, No.9.
22. See Patenaude, "L'extension territoriale," pp. 1, 71; Brun, *Le territoire du Québec* pp. 19–20.

23. The unreported decision was embodied in an Imperial order in council made on August 11, 1884, printed in *The Proceedings before the ... Privy Council ... Respecting the Westerly Boundary of Ontario* (Toronto: Warwick & Sons, 1889), pp. 416–18: see McNeil, *Native Rights*, pp. 26–33.
24. See McNeil, *Native Rights*, pp. 20–6.
25. 14 Geo. III, c.83 (U.K.), s.1.
26. *Proceedings before the ... Privy Council*, p. 362.
27. See McNeil, *Native Rights*, pp. 28–32.
28. See Geoffrey S. Lester, "The Territorial Rights of the Inuit of the Canadian Northwest Territories: A Legal Argument" (D. Jur. thesis, Osgoode Hall Law School, York University, 1981), pp. 1309–73. The Privy Council accordingly favoured a "dominative code," requiring effective occupation, over a "pre-emptive code" of territorial acquisition: on the distinction between these, see John T. Juricek, "English Territorial Claims in North America under Elizabeth and the Early Stuarts," *Terrae Incognitae 7* (1976): 7–22.
29. See generally J. E. Chamberlin, *The Harrowing of Eden: White Attitudes Toward North American Natives* (Toronto: Fitzhenry & Whiteside, 1975); Robert F. Berkhofer, Jr., *The White Man's Indian: Images of the American Indian from Columbus to the Present* (New York: Alfred A. Knopf, 1978). Ample evidence of these attitudes in Canada can be found in the parliamentary debates of the period: e.g., see *House of Commons Debates*, 1883, Vol. XIV, 1101–8; 1884, Vol. XVI, 1397–1404. See also the judgment of Boyd C. in *R. v. St. Catharines Milling and Lumber Company* (1885) 10 O.R. 196, esp. 206, 210–11, 227–9.
30. See *Proceedings before the ... Privy Council*, esp. pp. 53–63, where both counsel and Privy Council members discounted the possession of "savages" or "wild Indians."
31. *R. v. Syliboy* [1929] 1 D.L.R. 307, at 313, quoted [1985] 2 S.C.R. 387, at 399.
32. [1985] 2 S.C.R. 387, at 399.
33. [1990] 1 S.C.R. 1025.
34. *Ibid.*, 1052–53. See also Slattery, "Aboriginal Sovereignty and Imperial Claims."
35. This conclusion reflects a change in my own thinking since 1982 when I wrote the monograph on the boundaries of Rupert's Land, (see *Native Rights*, n. 11). At that time, I thought that Rupert's Land could be defined by subtracting the territory occupied and controlled by France prior to 1763 from the Hudson watershed. In light of *Simon* and *Sioui*, and my own reassessment of the colonial attitude implicit in my earlier view, I now realize

that territories occupied and controlled by aboriginal nations must be subtracted as well.
36. 8 Wheat. 543 (1823), at 580.
37. See McNeil, *Common Law Aboriginal Title*, pp. 236–37.
38. 6 Pet. 515 (1832), at 544–45.
39. *Ibid.*
40. *Ibid.*, p. 546. Note that *Worcester* v. *Georgia* was relied on by Monk J. in *Connolly* v. *Woolrich* (1867) 17 R.J.R.Q. 75, at 84–87, to conclude that "the Indian political and territorial right, laws, and usages remained in full force both at Athabaska and in the Hudson Bay region, previous to the Charter of 1670, and even after that date."
41. January 24, 1899, reproduced in Stephen Allan Scott, "The Prerogative of the Crown in External Affairs and Constituent Authority in a Commonwealth Monarchy" (D. Phil. thesis, Oxford University, 1968), App. I.
42. 53 & 54 Vict., c.37 (U.K.).
43. *Staples* v. *R.*, *supra* n. 41, p. 41. Although the Hudson's Bay and British South Africa charters were separated by over 200 years, and contained very different terms, the general principle that the Crown cannot acquire sovereignty by grant over a territory where it has no control is applicable to both. On the uncertainty of the British Colonial Office regarding this matter in the 1880s, see Claire Palley, *The Constitutional History and Law of Southern Rhodesia 1888–1965* (Oxford: Clarendon Press, 1966), pp. 18–21.
44. *Staples* v. *R.*, *supra* n. 41, p. 45. The other members of the Privy Council evidently agreed with the Lord Chancellor, as they decided that Matabeleland was a foreign state: *ibid.*, pp. 47–49.
45. The assumption has, nonetheless, been relied on in some cases: e.g., see *Re Labrador Boundary* [1927] 2 D.L.R. 401, at 403, 416–17; *Re Eskimos* [1939] 2 D.L.R. 417, esp. 418–22; *Baker Lake* v. *Minister of Indian Affairs* [1980] 1 F.C. 518, at 532–33; *La Société de Développement de la Baie James* v. *Kanatewat* [1975] Que. C.A. 166, at 170, 172. However, these decisions cannot be regarded as authoritative in this respect, as they were made *per incuriam*, without analysis of the issues and without reference to the *Ontario Boundaries* and *Staples* cases.
46. I am in agreement here with Lester, "Territorial Rights of the Inuit," pp. 1364–73, where it is also suggested that the Charter may have been void for uncertainty.
47. This conclusion is not inconsistent with judicial decisions holding that an unambiguous assertion of sovereignty by the Crown cannot be questioned by the courts: e.g., see *The Fagernes* [1927] P. 311, esp. 324; *R.* v. *Kent Justices* [1967] 1 All E.R. 560, esp. 564;

Post Office v. Estuary Radio [1967] 3 All E.R. 663, at 680; Adams v. Adams [1970] 3 All E.R. 572, at 583, 585. Those cases are all distinguishable, as none of them involved acquisition of sovereignty by the Crown over territory occupied by aboriginal nations where the Crown exercised no jurisdiction: see Ng, "Sovereignty and the Rupert's Land Charter." Moreover, even if Charles II intended to assert sovereignty over the whole of the Hudson watershed when he issued the 1670 charter, that claim could hardly be effective in regions which the Company still did not control 200 years later: see McNeil, Native Rights, pp. 30–32.

48. On aboriginal occupation prior to 1670, see Gros-Louis v. La Société de Développement de la Baie James [1974] Que. P.R. 38, at 45–47, 59–60; Jean Malaurie and Jacques Rousseau, eds., Le Nouveau-Québec: Contribution à l'étude de l'occupation humaine (Paris: Mouton, 1964), esp. William E. Taylor, "The Prehistory of the Quebec-Labrador Peninsula," pp. 181–210, and E. S. Rogers, "The Eskimo and Indian in the Quebec-Labrador Peninsula," pp. 211–49, at 214–19; J. V. Wright, Quebec Prehistory (Toronto: Van Nostrand Reinhold, 1979), pp. 77–85, 103–12; Daniel Francis and Toby Morantz, Partners in Furs: A History of the Fur Trade in Eastern James Bay 1600–1870 (Montréal: McGill–Queen's University Press, 1983), pp. 13–15; Harris, Historical Atlas of Canada, Plates 9, 11, 18. The royal charter was of course granted primarily so that furs could be obtained from the aboriginal nations living around Hudson Bay, with whom the Company's backers had already traded in 1668–69: see McNeil, Native Rights, pp. 6–7; Peter C. Newman, Company of Adventurers (Markham, Ont.: Penguin Books, 1986), Vol. 1, pp. 108–10. On the sufficiency of the territorial occupation by the aboriginal nations, analogous common law principles relating to land reveal that occupation is a relative matter, depending not only on the nature and location of the land involved, but also on the conditions of life, traditions and ideas of the people living there: see Lord Advocate v. Lord Lovat (1880) 5 App. Cas. 273, at 288; Kirby v. Cowderoy [1912] A.C. 599, at 603; Cadija Umma v. S. Don Manis Appu [1939] A.C. 136, at 141–42. In Mitchel v. United States, 9 Pet. 711 (1835), at 746, Baldwin J., delivering the opinion of the United States Supreme Court, said that Indian possession "was considered with reference to their habits and modes of life; their hunting-grounds were as much in their actual possession as the cleared fields of the whites." Moreover, in the Gros-Louis case, at 76–93, Malouf J. decided that the Cree and Inuit east of Hudson Bay have been in possession from time immemorial of the lands on which they hunt, trap and fish.

49. See K. G. Davies, ed., *Northern Quebec and Labrador Journals and Correspondence 1819–35* (London: Hudson's Bay Record Society, 1963); Alan Cooke, "The Exploration of New Quebec," in Malaurie and Rousseau, *Le Nouveau-Québec*, pp. 137–79, at 139–51; Francis and Morantz, *Partners in Furs*, esp. pp. 101–20; Harris, *Historical Atlas of Canada*, Plates 58, 62.
50. See Francis and Morantz, *Partners in Furs*, esp. pp. 77, 112–13, 117–18, 140–41, 158–60, 170; Diamond Jenness, *Eskimo Administration: II. Canada* (Montréal: Arctic Institute of North America, 1964), pp. 7–17; William Ashley Anderson, *Angel of Hudson Bay: The True Story of Maud Watt* (Toronto: Clark, Irwin & Company, 1961), esp. pp. 61–62.
51. *Report of the Select Committee on the Hudson's Bay Company* (London: House of Commons, 1857), Minutes of Evidence, pp. 91–92.
52. Deed of Surrender, 19 Nov. 1869, Schedule C to Rupert's Land and North-Western Territory Order, 1870, R.S.C. 1985, App. II, No.9.
53. *Ibid.* On the historical background and the provisions of the transfer, see Kent McNeil, *Native Claims in Rupert's Land and the North-Western Territory: Canada's Constitutional Obligations* (Saskatoon: University of Saskatchewan Native Law Centre, 1982). The location and supposed extent of the North-Western Territory are discussed in McNeil, *Native Rights*, esp. pp. 4–6, 43–45.
54. The *Rupert's Land Act, 1868,* 31–32 Vict., c.105 (U.K.), which had authorized the surrender and transfer of that territory, in s.2 defined Rupert's Land for the purposes of the Act as including "the whole of the Lands and Territories held or claimed to be held by the said Governor and Company." In the *Ontario Boundaries* case, the Privy Council did not regard that definition as bringing the whole of the Hudson watershed within Rupert's Land, despite the Company's claims to that effect. The words "claimed to be held" apparently related to the unresolved issue of the charter's validity, rather than to the geographic extent of Rupert's Land: see McNeil, *Native Rights*, 48–49.
55. However, within territory the Company did control, aboriginal nations would still have land claims based on aboriginal title, which Canada was constitutionally obliged to settle by the terms of the 1870 Order: see McNeil, *Native Claims*. When Canada extended Québec's boundaries in 1912, an equivalent obligation was imposed on the province: S.C. 1912 (2 Geo. V), c.45, s.2. This constitutional obligation was in fact ignored by Québec when it undertook the James Bay hydro-electric project, obliging the Cree and Inuit to go to court to enforce their rights: see *Gros-Louis v. La Société de Développement de la Baie James* [1974] Que. P.R. 38,

esp. 58–59, reversed *La Société de Développement de la Baie James* v. *Kanatewat* [1975] Que. C.A. 166; Boyce Richardson, *Strangers Devour the Land* (Toronto: Macmillan, 1975); *Sparrow* v. *The Queen* [1990] 1 S.C.R. 1075, at 1103–4.

56. Aboriginal occupation and control would, of course, effectively limit the size of Rupert's Land prior to 1870 as well. It will be remembered that the Québec Act of 1774 extended the boundaries of Québec on the north to the territory granted to the Hudson's Bay Company: see p. 118. This raises the possibility that territory excluded from Rupert's Land by aboriginal occupation and control in 1774 would have become part of Québec at that time. However, this could only have happened if that territory was under British sovereignty in 1774, as s.1 of the Act annexed to Québec "all the Territories, Islands, and Countries in *North America*, belonging to the Crown of Great Britain," lying within the defined boundaries. There was clearly no intention to extend the Crown's sovereignty over *new* territory, but only to include within Québec the "very large Extent of Country, within which there were several Colonies or Settlements of the Subjects of France, ... [which by the Royal Proclamation of 1763 had been] left, without any Provision being made for the Administration of Civil Government therein" (14 Geo.III, c.83 (U.K.), preamble). If the sovereignty of the aboriginal nations is to be taken seriously, as I have argued it must be, then territory excluded from Rupert's Land by aboriginal occupation and control would not have "belong[ed] to the Crown" in 1774, and therefore would not have been included in Québec at that time.

57. Note that, by the Adjacent Territories Order, 1880, R.S.C. 1985, App. II, No. 14, the British Crown annexed to Canada "all British Territories and Possessions in North America, not already included within the Dominion of Canada, and all Islands adjacent to any such Territories or Possessions, ... (with the exception of the Colony of Newfoundland and its dependencies)." This order was apparently made because doubts had been raised over Canada's claim to the Arctic Islands: see Nicholson, *Boundaries of the Canadian Confederation*, pp. 57–60; W. F. King, *Report upon the Title of Canada to the Islands North of the Mainland of Canada* (Ottawa: Government Printing Bureau, 1905). However, given the absence of any definition of the territories being transferred, the effect of the order remains uncertain: see McNeil, *Native Rights*, pp. 44–45. Clearly it could not have transferred territory which was not British at the time, notwithstanding the inclusion of adjacent islands. More likely, the Crown regarded those islands as appendant to its mainland possessions. In any case,

territories which were occupied and controlled by aboriginal nations, east of Hudson Bay and elsewhere, would not have been Crown possessions, and so could not have been included in the transfer.

58. See *supra* n. 20. The Crown's power to annex new territory by act of state is part of the royal prerogative over foreign affairs: see *Halsbury's Laws of England*, 4th ed. (London: Butterworths, 1973–91), Vol. XVIII, par. 1406, 1413; Kenneth Roberts-Wray, *Commonwealth and Colonial Law* (New York: Frederick A. Praeger, 1966), p. 116; McNeil, *Common Law Aboriginal Title*, pp. 111, 131, 162.

59. 52 & 53 Vict., c.28 (U.K.): see McNeil, *Native Rights*, pp. 33–34.

60. See Nicholson, *Boundaries of the Canadian Confederation*, p. 105. The fact that the boundary did intersect the bay had to be established by a survey, conducted by William Ogilvie in 1890: see Burgess to Daly, *supra* n. 13, p. 4.

61. As quoted in Nicholson, *Boundaries of the Canadian Confederation*. See also Burgess to Daly, *supra* n. 13, p. 4.

62. Nicholson, *Boundaries of the Canadian Confederation*, pp. 105–6. However, even after these expeditions, Burgess reported that "it would take many years of exploration and the expenditure of a good deal of money to settle what are the true sources of the East Main and Hamilton Rivers respectively": Burgess to Daly, *supra* n. 13, p. 5.

63. On Canadian expeditions into these regions from 1870 to 1914, see Cooke, *Exploration of New Quebec*, 152–57; Dorion *et al.*, *Rapport de la Commission d'étude*, Vol. 1, pp. 115–24. See also J. W. Anderson, *Fur Trader's Story* (Toronto: Ryerson Press, 1961), p. 56; Rolf Knight, *Ecological Factors in Changing Economy and Social Organization among the Rupert House Cree* (Ottawa: Queen's Printer, 1967), p. 19; Daniel Ashini, "David confronts Goliath: the Innu of Ungava versus the NATO Alliance," in Boyce Richardson, ed., *Drumbeat: Anger and Renewal in Indian Country* (Toronto: Summerhill Press, 1989), pp. 45–70, esp. 51–56. On explorations by private adventurers and scientists from the 1880s to 1950, see Cooke, pp. 158–69.

64. Jenness, *Eskimo Administration*, p. 17.

65. *Ibid.*, pp. 18–28.

66. *Ibid.*,; Anderson, *Fur Trader's Story*, esp. p. 203; Corporation des enseignants du Québec, "Le Nouveau-Québec, ou comment des colonisés traitent leur colonie ... ," Mémoire adressé au ministre de l'Éducation et à l'Assemblée nationale du Québec, janvier 1973, pp. 7–11.

67. See *supra* n. 20.

266 Negotiating with a Sovereign Québec

68. See generally Jenness, *Eskimo Administration;* Knight, *Ecological Factors,* esp. pp. 29–37; Québec, *Le Nord du Québec: profil régional* (Québec: Gouvernement du Québec, 1983), esp. pp. 9–10, 20, 45.
69. With respect to the 1898 Acts, this conclusion is of course subject to our earlier discussion regarding the boundary between New France and the Hudson's Bay Company territory: see p. 116. The validity of French claims to sovereignty over the aboriginal nations of the region would also have to be considered in this context: see *supra* n. 9. Moreover, as a matter of fact the government of Québec made little effort until the 1960s to exercise jurisdiction in the territories purportedly included within its boundaries by the 1898 and 1912 Acts: see Jenness, *Eskimo Administration;* Corporation des enseignants du Québec, *Le Nouveau-Québec,* pp. 11–14; Québec, *Le Nord du Québec,* esp. p. 20. In the 1930s, however, Québec did support James and Maud Watt, the Hudson's Bay Company factor at Rupert House and his wife, in their remarkably successful efforts to create beaver preserves for the Cree trappers of James Bay: see Anderson, *Angel of Hudson Bay,* pp. 163–92; Knight, *Ecological Factors,* pp. 26–31. Maud Watt lobbied Louis A. Richard, Deputy Minister of Colonisation, Game and Fisheries for the province (the name of this ministry is worth noting) to accomplish this, pointing out to him that the Québec government had no presence whatever in the region at the time (1932), and that she was "the only French-speaking person in the Rupert House territory!" (Quoted in Anderson, p. 176.) Québec responded by leasing 7,200 square miles to her for the creation of a beaver preserve, on the evident assumption that Québec owned the land. See also Robert Rumilly, *Histoire de la Province de Québec,* Vol. 29, *Vers l'age d'or* (Montréal: Fides, 1955), p. 42, on Québec's complete absence in 1927 from the territory "so triumphantly annexed" to it in 1912.
70. Nor would it have been corrected by the *Statute of Westminster, 1931,* 22 Geo. V., c.4 (U.K.). In *Croft* v. *Dunphy* [1933] A.C. 156, it was argued that s.3 of that statute, giving the Dominion Parliaments power to make extra-territorial laws, had retroactive effect, but the Privy Council found it unnecessary to decide the question. To deal with this uncertainty, Canada enacted the *Extra-territorial Act, 1933,* S.C. 1932–33 (23–4 Geo. V), c. 39, which provided in s.2 that "[e]very Act of the Parliament of Canada now in force enacted prior to the eleventh day of December, 1931, which in terms or by necessary or reasonable implication was intended, as to the whole or any part thereof, to have extra-territorial operation, shall be construed as if at the date of its enactment the Parliament of Canada then had full power to

make laws having extra-territorial operation as provided by the Statute of Westminster, 1931." However, this Act cannot have made the 1898 and 1912 Acts effective to include territory in Québec which was not part of Canada at the time, for two reasons: (1) the *Extra-territorial Act* did not give Canada retroactive capacity over foreign affairs generally, including the power to annex territory, which Canada would have needed to make the 1898 and 1912 Acts effective (see n. 20, *supra*); and (2) the 1898 and 1912 Acts were not "intended," as s.2 of the *Extra-territorial Act* says, to have extra-territorial operation, as they were enacted on the mistaken belief that all of the territory which they purported to include in Québec was already part of Canada. Moreover, annexation by statute of territories Canada did not effectively control in 1898 and 1912 would probably have been in violation of international law, so an interpretation of the *Extraterritorial Act* which avoids that effect is to be preferred: see P. St. J. Langan, *Maxwell on the Interpretation of Statutes*, 12th ed. (London: Sweet & Maxwell, 1969), pp. 183–86, and S. G. G. Edgar, *Craies on Statute Law*, 7th ed. (London: Sweet & Maxwell, 1971), pp. 69, 469, on the rule that statutes are to be interpreted if possible in a manner consistent with international law.

71. *Reference re Manitoba Language Rights* [1985] 1 S.C.R. 721.
72. E.g., see Canada, Justice Information, "Notes for an Address by the Honourable Kim Campbell to the Standing Committee on Aboriginal Affairs regarding Oka," Jan. 31, 1991, esp. pp. 1–3.
73. See Noel Lyon, *Aboriginal Peoples and Constitutional Reform in the 1990s* (North York, Ont.: York University Centre for Public Law and Public Policy, 1991), esp. pp. 13–16; "Cree consent necessary for separation, study says," *The Globe and Mail*, Feb. 24, 1992, p. A6; Rhéal Séguin, "Crees demand role in charter changes," *ibid.*, Feb. 26, 1992, p. A8.
74. See discussion by Mary Ellen Turpel, "Does the Road to Québec Sovereignty Run through Aboriginal Territory?" in this book.

Chapter 9
1. For example, if Québec's currency appeared to be on the verge of falling below the bottom end of the target range for its value relative to the Canadian dollar, Québec's central bank could either push up interest rates relative to those in Canada or intervene directly in the foreign exchange market by selling Canadian dollars and buying Québec's currency. Either action might be sufficient to prop up the value of Québec's currency *vis-à-vis* the Canadian dollar.

2. If the central banks of Canada and Québec were to share the commitment to keep the exchange rate between their currencies within a certain range, they would have to co-ordinate their interest-rate policies so as to ensure that the interest-rate differential was adequate to support the exchange rate. Or the two banks would have to co-ordinate their intervention in the foreign exchange market.

3. Carlos Costa has pointed out: "The efficiency of floating exchange rates in making adjustments in response to specific disturbances depends upon their effectiveness in promoting competitiveness or switching expenditures. This effectiveness is inversely related to the openness of the national economy to integration into a wider area ... We must also consider the adverse effects of exchange rate variations on interest rates' risk premiums in a fully integrated financial market. It will increase real interest rates which will hurt investment and reduce room for manoeuvre in budget policy." See C. Costa, "EMU: The Benefits Outweigh the Costs," *European Affairs* no. 3 (1990): 24, 25.

4. See, for example, G. Tootell, "Central Bank Flexibility and the Drawbacks to Currency Unification," *New England Economic Review* (May/June 1990); R. A. Mundell, "A Theory of Optimum Currency Areas," *American Economic Review* (September 1961); R. I. McKinnon, "Optimum Currency Areas," *American Economic Review* (September 1963).

5. Examples of alternative adjustment mechanisms include: factor mobility between the regions; price flexibility other than through real-exchange-rate adjustments; and regional development or adjustment funds.

6. *Report of the Delors Committee* (Brussels: European Council, April 1989).

7. See, for example, H. D. Smeets, "Interest Rate Linkages Within the EMS," Discussion Paper, University of Bayreuth (1989).

8. In this example, the Québec customer is committed to paying a fixed price in Canadian dollars at a specified future date. Unfortunately, the price at that date in terms of the Québec currency is unknown. If the Québec currency depreciates in value relative to the Canadian dollar between the delivery date and the payment date, the Québec customer will face a higher price in the Québec currency. On the other hand, an appreciation will result in a lower price. The risk facing the Québec customer stems from the uncertainty regarding the Québec currency cost of the transaction.

9. Costa, "EMU," pp. 23, 24.

10. M. van Meerhaeghe, "Capital Mobility and Currency Policy in the EC," *European Affairs* no. 3 (1988): 139.

Chapter 10

1. The 395,000 figure for potential employment gains was arrived at as follows: GNP per worker in Canada in the third quarter of 1991 was $55,600. Dividing the $22 billion current account deficit in 1990 by this figure yields the potential employment gains. The monthly average number of unemployed in Canada in the third quarter of 1991 was 1.4 million. The potential employment gains represent approximately 28 percent of the number of unemployed and so if these jobs materialized to absorb an equal number of the unemployed, the unemployment rate would have been 28 percent lower, or approximately 7.3 percent in the third quarter of 1991.
2. M. Porter, *Canada at the Crossroads: The Reality of a New Competitive Environment* (Ottawa: BCNI, 1990), p. 4.
3. Department of Finance, *Budget Papers* (February 1992), pp. 22, 25.
4. Section 301 of the U.S. 1974 Trade Act (amended in 1988) lies outside of the GATT. Thus, the United States is able to initiate investigations under section 301 against policies of other governments, policies that do not violate any of the provisions of the GATT.
5. During the present Uruguay Round of the GATT, there has been much discussion of negotiating a green-, yellow- and red-light classification of subsidies. Green-light subsidies would be free from countervail actions. Yellow-light subsidies would be subject to countervail investigations. Red-light subsidies would be automatically subject to countervail. The group of subsidies proposed by Dunkel were to be the only green-light subsidies in the GATT.
6. R. J. Krommenacker, "The Impact of Information Technology on Trade Interdependence," *Journal of World Trade Law* 20 (1986): 394.
7. A free trade area involves only the elimination of tariffs on all goods and services that are traded among the members of the area. A customs union extends beyond a free trade area to include a common set of tariffs, among all the members of the union, on imports from other countries. A common market is a customs union that allows for the free movement of services, labour and capital in addition to goods among the members of the market.
8. See chapters 14, 16 and 17 in the FTA.
9. Listed in article 1408 of the FTA.

10. "National treatment" is defined, in the case of services, as treatment no less favourable than that accorded in like circumstances to a party's own service providers; and "no less favourable" means no less favourable than the most favourable treatment a party accords to any domestic provider of like services.

11. Article 57 (1) of the Treaty of Rome enables the Council of the European Community, on a proposal of the European Commission, to issue directives for the mutual recognition of diplomas, certificates or other national qualifications. A number of directives have been adopted under the authority of this article to make it easier for individuals to practise their professions, as self-employed persons, throughout the EC. The directives are binding on the member states of the EC insofar as the results to be attained are concerned, but they allow the member states to decide the ways and means to obtain the results.

12. The right of establishment is not a formal GATT principle at the present time, but it is included in the Treaty of Rome and the free trade agreement between Canada and the United States. According to the Treaty of Rome, the right of establishment implies a right to set up a business base within any member state and to be treated without discrimination according to the rules of the host country.

13. Transparency requires that all judicial decisions and administrative rulings, and all other measures which pertain to or affect trade in services or goods, be made public promptly.

Chapter 11

1. There have already been a number of quite useful attempts to assess the question of the division of assets and liabilities. Among those that have been published, the following will be considered briefly: the background report of the Bélanger-Campeau commission, the report of the C. D. Howe commission and the report of the John Deutsch Centre at Queen's University. Each of these documents considers the issue in careful detail, adopts a particular methodology and proposes solutions (all three reports propose more than one solution). On the whole, although they differ in the solution proposed, the methodology is sufficiently close that the basis of a rational negotiation can be foreseen.

2. *Rapport de la Commission sur l'avenir politique et constitutionnel du Québec* (Québec: Gouvernement du Québec, 1991).

3. *Ibid.*, p. 476 Table 28.

4. *Ibid.*, pp. 422–16.

5. R. Boadway, T. Courchene, and D. Purvis, *Economic Dimensions of Constitutional Change*, Vols. 1 and 2 (Kingston: John Deutsch Institute for the Study of Economic Policy, Queen's University, 1991); P. Boothe *et al.*, *Closing the Books: Dividing Federal Assets and Debt if Canada Breaks Up* (Toronto: C. D. Howe Institute, 1991).

6. Contrary to the conventional wisdom, the anglophone minority consists of a community of between 500,000 and 750,000 people located principally but not exclusively in the western sectors of Montréal and its suburbs. In addition there are a substantial number of anglophones in the Eastern Townships, the Gaspé Peninsula and western Québec close to the Ottawa river. If one adds to this community the allophone Canadians of Québec who regard themselves as Canadians and federalists and not just Québécois, the total probably approaches one million people.

    In other words, the federalist anglophone and allophone population of Québec is larger than the population of any of the Atlantic provinces and as large as that of two of the Western provinces, Saskatchewan and Manitoba. In addition, of course, there is the federalist population of French Québec, principally but not exclusively in Montréal, who, depending on the circumstances, number perhaps as much as 30 to 35 percent of the francophone population of the province. Of these, a small but significant minority would probably prefer to remain in Canada if Québec were to separate, provided this did not entail leaving the present boundaries of Québec.

7. H. Chorney, "A Regional Approach to Monetary and Fiscal Policy," in *The Constitutional Future of the Atlantic and Prairie Regions, Conference Proceedings* (Regina, Sask.: Canadian Plains Research Centre and Gorsebrook Research Institute, 1992).

8. Daniel Desjardins and Claude Gendron, "Legal Issues Concerning the Division of Assets of Debt in State Succession," in *Closing the Books*, edited by Paul Boothe *et al.* (Toronto: C. D. Howe Institute, 1991).

9. *Ibid.*

Chapter 12

1. These data are adjusted Statistics Canada data, as reproduced in Commissioner of Official Languages, *Annual Report, 1990* (Ottawa: Minister of Supply and Services, 1991), p. 312. We have calculated the results for "Canada."

2. As calculated from *ibid.*

3. As calculated from *ibid.* and from Marc Termote, "L'évolution démolinguistique du Québec et du Canada," in Commission sur

l'avenir politique et constitutionnel du Québec, *Éléments d'analyse institutionnelle, juridique et démolinguistique pertinents à la révision du statut politique et constitutionnel du Québec*, Document de travail, numéro 21, 1991, Table 7.

4. Statistics Canada, *Census of Canada, 1986*, No. 94–110.
5. Calculated from Commissioner of Official Languages, *Annual Report*.
6. Statistics Canada, *Census of Canada, 1986*, No. 94–108 and 94–112.
7. Termote, "L'évolution démolinguistique," Table 17.
8. *Ibid.,*, Table 18.
9. As calculated from *ibid.*, Table 21. These calculations do indeed produce identical results for 1966–71 and 1971–76!
10. Calculated from *ibid.*
11. Réjean Lachapelle and Jacques Henripin, *La situation démolinguistique au Canada: Évolution passée et prospective* (Montréal: Institut de recherches politiques, 1980), Table 8.2. To be precise, they produce four percentages (based upon different economic and linguistic conditions) ranging from 2.2 percent to 3.5 percent.
12. Marc Termote and Danielle Gauvreau, *La situation démolinguistique du Québec* (Québec: Conseil de la langue française), as reported in Termote, "L'évolution démolinguistique," p. 266.
13. Mario Fontaine, "L'indépendance ferait fuir 1 anglophone sur 2," *La Presse*, April 27, 1991, p. A1.
14. Termote, "L'évolution démolinguistique," p. 266.
15. Calculated from Termote, "L'évolution démolinguistique," Table 39.
16. *Census of Canada, 1986*, pp. 93–156, Table 8.
17. Calculated from *Census of Canada, 1981*, 92–910, Table 7, 92–911, Table 2, and 95–943, Table 1.
18. Termote, "L'évolution démolinguistique," Tables 5 and 6.
19. Donald J. Savoie, *The Politics of Language* (Kingston: Institute of Intergovernmental Relations, 1991), pp. 10–15.
20. Parti Québécois, *Programme officiel du Parti québécois*, 1978 edition, p. 44. By the same token, the PQ government's 1979 White Paper declared: "Le gouvernement assure à la minorité anglophone du Québec qu'elle continuera à jouir des droits qui lui sont actuellement accordés par la loi." (See Gouvernement du Québec, *La nouvelle entente Québec-Canada* (Québec: Éditeur officiel, 1979), p. 61.
21. Parti Québécois, *Programme du Parti québécois*, 1991 edition (Montréal: Parti québécois, 1991), Préface.

22. "Le PQ s'engage à faire une place aux anglophones," *Le Devoir*, September 23, 1991.

23. José Woerhling, "Les aspects juridiques de la redéfinition du statut politique et constitutionnel du Québec", in Commission sur l'avenir politique et constitutionnel du Québec, *Élements d'analyse institutionnelle, juridique et démolinguistique pertinents à la révision du statut politique et constitutionnel du Québec*, Document de travail, numéro 2, 1991, pp. 71–72.

24. See the discussion in David J. Bercuson and Barry Cooper, *Deconfederation: Canada Without Quebec* (Toronto: Key Porter, 1991), pp. 149–56.

25. Allan Blakeney, unpublished address to Osgoode Hall Law School Convocation, June 14, 1991. Quoted in Patrick Monahan and Lynda Covello, *An Agenda for Constitutional Reform*, Final Report of the York University Constitutional Reform Project (North York: Centre for Public Law and Public Policy, York University, 1992), p. 102. This position was in fact the majority position of the York University Constitutional Reform Project. To be sure, "a number of members" of the project team opposed this recommendation, claiming that instead of raising the issue negotiators should pursue a joint protocol (*ibid.*, p. 103).

26. Ian Ross Robertson, "The Atlantic Provinces and the Territorial Question," in J. L. Granatstein and Kenneth McNaught, eds., *"English Canada" Speaks Out* (Toronto: Doubleday, 1991), p. 165.

27. Robertson, "The Atlantic Provinces," p. 168.

28. *Census of Canada, 1986.*

29. Québec, National Assembly, *Journal de débats*, Commission d'étude des questions afférentes à l'accession du Québec à la souveraineté, pp. 296–97.

30. Article 86: "Le gouvernement peut faire des règlements pour étendre l'application de l'article 73 aux personnes visées par une entente de réciprocité conclue entre le gouvernement du Québec et le gouvernement d'une autre province."

31. José Woerhling, "Les aspects juridiques," p. 63.

32. Québec, National Assembly, Commission d'étude des questions afférentes à l'accession du Québec à la souveraineté, *L'accession à la souveraineté: les droits des minorités*, p. 7.

33. National Assembly, *Journal de débats*, p. 292.

34. Jean-Pierre Charbonneau and Gilbert Paquette, *L'option* (Montréal: Les Éditions de l'homme, 1978), p. 456.

35. *Ibid.*

Chapter 13

1. G. Hardin, "The Tragedy of the Commons," *Science* 162 (1968): 1243–48. The basic premise underlying this concept is that if each person maximizes his or her use of a common good, such as the environment, the result is the destruction of that good to the detriment of all users.

2. W. Ophuls, *Ecology and the Politics of Scarcity* (W.H. Freeman and Company, 1978) p. 226.

3. Government of Canada, *Canada's National Report* (August 1991): 8.

4. As much as is practical, this essay will discuss the general issues raised from the perspective of the province of Ontario, bearing in mind the global nature of most present-day environmental problems.

5. Although the September 1991 constitutional proposals of the federal government and the February 1992 Beaudoin-Dobbie report appear to give some thought to the protection of the environment, they are disappointing. See the author's submission to the Standing Committee on the Environment, co-written with Paul Muldoon of Pollution Probe, *Environment and the Constitution* (Canadian Environmental Law Association, 1991).

6. "Power Play," *Northern Perspectives 19*, no. 3 (Autumn 1991): 2–3, published by the Canadian Arctic Resource Committee.

7. *Ibid.*, pp. 3 and 4.

8. A. Dwyer, "The Trouble at Great Whale" *Equinox* no. 61 (February 1992).

9. *Canada's National Report* (August 1991): 26, 49.

10. At the time of writing, a federal government report was released which confirmed that Canada's fresh water is under stress from coast to coast and its deterioration is a major health concern. "More than 360 chemical contaminants have been detected in the Great Lakes. Studies have found that exposure to a mixture of toxic substances can have a greater effect than the sum of the effects of each substance individually." "Pollutants threaten nation's fresh water," *The Globe and Mail*, April 9, 1992, p. A4.

11. Ontario Waste Management Corporation, *Environmental Assessment, Volume I. The OWMC Undertaking*, November 1988, pp. 4–54; and Ministry of the Environment, Waste Management Branch, *Manifest Information System — Report from All Manifests: Report on Receiver Sites for the Period from 890101 to 891231*, April 18, 1990.

12. The World Commission on Environment and Development, *Our Common Future* (Oxford: Oxford University Press, 1987), p. 27.

13. R. Howse, "Sell Out or Give Away? The Federal Proposals on the Division of Powers." Paper originally presented at the Queen's Institute for Intergovernmental Relations, Rev. 27, November 1991.
14. S. Shrybman, "Poverty and Pollution," (CELA, 1987).
15. The treaties concerning environmental matters to which Canada is a party or a signatory are too numerous to mention. See M. J. Bowman, *Multi-Lateral Treaties — Index and Current Status* (London: Butterworths, 1984) for a comprehensive list, and see also Kindred *et al.*, *International Law*, 4th ed. (Edmond Montgomery Publications Limited, 1987) for legal analysis, pp. 789–872.
16. For the view of the National Assembly see Commission sur l'avenir politique et constitutionnel du Québec, *L'accession à la souveraineté* (Québec: Gouvernement du Quebec, 1991).
17. World Commission on Environment and Development, *Our Common Future*, pp. 312–13; J. A. Gallob, "Birth of the North American Transboundary Plaintiff: Transboundary Pollution and the 1979 Draft Treaty for Equal Access and Remedy," *Harvard Environmental Law Review* 15, no. 1 (1991): 85–148; A. E. Boyle, "Saving the World? Implementation and Enforcement of International Environmental Law Through International Institutions," *Journal of Environmental Law* 3, no. 2 (1991) 229-245; P. H. Sand, "Innovations in International Environmental Governance," *Environment* 32, no. 9 (November 1990); W. W. Wood *et al.*, "Ecopolitics in the Global Greenhouse," *Environment* 31, no. 7 (September 1989).
18. *Declaration of the United Nations Conference on the Human Environment*, June 16, 1972, Principle 1.
19. Boyle, "Saving the World?" p. 230.
20. Boundary Waters Treaty, January 11, 1909, United States–United Kingdom, 36 Stat. 2448, T.S. No. 548.
21. Gallob, "Transboundary Environmental Plaintiff," p. 119.
22. "Pollutants threaten nation's fresh water," *The Globe and Mail*, April 9, 1992, p. A4.
23. Gallob, "Tranboundary Environmental Plaintiff," p. 113.
24. D. A. Westbrook, "Environmental Policy in the European Community: Observations on the European Environment Agency," *Harvard Environmental Law Review* 15 (1991): 257.
25. The environmental amendments to the Treaty of Rome are contained in Title VII, added by the *Single European Act*.
26. H. F. French, "The EC: Environmental Proving Ground," *Worldwatch* (Nov./Dec. 1991): 27. For further discussion of EC legal initiatives and a comparison to Canadian jurisdictional

matters, see A. R. Lucas, "Environmental Law: Lessons From the European Community," *Resources* no. 32 (Fall 1990).

27. W. Ophuls, *Ecology and the Politics of Scarcity*, p. 148.

28. It is entirely possible that the FTA (and/or NAFTA, if it is successfully negotiated and implemented prior to Québec's secession) would have to be renegotiated in the event of Québec's separation. It appears likely that NAFTA will replace the FTA.

29. S. Shrybman, *Selling the Environment Short: An Environmental Assessment of the First Two Years of Free Trade Between Canada and the United States* (CELA: May 1991), citing *In the Matter of Canada's Landing Requirement for Pacific Coast Salmon and Herring* (Canada–United States Trade Commission Panel, October 16, 1989, 2TCT 7162).

30. *Corrosion Proof Fittings* et al. v. *Environmental Protection Agency* (in the United States Court of Appeals for the Fifth Circuit, May 22, 1990).

31. *The Globe and Mail*, October 22, 1991.

32. "U.S. Companies Use FTA to Attack Regional & Environmental Aid," *GATT FLY* (Toronto: September 1989).

33. This phenomenon is probably exacerbated in the current political climate as our governments struggle to counter the popular sentiment that the FTA is responsible for layoffs and relocation of industry south of the border.

34. J. Ferretti (Pollution Probe), Z. Makuch (CELA), and Ken Traynor (Common Frontiers), *Issue Paper: International Trade and the Environment* (CELA: October 1991).

35. Throughout this discussion, the author is purposely not addressing the question of the federal government's fiduciary duty towards aboriginal peoples residing in Québec.

36. Government of Canada, Federal-Provincial Relations Office, *Federal-Provincial Programs and Activities: A Descriptive Inventory 1990–91* (Ottawa: December 1991), Chapter 11.

37. One interesting option for dispute resolution for transboundary pollution is to allow "transboundary plaintiffs" to sue locally where the pollution originates. See "Tranboundary Environmental Plaintiff."

38. CELA and other environmental groups, as well as the Brundtland Commission, advocate strong national standards, which obviously curtail the autonomy of the Canadian provinces. See Barbara Rutherford and Paul Muldoon, *Environment and the Constitution*.

Chapter 14

1. Canada, *National Defence Act*, RSC 184 S.I. Section 236.

2. Douglas Bland, *The Administration of Defence Policy in Canada 1947–1985* (Kingston, Ont.: R. P. Frye, 1985).
3. All figures are approximations drawn from the Defence Estimates (1991) and from Department of National Defence, "Making Sense of Dollars" (1990–91).
4. Douglas Bland, *The Military Committee of the North Atlantic Alliance: A Study of Structure and Strategy* (New York: Praeger, 1990).
5. Christopher Conliffe, "The Permanent Joint Board on Defence: 50 years after Roosevelt's Kingston Declaration" *Canadian Defence Quarterly* 18, no. 1 (Summer 1988), 54–60.

Chapter 15

1. What follows is only the briefest summary of a position which is developed at length in Michael Mandel, *The Charter of Rights and the Legalization of Politics in Canada* (Toronto: Wall and Thompson, 1989).
2. Charters continue to this day to play this same role of reconciling a dangerously expanded suffrage with private power, as for example in South Africa, where the African National Congress, in order to overcome white resistance and gain international legitimacy, had to give in to the demand for an enforceable Bill of Rights with guarantees to the powerful white minority that is *socially* powerful beyond its numerical, one-person-one-vote weight, by virtue of its ownership of 87 percent of the land and 95 percent of the capital in the country, despite constituting less than 15 percent of the population. The ANC had earlier opposed judicial review as an entrenchment of white social and economic power at the very moment the black majority would finally achieve the goal of universal suffrage. See Albie Sachs, "A Bill of Rights for South Africa — Areas of Agreement and Disagreement," *Columbia Human Rights Law Review* 2 (1989): 13. Now an entrenched, judicially administered Bill of Rights plays an important role in Nelson Mandela's attempts to reassure investors that despite the enormous property inequality in South Africa there will be no nationalization, and a state sector no bigger than that in Western Europe. See *The Globe and Mail*, February 3, 1992, p. A3; Albie Sachs, "The Constitutional Position of White South Africans in a Democratic South Africa," *Social Justice* 18 (1991): 1; African National Congress Constitutional Committee, "A Bill of Rights for a Democratic South Africa — Working Draft for Constitution," *Social Justice* 18 (1991): 49.
3. Other important examples of the conservatism of legal politics in practice include the boost given by the Charter to the free trade agreement by the 1984 Alberta court decision — which is

still binding — holding that any limits on campaign spending were a denial of "freedom of expression" (*National Citizens' Coalition* v. *Attorney General*, 1984); this allowed a business spending spree in support of free trade such as had never been seen in Canadian electoral history. The commercialization of Sundays received an assist from the Supreme Court of Canada (*R.* v. *Big M Drug Mart*, 1985), which has also decided that business advertising is a fundamental human right (*Ford* v. *Quebec*, 1988), but the right to strike is not (*Public Service Alliance of Canada et al.* v. *The Queen in Right of Canada et al.*, 1987).

4. We also find that procedural guarantees are of much greater benefit to organized and corporate crime than to the mass of powerless offenders. For a more detailed explication of these questions, see Mandel, *The Charter of Rights*, pp. 128 ff.

5. *Morgentaler, Smoling and Scott* v. *The Queen* (1988), 37 C.C.C. (3d) 449; *R.* v. *Seaboyer; R.* v. *Gayme* (1991), 66 C.C.C. (3d) 321.

6. Michel Foucault, *Discipline and Punish: The Birth of the Prison*, trans. Alan Sheridan (New York: Pantheon Books, 1977), p. 26.

7. Government of Canada, *Shaping Canada's Future Together: Proposals* (Ottawa: Minister of Supply and Services Canada, 1991).

8. Other less far reaching, but consistently pro-business, features of the proposals include amendments to the Charter which would strengthen its deregulatory thrust: the entrenchment of property rights and an enhanced majority provision for the use of the "notwithstanding" clause. And of course, there is the businessman's dream of a zero-inflation mandate for the Bank of Canada.

9. The Tories have offered a "general justiciable right to self-government" but have provided for it to be "delayed-action" in nature, contemplating ten years of negotiations before any justiciability would take effect. Native representatives have counter-proposed an immediately justiciable "inherent" right to self-government. As will immediately be seen, this basically amounts to wrangling about how soon a blank cheque will be handed over to the courts, i.e., full admission to the world of legalized politics. In a revealing subplot, divisions have broken out between the male-dominated native leadership and native women's groups over whether the new right to self-government or the old Charter guarantees of sexual equality would be supreme. Unfortunately, the differences between all of these positions are only in their empty symbols, because each proposal would leave the courts equally free to determine the outcome according to their view of prevailing political power realities.

10. For "repressive," see Michael Mandel, "The Great Repression: Criminal Punishment in the Nineteen-Eighties," in Les Samuelson and Bernard Schissel, eds., *Criminal Justice: Sentencing Issues and Reforms* (Toronto: Garamond Press, 1991). It is unequal both in terms of the concentration of property in fewer hands and the increase in poverty, itself a measure of inequality. In 1986, the richest twenty-five non-financial enterprises in Canada controlled 35 percent of the total enterprise assets, up from 29 percent in 1975; the top 1 percent of corporations controlled 80 percent of all corporate assets; the top .01 percent owned 44.9 percent. See *Annual Report of the Minister of Supply and Services Canada under the Corporations and Labour Unions Returns Act, Part I — Corporations 1986* (Ottawa: 1988). In the United States, asset concentration was higher in 1983 than at any time since 1929. See L. J. Davis, "The Next Panic: Fear and Trembling on Wall Street," *Harper's Magazine* 274, p. 36. Between 1977 and 1989, the wealthiest 1 percent of American families reaped 60 percent of the growth in after-tax income and the bottom 80 percent received only 6 percent, with the bottom 40 percent posting actual declines (*The Globe and Mail*, March 6, 1992, p. B5). Ontario welfare rolls are double what they were at the beginning of the decade (*The Toronto Star*, November 14, 1991, p. A1). Food banks are frequented by hundreds of thousands in Toronto alone (*The Toronto Star*, January 8, 1992, p. B3). One out of every six or seven children live below the poverty line (*The Globe and Mail*, December 16, 1991, p. A14); twice as many young families are poor than were poor in 1973 (*The Toronto Star*, October 31, 1991, p. A5).

11. Ontario Ministry of Intergovernmental Affairs, *A Canadian Social Charter: Making Our Shared Values Stronger. A Discussion Paper* (September 1991), p. 3.

12. *The Toronto Star*, October 31, 1991, p. A5.

13. James Laxer, "Teaching old leftists some new tricks," *The Globe and Mail*, December 20, 1991, p. A17.

14. Stephen J. Silvia, "The Social Charter of the European Community: A Defeat for European Labor," *Industrial and Labor Relations Review* 44 (1991): 639.

15. Ontario Ministry of Intergovernmental Affairs, *A Canadian Social Charter*, p. 17.

16. *The Globe and Mail*, February 6, 1992, p. A1.

17. *The Toronto Star*, February 14, 1992, p. A21.

18. *Ibid.*, February 7, 1992, p. A22.

19. *Public Service Alliance of Canada*, 1987.

20. Ontario Ministry of Intergovernmental Affairs, *A Canadian Social Charter*, p. 5.

21. *The Financial Post*, February 19, 1992, p. 11; *The Globe and Mail*, February 1, 1992, p. A1, February 24, 1992, p. A5.
22. *The Globe and Mail*, February 22, 1992, p. A5.

Chapter 16

1. The National Action Committee adopted a position recognizing the right of self-determination of aboriginal peoples, Québécois and Canadians outside of Québec at its Annual General Meeting in June 1991. A variation on this position was adopted in the fall of 1991 by the Action Canada Network and the Council of Canadians.
2. Citizens' Forum on Canada's Future, *Report to the People and Government of Canada* (Ottawa: Minister of Supply and Services, 1991). On page 24 of the *Report*, members of the Forum describe their process as follows: "It was an honest process. It worked because citizens themselves *wanted* it to work. Except among French-speaking Quebecers and the aboriginal peoples, the people took ownership of the process."
3. Philip Resnick outlines the argument for two sociological nations in Chapter Two of his *Toward a Canada-Quebec Union* (Montréal and Kingston: McGill–Queen's University Press, 1991). He considers only Québec and English Canada and omits the aboriginal societies.
4. Special Joint Committee of the Senate and the House of Commons, *Report: A Renewed Canada*, February 28, 1992.
5. Special Joint Committee, *Report*, pp. 122–23. The proposal is to add two new clauses to the existing section 36 of the Constitution Act, 1982, which commit Parliament and the provincial governments to the principle of equal opportunities and the provision of essential public services, and the federal government to the principle of equalization payments.

   The proposed amendment 36.1 would add a Social Covenant, which would jointly commit Parliament, the provincial legislatures and the territorial councils to (1) provide a health care system that is comprehensive, universal, portable, publicly administered and accessible; (2) provide adequate social services and benefits to ensure reasonable access to housing, food and other basic necessities; (3) provide high-quality public primary and secondary education and reasonable access to post-secondary education; (4) protect the rights of workers to organize and bargain collectively; (5) preserve "the integrity of the environment in an economically sustainable manner."

   The proposed amendment 36.2 would commit Parliament, the legislatures and territorial councils to (1) work together to strengthen the Canadian economic union; (2) ensure the free movement of persons, goods, services and capital; (3) meet the goal of full employment; (4) ensure that all Canadians have a reasonable standard of living.

To monitor the performance of government in implementing these new clauses, separate intergovernmental agencies would be established for each of section 36.1 (the Social Covenant) and section 36.2 (the Economic Union). The only power of these agencies would be to lay reports before Parliament, the provincial legislatures and the territorial councils.

6. Special Joint Committee, *Report*, p. 121.

The existing section 121 of the Constitution Act, 1867, provides that "all articles of the growth, produce, or manufacture of any of the provinces shall, from and after the union, be admitted free into each of the other provinces." The proposed new section 121 would extend free movement of goods to include as well the free movement of services, capital and persons. Unlike section 121, which has been in the constitution since 1867, the wording of the proposed amendment would make possible legal challenges to federal or provincial legislation that interfered with the free movement of goods, services, capital and persons.

The version of an amended section 121 which appears in the Beaudoin-Dobbie report is an improvement on the wording contained in the fall 1991 federal proposals in that it makes it clearer that the intention of the legislation must be to restrict trade. A longer list of exemptions is also contained in the Beaudoin-Dobbie report, which includes laws directed at promoting equalization or regional development; public protection, safety or health; government-owned corporations exercising monopolies in the public interest; the preservation of existing marketing and supply management systems.

7. Special Joint Committee, *Report*, pp. 114–16.

A new section 95A would allow for the delegation of powers between the Parliament of Canada and the legislature of a province. This section stipulates a clear and public process for the delegation of power from one level of government to another. Any act delegating power would expire within five years; however, it could be re-enacted within that five-year period without going through the public process.

The proposed new section 95AA does not contain the same procedures for public hearings nor the same one-year delay between notice of the proposed delegation and enactment. Instead, it gives special constitutional status to any agreement, contract or other arrangement between the government of Canada and the government of a province, once it has been approved by the legislature of the province and the Parliament of Canada. A resolution approving the agreement which is laid before Parliament or a provincial legislature will be deemed adopted after twenty-one sitting days, unless at least two members of the house or legislature move that the resolution be debated. Any agreement, contract or other arrangement so approved may not be amended or revoked except in accordance with its terms or by a further agreement of some sort. No limitations are placed on what the terms of such an agreement, contract or other arrangement would be. The effect of this amendment would be to bind future Parliaments or legislatures to the terms agreed to.

8. Special Joint Committee, *Report*, p. 120. The proposed amendment 106A is identical to the Meech Lake proposal with the exceptions that the term *Canada-wide* is used instead of *national* to describe a "shared-cost program," and the opting out with compensation is available "if the province carries on a program or initiative that *meets the objectives* of the Canada-wide program," rather than being "compatible with the national objectives."

9. This special constitutional status for bilateral agreements is provided for in the proposed section 95AA, discussed in note 7. Special Joint Committee, *Report*, p. 116.

10. "Triple-E or No Deal, Getty Warns," *The Globe and Mail*, March 30, 1992.

11. Remarks by Judy Rebick, President of the National Action Committee on the Status of Women, to the "Workshop on Beaudoin-Dobbie" co-sponsored by the Canadian Studies Program, University College, University of Toronto, and the Phoenix Community Works Foundation, March 7 and 8, 1992.

12. *The Globe and Mail*, March 30, 1992.

13. Personal communication with Shelagh Day, Vice-President, National Action Committee on the Status of Women.

The existing section 28 of the Charter of Rights and Freedoms reads, "Notwithstanding anything in this Charter, the rights and freedoms referred to in it are guaranteed equally to male and female persons." Day's criticism is that the section is based on a gender-neutral or "same-treatment" model of equality. Feminists have specifically rejected this notion over the past decade and have argued instead that equality means equality of condition, and that creating equality requires doing whatever is necessary to put a subordinated group on an equivalent footing with the dominant group in society. An improved section 28 would state specifically that women have been historically disadvantaged by discrimination and that overcoming the inequality of women requires changing the material conditions of women.

14. Coalition of Provincial Organizations of the Handicapped, "COPOH's Position on the Constitutional Challenge," August 6, 1991, mimeo. On page 4 of this paper, COPOH proposes adding a new section 15(2) to the equality rights clause of the Charter of Rights and Freedoms which would read: "In order to ameliorate the conditions of disadvantaged individuals or groups the use of subsection (1) is limited to those who are members of disadvantaged groups."

15. National Anti-Poverty Organization and the Charter Committee on Poverty Issues, "Draft Social Charter," February 21, 1992, mimeo.

16. Special Joint Committee, *Report*, p. 106. Emphasis added.

17. *Ibid.*, p. 37.

18. Citizens' Forum, *Report*, p. 47.

19. Special Joint Committee, *Report*, p. 46. The proposals relating to reform of the Senate appear in the text of the report but not in the list of Draft Constitutional Amendments presented in Appendix A to the report.

20. *Ibid.*, p. 123.

Bibliography

Assembly of First Nations. 1991. *First Nations and the Constitution: Discussion Paper*. Ottawa.

Balthazar, Louis, Guy Laforest and Vincent Lemieux, eds. 1991. *Québec et la restructuration du Canada, 1980–1992: Enjeux et perspectives*. Québec: Septentrion.

Bell, David V. J. 1992. *The Roots of Disunity*. Toronto: Oxford U.P.

Bercuson, David J. and Barry Cooper. 1991. *Deconfederation: Canada without Quebec*. Toronto: Key Porter Books.

Boothe, Paul et al. 1991. *Closing the Books: Dividing Federal Assets and Debt If Canada Breaks Up*. Toronto: C.D. Howe Institute.

Broadway, Robin W. and Douglas D. Purvis, eds. 1991. *Economic Aspects of the Federal Government's Constitutional Proposals*. Kingston: Queen's University.

Broadway, Robin W., Thomas J. Courchene and Douglas D. Purvis, eds. 1991. *Economic Dimensions of Constitutional Change*. Kingston: Queen's University.

Brossard, J. 1976. *L'accession à la souveraineté et le cas du Québec*. Montréal: Les Presses de l'Univ. Montréal.

Business Council on National Issues. 1991. *Canada and the 21st Century: Towards a More Effective Federalism and a Stronger Economy*. Ottawa: BCNI.

Business Council on National Issues. 1992. *Canada's Constitutional Future: A Response by the Business Council on National Issues to the Government of Canada Proposals "Shaping Canada's Future Together."* Ottawa: BCNI.

Cairns, Alan. 1991. *Disruptions: Consititutional Struggles from the Charter to Meech*. Toronto: McClelland and Stewart.

Cameron, Duncan and Miriam Smith, eds. 1992. *Constitutional Politics*. Toronto: James Lorimer.

Canada. 1991. *Canadian Federalism and the Economic Union: Partnership for Prosperity*. Ottawa: Ministry of Supply and Services.

————1991. *Shaping Canada's Future Together: Proposals*. Ottawa: Minister of Supply and Services.

————Citizens' Forum on Canada's Future (The Spicer Report). 1991. *Citzens' Forum on Canada's Future: Report to the People and Government of Canada*. Ottawa: Supply and Services.

————Special Joint Committee Beaudoin-Dobbie. 1992. *Report of the Special Joint Committee on a Renewed Canada*. Ottawa: Queen's Printer.

Cloutier, Edouard, Jean H. Guay and Daniel Latouche. 1992. *L'évolution de l'opinion publique au Québec depuis 1960.* Montréal: Québec/Amérique.

Commission sur l'avenir politique et constitutionel du Québec. 1991. *Élements d'analyse économique pertinents à la révision du statut politique et constitutionel du Québec.* Québec: Éditeur Officiel.

Courchene, Thomas J. 1991. *In Praise of Renewed Federalism.* Toronto: C. D. Howe Institute.

Drache, Daniel and Meric Gertler, eds. 1991. *The New Era of Global Competition.State Policy and Market Power.* Montreal: McGill–Queen's U.P.

Economic Council of Canada. 1991. *A Joint Venture.* Ottawa: Minister of Supply and Services.

———1991. *Transitions for the 90s.* Twenty-Seventh Annual Review. Ottawa: Minister of Supply and Services.

Fournier, Pierre. 1991. *A Meech Lake Post-Mortem.* Montréal: McGill–Queen's U.P.

Gagnon, Alain-G. and Daniel Latouche, eds. 1991. *Allaire, Bélanger, Campeau et les autres.* Montréal: Québec/Amérique.

Gagnon, Alain-G. and François Rocher, eds. 1992. *Répliques aux détracteurs de la soveraineté du Québec.* Montréal: vlb éditeur.

Grady, Patrick. 1991. *The Economic Consequences of Quebec Sovereignty.* Vancouver: Fraser Institute.

Granatstein, J. L. and Kenneth McNaught, eds. 1991. *'English Canada' Speaks Out.* Toronto: Doubleday.

Grand Council of the Crees of Québec. 1992. *Status and Rights of the James Bay Crees in the Context of Quebec's Secession from Canada. Submission to the United Nations Commission on Human Rights, 48th Session, February 21, 1991.* Ottawa: Grand Council of the Crees of Québec.

Laidler, David E. W. 1991. *How Shall We Govern the Govenor? A Critique of the Goverance of the Bank of Canada.* Toronto: C. D. Howe Institute.

Laidler, David E. W. and William B. P. Robson. 1991. *Two Nations, One Money?: Canada's Monetary System Following a Québec Secession.* Toronto: C. D. Howe Institute.

Leslie, Peter M. 1991. *The European Community: A Political Model for Canada?* Ottawa: Minister of Supply and Services.

Mandel, Michael. 1989. *The Charter of Rights and the Legalization of Politics in Canada.* Toronto: Wall and Thompson.

McCall, Christina *et. al.* 1992. "Three Nations," *Canadian Forum.* March.

McCallum, John and Chris Green, eds. 1991. *Parting as Friends: The Economic Consequences for Quebec.* Toronto: C. D. Howe Institute.

McNeil, Kent. 1982. *Native Claims in Rupert's Land and the North-West Territory: Canada's Constitutional Obligations*. Saskatoon: University of Saskatchewan Native Law Centre.

McRoberts, Kenneth. 1988. *Quebec: Social Change and Political Crisis*. 3rd ed. Toronto: McClelland and Stewart.

Miller, J. R., ed. 1991. *Sweet Promises: A Reader on Indian-White Relations in Canada*. Toronto: University of Toronto Press.

Monahan, Patrick and Lynda Covello. 1992. *An Agenda for Constitutional Reform*. North York: Centre of Public Law and Public Policy, York University.

National Action Committee on the Status of Women 1991. *NAC Response to Federal Constitutional Proposals*. Ottawa: NAC.

Ontario. Ministry of Intergovernmental Affairs. 1991. *A Canadian Social Charter: Making Our Shared Values Stonger*. Toronto: Intergovernmental Affairs.

Quebec. Commission on the Political and Constitutional Future of Quebec. 1991. *The Political and Constitutional Future of Quebec*. Quebec: St.-Romuald: Imprimerie St. Romuald.

The Quebec Liberal Party of Quebec. 1991. *A Quebec Free to Choose. (The Allaire Report)*. Québec: Liberal Party.

Resnick, Philip. 1991. *Toward a Canada-Quebec Union*. Montreal: McGill–Queen's U.P.

Richardson, Boyce, ed. 1989. *Drumbeat: Anger and Renewal in Indian Country*. Toronto: Summerhill Press.

Ritchie, Gordon, ed. 1991. *Broken Links: Trade Relations after a Quebec Secession*. Toronto: C. D. Howe Institute.

Royal Commission on Aboriginal Peoples. 1992. *The Right of Aboriginal Self-Government and the Constitution: A Commentary*. Royal Commission on Aboriginal Peoples, Ottawa.

The Group of 22. 1991. *Some Practical Suggestions for Canada: Report of the Group of 22*. Toronto.

Watts, Ronald L. and Douglas M. Brown, eds. 1991. *Options for a New Canada*. Toronto: University of Toronto Press.

Weaver, Kent, ed. 1992. *The Collapse of Canada?* Washington: The Brookings Institute.

Western Centre for Economic Research. 1991. *Alberta and the Economics of Constitutional Change*. Alberta: University of Alberta.

Whitaker, Reg. 1991. *A Sovereign Idea: Essays on Canada as a Democratic Community*. Montréal: McGill–Queen's U. P.

Young, Robert, ed. 1991. *Confederation in Crisis*. Toronto: James Lorimer.

Contributors

DAVID BELL is Professor of Political Science, York University. His latest book is entitled *The Roots of Disunity* and is published by Oxford University Press.

DOUGLAS BLAND holds a doctorate from Queen's University, Kingston, and is a noted military and security expert. He is the author of *The Military Committee of the North Atlantic Alliance: A Study of Structure and Strategy*, published by Praeger.

BARBARA CAMERON has worked extensively with the National Action Committee on the Status of Women on consititutional issues. She is a specialist on women and public policy and teaches political science at Atkinson College, York University.

HAROLD CHORNEY is Professor of Economics, Concordia University, and a noted authority on public finance.

ARTHUR DONNER is one of Canada's leading macro-economists and a private consultant to government and the private sector.

DANIEL DRACHE is Associate Professor of Political Science, Atkinson College, York University. He has written widely on public-policy issues. His most recent book, *Getting on Track: Social Democratic Strategies for Ontario*, was published by McGill–Queen's University Press.

FRED LAZAR is Associate Professor of Economics, York University. He has written extensively on trade and macro-economic questions.

MICHAEL MANDEL is Professor of Law, Osgoode Hall Law School. He is the author of *The Charter of Rights and the Legalization of Politics in Canada*, published by Wall and Thompson.

KENT McNEIL is Associate Professor of Law, Osgoode Hall Law School. He has written *Common Law Aboriginal Title*, published by the Clarendon Press.

KENNETH McROBERTS is Professor of Political Science, York University. He is the author of numerous studies on Québec politics, his most recent being *English Canada and Quebec*, published by the Robarts Centre for Canadian Studies, York University.

ROBERTO PERIN is Associate Professor of History, Atkinson College, York University. He has written widely on Québec history. His latest book is *Rome in Canada: The Vatican and Canadian Affairs in the Late Victorian Age*, published by University of Toronto Press.

PHILIP RESNICK is Professor of Political Science at the University of British Columbia. His numerous books include *Toward a Canada-Quebec Union*, published by McGill–Queen's University Press.

BARBARA RUTHERFORD is a legal counsel to the Canadian Environmental Law Association.

MIRIAM SMITH is Associate Professor of Political Science, Carleton University. With Duncan Cameron, she has co-edited *Constitutional Politics*, published by Lorimer.

MARY ELLEN TURPEL is Assistant Professor of Law, Dalhousie University, a member of the Native Bar Association, and a constitutional advisor to the Assembly of First Nations.

REG WHITAKER is Professor of Political Science, York University. Author of numerous political studies, his latest book is *A Sovereign Idea: Essays on Canada as a Democratic Community* published by McGill–Queen's University Press.

Index

DATE DUE

Printed by
Ateliers Graphiques Marc Veilleux Inc.
Cap-Saint-Ignace, Qué.
in September 1992